Architectural Guide
Lima

Architectural Guide
Lima

Laura Torres Roa
Jorge Álvarez-Builla

DOM
publishers

Contents

Foreword

Guillermo Velaochaga
CEO
Los Portales

During its 488 years of existence, Lima has undergone a profound transformation that has seen it emerge as one of the most important cities in Latin America. Founded on 18 January 1535 as the Ciudad de los Reyes, or 'City of Kings,' today the capital of the Republic of Peru is a lively, modern and cosmopolitan city that celebrates its cultural diversity, manifested in its fascinating history, in its ancestral customs, in its exquisite cuisine and in what brings us here today: its outstanding architecture.

In recent years, Los Portales has been part of this change, as a key player in the urban development and controlled growth of the city, in keeping with our aim of improving the quality of life of the people who live in the cities in which we operate.

As part of this commitment and with the desire for more and more people to understand how the Peruvian capital has evolved through the ages, we are pleased to present the *Architectural Guide Lima* in partnership with DOM publishers. This guide joins three other publications by Los Portales that have a similar aim:

Memorias de Lima (Juan Gunther, 2011), a historical portrait of a Lima that no longer exists; *Lima Más Arriba* (Evelyn Merino, 2014), a bird's-eye view of the city; and *La Lima de Ribeyro* (2016), a journey back in time to the 1950s through ten short stories by acclaimed writer Julio Ramón Ribeyro.

We hope this guide, which showcases the architecture of Lima and the nuances that have characterised it during each period in its history, from pre-Columbian times to the present, will take readers on an enlightening journey and encourage them to look at the city in a different way, focusing in particular on its main architectural and urbanistic attractions.

The book features more than 160 works from every district in Metropolitan Lima, from Ancón to Santa María del Mar, and is organised into eight routes designed to explore the city by boat, electric train, car, bus, bike and on foot.

Undoubtedly, this guide will contribute to the appreciation of a city that has not always been portrayed attractively and that still has so much to offer.

Lima's Costa Verde

Lima and El Callao

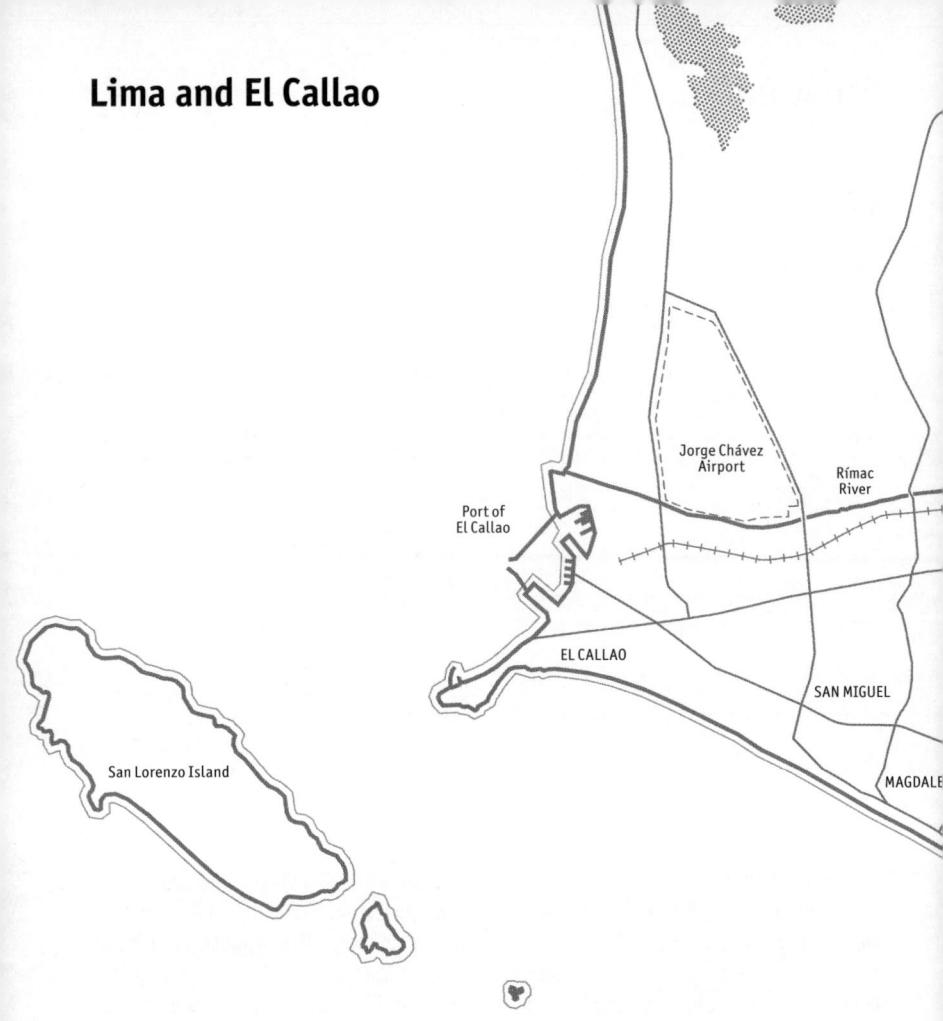

Jorge Chávez
Airport

Rímac
River

Port of
El Callao

EL CALLAO

SAN MIGUEL

San Lorenzo Island

MAGDALE

MAP KEY

+ Cerro San Cristóbal viewpoint
— Roads
— Pacific Ocean
▦ Hills

km

0   5   10

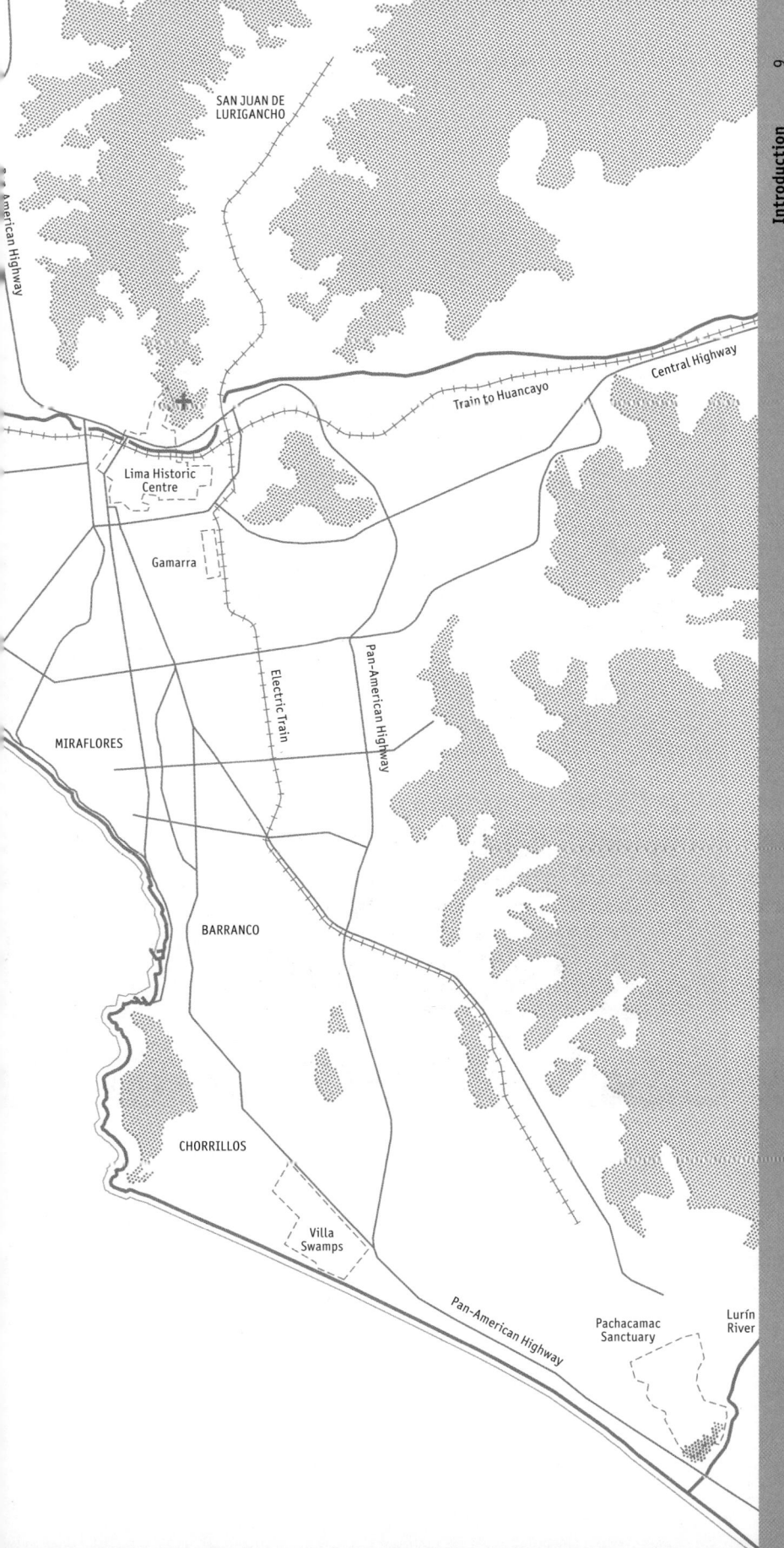

SAN JUAN DE
LURIGANCHO

American Highway

Train to Huancayo

Central Highway

Lima Historic
Centre

Gamarra

Electric Train

Pan-American Highway

MIRAFLORES

BARRANCO

CHORRILLOS

Villa
Swamps

Pan-American Highway

Pachacamac
Sanctuary

Lurín
River

Villa María del Triunfo

Introduction

The capacity for surprise upon arriving in a new city from a different culture is what inspired this guide. Our original intention was to highlight the places that had interested us during our early years in Lima and that would rarely be found in Europe, our own place of origin as well as that of the publisher. Although the viceregal and republican architecture of the historic centre has unquestionable value and was already featured in our first selection, its ties to our own – Spanish – culture and its documentation in existing publications persuaded us, instead, to emphasise other aspects that had caught our attention: the pre-Columbian ruins, interspersed with the urban fabric in a manner that, elsewhere, can only be found in Cairo; a modernist movement more cheerful than that of the old continent, midway between that of Brazil and

that of California; and the informality, a heterodox phenomenon that acquires a radical and all-pervasive dimension in Lima, generating unexpected and astonishing new forms of urban development.

That first foreigner's gaze was gradually enriched by our professional practice during the years we lived in the city, where we worked on architecture and engineering projects at the Port of Callao, the Cuartel San Martín, the Pampilla refinery, the industrial zone of Lurín, the farming valley of Cieneguilla, a former mine and the Jorge Chávez Airport. All of these projects and the people we met through our work – architect Daniel Danés, in particular – enabled us to gain a much more meaningful appreciation of the city, through the infrastructures that articulate it, the ownership structures that govern it and the legal bureaucracy that administers it. In short, we learnt about the social mechanisms that have shaped the construction of Lima and that are referenced – both implicitly and explicitly – in the texts that follow.

Edi Hirose

Lomas de Villa María del Triunfo

Naturally, we consulted other guides and catalogues that have been published to date: the *Catálogo de Arquitectura del Movimiento Moderno del Perú* by Michelle Llona and Alejandra Acevedo (2018), comprising studies of 60 buildings and references to 400, perhaps the best publication that exists on the modern period. The comprehensive and extremely detailed *Inventario del Patrimonio Monumental Inmueble de Lima* by Víctor Pimentel, José Beingolea and Enrique Guzmán (1994), which examines more than 600 buildings from the viceregal, republican and contemporary eras. And the *Guía de Arquitectura y Paisaje: Lima y El Callao*, edited by Enrique Bonilla (2009), the most recent guide with a particular focus on the historic centre. We also included works that have won the Chavín Prize, the Hexágono de Oro from the Colegio de Arquitectos del Perú and the Oscar Niemeyer Award for Latin American Architecture granted by the Network of Latin American Architecture Biennials. Additionally, we considered works that have been featured on the front cover of major indexed journals in Peru: *El Arquitecto Peruano*, founded by Fernando Belaúnde Terry and continued by Miguel Cruchaga; *Arkinka*, run by Frederick Cooper; and *Revista A*, edited by Sharif Kahatt. Although it was not a criterion for exclusion, we also took into account the current state of conservation and the possibility of visiting works, which ruled out many single-family homes and other buildings included in private condominiums.

Once we had drawn up our first list, we sought the opinion of urban planners, historians and architects of different ideological trends who have played a role in the construction of the city. They talked at length about their areas of expertise, providing us with new ideas and angles. Sometimes they would express surprise at an omission or inclusion on the list. After narrowing the selection down to 200 buildings, we organised the works by style and historical period (pre-Columbian, viceregal, republican, eclectic, modern, postmodern, contemporary and informal) to ensure balance. We also considered the building type, use (residential, tertiary, commercial or civic), whether public or private, and location. The synthesis of this knowledge reveals a city of contrasts, a snapshot of what is considered important or relevant in Lima's built heritage, reflecting the interests and contradictions of Peruvian society at this moment in time.

In writing the texts, we consulted archives at institutions such as the Universidad Nacional de Ingeniería

(UNI), the Pontificia Universidad Católica del Perú (PUCP), the Centro Canadiense de Arquitectura, the Museo de Arte Moderno de Lima, the Museo Naval de Madrid and the Biblioteca Nacional de España. We supplemented this by reading various monographs and essays, most notably those released by the publication departments of the PUCP, Universidad de Lima, Universidad Ricardo Palma and UNI, and we consulted online publications such as *Bitácora de Arquitectura Peruana* by Claudia María Delgado, the blog *La Forma Moderna en Latinoamérica* by Fernando Freire, and *ArchDaily*, founded by David Basulto and David Assael.

Also present in the book, albeit indirectly, are the academics who have shed a meaningful light on the city's history: Ruth Shady for explaining the role of hydraulic infrastructure in the development of coastal settlements; José Matos Mar for describing what happens when a government is overwhelmed by a new social reality; and Hernando de Soto for revealing the commercial activities behind a seemingly chaotic informality.

At the core of this guide is architect Margaux Eyssette's perspective on the development of the city, its markets and its informality, while photographers such as Gonzalo Cáceres, Evelyn Merino, Edi Hirose, Billy Hare, Leonardo Finotti,

Renzo Rebagliati, Gladys Alvarado and others have kindly offered images from their archives to provide a vital visual narrative for the book.

The final result is a selection of more than 160 buildings and places – some of them grouped into urban ensembles – organised into eight categories, each intended to be explored with different modes of transport: the coast by boat, the Pan-American and Central Highway by car, the Electric Train by metro, the Vía Expresa by metropolitan bus, the Arequipa-Larco axis and West Lima by bicycle, and San Isidro and the historic centre on foot. Some of the works excluded during the selection process are referenced at the end of each chapter and are included on the maps, forming part of an additional list of more than 100 buildings to offer a more complete vision of the city.

Until now, Lima has shown the world a gloomy and unattractive ambience. Writer Herman Melville described it as 'the strangest, saddest city thou can'st see,' poet César Moro as 'Lima, the horrible' and architect Héctor Velarde as 'Lima, the grey.' Our intention in this guide is to offer a different picture: one of a vibrant and cheerful city, with sunny and brightly coloured photographs that invite visitors and residents to see it in a new light.

Pampas de Lurín

Latin Case Study Houses

Until 1945, only historicist houses were built in Lima. The Casa Huiracocha was completed in 1946 and in 1947 the daily newspaper *El Comercio* published the principles of Agrupación Espacio as the first of several articles criticising eclecticism and advocating the tenets of the modernist movement. The Second World War had ended and the country was looking towards the United States – and the West Coast in particular.

In Southern California, John Entenza, editor of the magazine *Arts & Architecture*, had published photographs of houses with swimming pools, images that came to represent a hedonistic version of modernity. Soon, these ideas took root in a city that, like Los Angeles, shared the Pacific Ocean, a desert landscape and an original Spanish layout. The absence of rain and the mild temperatures facilitated the construction of flat roofs and open spaces, combined with a local type of gardening that mixed tropical vegetation with horizontally-crowned desert trees,

generating exuberant but functional architecture: the Latin version of the Case Study Houses.

Floor plans were organised with Cartesian geometry, which became more organic towards the interior garden. Driveways were paved with black cement and pebbles and paths with Arequipa stone. Façades were finished with the same cladding, wooden strips or simple rendering adorned with a characteristic vertical burnish. Overhanging eaves and planters played with volumetry and demarcated the space for the wood or aluminium window frames, usually composed of a large fixed module and a smaller one with adjustable glass slats for ventilation. The ever-present grille was made of ultra-thin rounds of smooth steel placed behind the glass but in front of the curtains, forming evanescent latticework patterns.

The houses were published to great acclaim and repeated in their hundreds, not only in Lima but in Chiclayo, Trujillo and Piura. In La Molina, plots of land

Courtesy of Miguel Rodrigo Mazuré archive

Casa Chávez (Miguel Rodrigo Mazuré, 1958)

Chávez House in 1967

were sold with limited-edition designs for rationalist houses whose perspectives took the suburban landscape of this vice-regal city to another modern, cheerful and tropical place. Even Julius Schulman travelled to Peru to photograph them. In certain parts of the districts of Santiago de Surco, Miraflores and San Borja, the style multiplied in a simplified and more commercial version. It practically became the norm and generated suburban plots which, despite modifications, still preserve their horizontal emphasis and a certain beauty. Cycling through these areas is one of the finest experiences the city has to offer because the houses are generally not fronted by hedges and are therefore easily recognisable between the winding streets where one loses all sense of time and direction. Those willing to explore the tree-lined secondary streets, avoiding the wide boulevards where the traffic is usually intense, run the risk of unlearning the principles of European civilisation and ending up like Reyner Banham, embracing the American sprawl. Beyond the empty streets with no shops or metropolitan life, all kinds of interesting situations emerge, inside the houses and the gardens in particular,

establishing various degrees of privacy, sometimes resulting in realities far removed from social conventions.

The *Catálogo de Arquitectura del Movimiento Moderno del Perú* by Michelle Llona and Alejandra Acevedo, published by the Universidad de Lima, features some of these houses and mentions the poor condition in which they have reached us today due to the lack of adequate protection. Little by little, the modern fabric of villas and gardens is evolving into a landscape of multi-family dwellings. While this new density cannot be described as metropolitan, the architecture is disconnected from the climate, landscape and local vegetation. To date, municipal authorities have done little to protect this type of architecture, but there are certain administrative mechanisms for preserving fragments of the city – as has occurred with the *quinta* estates in Miraflores – transferring buildable areas to more suitable locations within the urban plan; an opportunity to preserve this modernist heritage.

Modernist houses included in this guide: B11, B12, B14, B15, D11, D12, I24, G01, G10, G11, G12, G14, G15, G18 and G20

The Urban Evolution of Metropolitan Lima

Ramiro Gil Serrate

Metropolitan Lima, the conurbation resulting from the amalgamation of Lima and Callao, has a population of more than 10 million people and, according to the United Nations, is one of the 35 megacities that currently exist in the world. As with other cities in the developing world, it is a place of stark contrasts, where buildings by international architects can be found in relative proximity to large areas of informal land occupation and self-built houses, which in Lima are known as *conos*. In recent decades, poor urban planning, with a notable lack of basic services, has failed to keep pace with the speed of growth in these areas. This institutional weakness has prompted numerous citizens to look for ingenious solutions that have left their mark on the city's urban structure and the habits of its population. Lima is the capital of what in this century has become Peru's open economy. As such, it is a magnet for immigration and direct foreign investment, the urban impact of

which is overcoming the economic and political crisis that plagued Peru in the last 30 years of the twentieth century. During the colonial period, Lima was the most important city in South America, as is amply demonstrated by its historic centre. Today, it looks to the future by addressing what are currently the most pressing urban problems for many megacities: economic inequality, pollution and unhealthy living conditions.

Lima has distinctly coastal characteristics, stretching from the resort of Ancón in the north, through the Costa Verde districts from La Punta to Chorrillos, to the more modern resorts of what is now known as Sur Chico. Together, these comprise a shoreline of approximately 130 kilometres, lined with apartment buildings and beach houses overlooking the Pacific Ocean. But the city is also expanding inland, up to the foothills of the central Andes, with a maximum distance from the coast of around 50 kilometres. As such, it occupies a desert area bathed by three

Panorama of Lima from Cerro de San Cristóbal

rivers: the Rímac, as well as the Chillón in the north and the Lurín in the south. The valleys of these rivers, especially the upper part of the Rímac along the Central Highway, where the climate is drier, are home to social clubs and numerous country houses. Metropolitan Lima extends across more than 2,800 square kilometres, making it one of the largest urban areas in Latin America. It is divided into 50 administrative districts, 43 belonging to Lima province and seven to the constitutional province of Callao, which vary enormously in size from less than one square kilometre in the case of La Punta to the 347 square kilometres of Carabayllo. These districts are organised into five sectors: North Lima, Central Lima, East Lima, South Lima and Callao Province. The metropolitan area makes up 35 per cent of the total population of Peru and represents 40 per cent of its GDP.

Maranga, nowadays a group of ruins in the San Miguel district, was one of the most populous areas of the Lima Valley during the pre-Hispanic period. From the times of the Lima (100–650) and Ychsma (900–1469) cultures, and throughout the Inca Empire (1470–1533), it was an important administrative and trading centre. The Spanish chose this site for the city we know today because of its proximity to the natural port at Callao and the existing network of irrigation channels, which made it a fertile valley.

The Lima district, popularly known as Cercado de Lima, has been the political, administrative and religious centre of the city since the viceregal period, organised around Plaza de Armas at the heart of the historic centre. The same cannot be said of economic and financial power, which during the course of the second half of the twentieth century gradually abandoned this part of the city in favour of more southern districts in the Central Lima sector. This process was particularly intense during the political and economic crisis that afflicted the country in the last 30 years of the century. The relocation of commercial and financial activities, coupled with significant urban development partly generated by the mass influx of migrants from other parts of the country, provoked a profound transformation at the time. In the absence of adequate urban planning, the city expanded horizontally and in a scattered manner, absorbing numerous

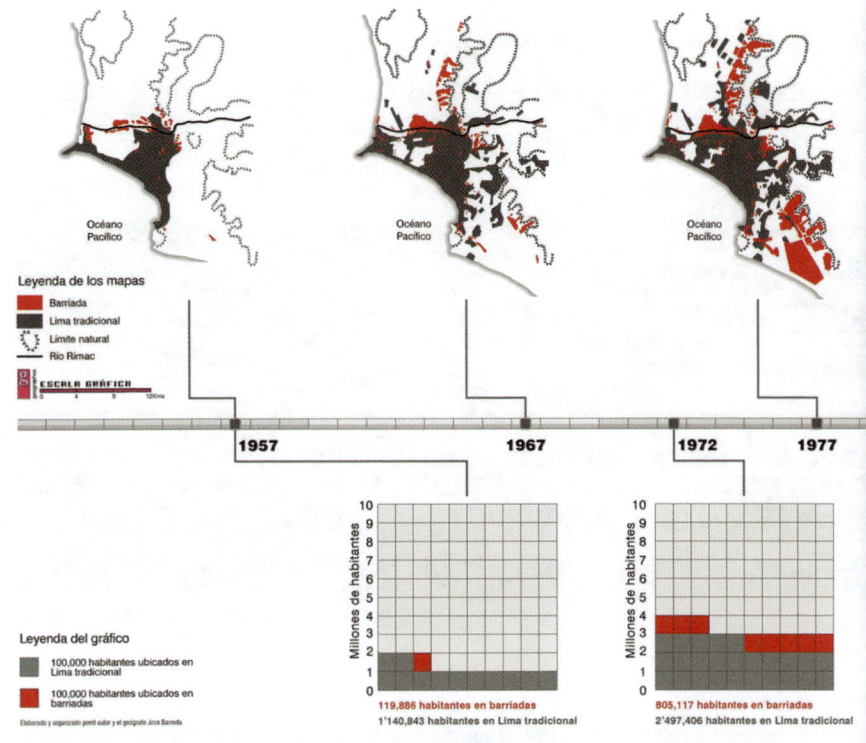

Leyenda de los mapas

■ Barriada
■ Lima tradicional
Límite natural
— Río Rímac

ESCALA GRÁFICA

1957   **1967**   **1972**   **1977**

Leyenda del gráfico

■ 100,000 habitantes ubicados en Lima tradicional
■ 100,000 habitantes ubicados en barriadas

Elaborado y organizado porel autor y el geógrafo Jose Barreda

119,886 habitantes en barriadas
1'140,843 habitantes en Lima tradicional

805,117 habitantes en barriadas
2'497,406 habitantes en Lima tradicional

The evolution of Lima (1957–2011). In grey, the traditional city. In red, the invasions. The maps show the geographical expansion and the tables show the demographic growth (each box represents 100,000 inhabitants).

nearby localities that had previously been physically separate. Some of these gave rise to new centres of activity and ultimately became districts in what is now Metropolitan Lima.

San Isidro, Miraflores and Barranco are cases in point. The first two, nowadays the city's main financial and commercial centres, emerged in the 1970s as alternatives to the gradual decay of the historic centre. By the end of the century, they had been fully consolidated, assisted by the favourable winds of the economic policies adopted in the country at that time to stimulate growth, especially in the service sector. Barranco, initially a fishing village and then a high-end resort for Lima's upper class, is nowadays the city's leisure hotspot and some of the more modest streets in the district are showing signs of an incipient gentrification. Today, neighbouring districts such as Santiago de Surco in the south and

Jesús María and Magdalena del Mar in the north accommodate some of these service activities, although more as a spillover rather than as genuine centres for such uses. This relocation and consolidation of financial, commercial and leisure areas is occurring entirely in zones once favoured by high-income citizens, which in turn is displacing this segment of the population to new residential developments, usually in the same districts. As part of this change, single-family housing tends to be replaced by multi-family apartment buildings, leading to a process of densification and the rise of private condominiums with no public access.

The migrants who moved to Lima from the provinces in the second half of the twentieth century initially occupied the fringes of the historic centre. Today, those areas correspond to the districts of San Martín de Porres – from which the Independencia district and Los Olivos

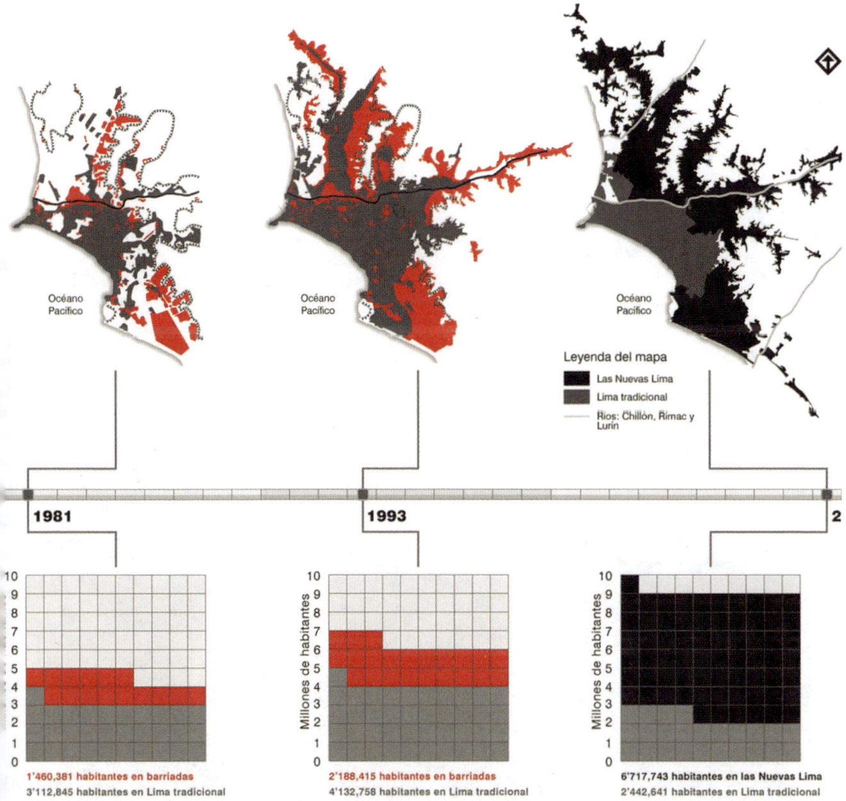

Océano
Pacífico

Océano
Pacífico

Océano
Pacífico

Leyenda del mapa

■ Las Nuevas Lima

■ Lima tradicional

— Ríos: Chillón, Rímac y Lurín

1981

1993

2

Millones de habitantes

Millones de habitantes

Millones de habitantes

1'460,381 habitantes en barriadas

3'112,845 habitantes en Lima tradicional

2'188,415 habitantes en barriadas

4'132,758 habitantes en Lima tradicional

6'717,743 habitantes en las Nuevas Lima

2'442,641 habitantes en Lima tradicional

Chart by José Matos Mar and José Barreda, published in *Perú Estado desbordado y sociedad nacional emergente*.
Courtesy of Editorial de la Universidad Ricardo Palma.

Servicio Aerofotográfico Nacional

Ciudad de Dios in 1957

El Agustino and Cerro San Cosme

A workshop in Villa El Salvador

emerged – and Comas in the north; San Juan de Lurigancho, El Agustino and Ate in the east; La Victoria and Lince in the south; and Breña, Pueblo Libre and San Miguel in the west. Part of this territory was already occupied by old mansions, farmland and even the first neighbourhood units that accommodated the urban working class. This process of densification intensified in the latter decades of the twentieth century due to terrorist attacks in the provinces and the economic crisis that afflicted the entire country, so that by the beginning of the 1980s a distinct phenomenon of conurbation was under way. The population of

Lima has grown from the 660,000 people recorded in the 1940 census to the more than 10 million who now live in the metropolitan area. In this respect, it is important to note the case of the district of Villa El Salvador. Located 25 kilometres south of downtown Lima, it emerged in the early 1970s as just another settlement but with an urban planning strategy that earned it the Prince of Asturias Award for Concord in 1987 as a 'practical example for organising a supportive and economically productive city.'

In addition to the different informal developments that have, primarily, defined the sprawl on the outskirts of the capital, a series of formal but clearly insufficient proposals have emerged to accommodate this new population. An idea imported from Mexico City, these proposals are known as *unidades vecinales* (neighbourhood units) and were first promoted in the 1940s by architect Fernando Belaúnde Terry, who would later became president of the Republic of Peru on two separate occasions. The initial units were Número 3 and Mirones in the Cercado de Lima district and Matute in La Victoria, with a second phase developed almost 30 years later. Neighbourhood units were also built in the Rímac and Miraflores

Party walls in Miraflores

districts and the constitutional province of Callao in the first phase. Although these developments were conceived from the outset as autonomous complexes and therefore included the provision of basic services and amenities, on numerous occasions they suffered the same problems as the informal developments in terms of their excessive distance from the economic and educational opportunities available at the time. As a result, the occupants were forced to bare this cost which, over time and exacerbated by a grossly inadequate transport system, would further widen the social and economic divide that now characterises the capital's population.

However, as mentioned above, new economic and social hubs emerged in certain parts of the city during the second half of the twentieth century, acquiring interdependent productive and, in certain cases, residential functions with the rest of the city. San Isidro and Miraflores have joined Cercado de Lima as strong centres of activities related to the advanced services and leisure sector aimed at the middle and higher segments of society, and today they attract a much larger population than the number of residents recorded in the census. Other centres of commercial activity can be found in the centre of Lima, in the vicinity of the central market, in the Barrio Chino and Mesa

Redonda areas, and around Alameda de las Malvinas. In the San Miguel and Los Olivos districts commercial hubs have also grown up around the modern shopping malls, although with a smaller degree of economic concentration and size. For example, Los Olivos is home to Mega Plaza Lima Norte, oriented to an emerging middle class and in terms of floor area and revenue second only to the country's largest mall, Jockey Plaza in Santiago de Surco, which caters to the more traditional middle and upper classes. The centres that have emerged in San Miguel and Los Olivos largely developed as a result of the neoliberal policies that the country has been pursuing since the 1990s to promote private investment, competitiveness and individual business initiatives. The ones located in the centre of Lima date back to an earlier period, although their expansion has also been stimulated by these policies.

In view of its characteristics, Gamarra in La Victoria is a unique case in this line of dynamic commercial places developed in these economically liberal years. This centre, initially informal like many of the previous ones, does not only sell textile products but makes them. It has also managed to harness a series of benefits typically associated with economic agglomeration, such as innovation, efficient organisation and cost savings. Thanks to the high degree of competitiveness achieved, it can target its products at both national and international markets. As well as accommodating thousands of retail outlets, Gamarra employs approximately 100,000 people in the textile industry. Another mixed commercial and industrial zone is the aforementioned Las Malvinas, where the manufacturers of large heavy goods are located. The industrial zones in the Ate district, in the eastern sector of the city, and in the southern districts of Chorrillos and Lurín are also expanding and consolidating their activities. These production and distribution centres obey the usual dynamics of seeking a location close to the principal transport connections with external markets – as in the case of Callao, home to the country's main port and airport – and the interior of Peru, as in the case of all the industrial plants along the Pan-American and Central Highway, the two

Edi Hirose

Unfinished building on Avenida Benavides (Miraflores)

Margaux Eyssette

Vía Expresa

most important land connections. These locations are sought to facilitate both supplies and the national and international commercialisation of the products concerned: primarily food, textiles, footwear, furniture, plastics, other chemical products and metals.

The Lima we see today has therefore emerged from the transfer of attributes and functions from the historic centre to other centres across the city, each with its own urban specialisation but all interdependent. Besides, these alternative centres are not too far away from the original centre and are quite close to each other, representing what might be described as a 'centralised decentralisation' of activity. This urban structure is undoubtedly related to the complete absence of an integrated public transport system that reduces personal costs, and to a type of coordination between the different levels of administration – districts, the Metropolitan Municipality of Lima, the Provincial Municipality of Callao, and even the central government – that is wholly inadequate for the optimal design of urban zoning policies. The result is enormous urban congestion and the excessive use of private vehicles, both of which are exacerbating the city's most pressing problems: pollution, unhealthy living conditions and economic inequality. In the Lima of today we find low levels of sanitation in the shanty towns on the fringes of the city, partly due to excessive densification and partly due to the fact that a significant proportion of the residents in these areas have to spend a large chunk of their time and income on commuting to their workplace. Most people use informal motorised modes of transport for these commutes, such as the famous *combis* (minivans) and an infinite number of taxis and mototaxis (three-wheeled motorbikes with a roof), which not only produce huge traffic congestion but also high levels of air pollution.

This is the urban reality of a city that was once the centre of the pre-Inca cultures and Spain's empire in South America, and as such the nexus between civilisations. Through the port of Callao, it received a constant influx of highly skilled Europeans from the mother country, including Jews and Moriscos expelled from the Iberian Peninsula. In 1551, it became home to the first university on the American continent, the present-day Universidad Nacional Mayor de San Marcos. For a large part of the colonial period, it was the centre of Spain's political and religious power on the continent, including the Inquisition. Just as this legacy shines through in the architecture and urban structure of the historic centre, it may have also left its mark on certain institutional dynamics and the rules governing the use of public space, preventing or hindering coordination between the civic powers today in their response to the aforementioned problems. Excessive and rigid regulation inherited from the past combines with significant institutional weakness, a product of the vicissitudes the country has experienced in the last half century.

The challenge facing Lima today is to improve its land management through a better articulation of the entire population, better coordination between the different levels of government, more flexible zoning and the development and promotion of an integrated public transport system. That is the only way to solve the current problems of congestion, pollution, overcrowding, waste management, poor sanitation and segregation. All of these problems have a severe negative impact on efficiency, insofar as they reduce productivity, and increase economic and social inequalities. As such, their resolution would improve the interaction between residents and therefore lead to other benefits.

Edi Hirose

Building in the Ate district

The Legacy of the Historic Centre

Luis Martín Bogdanovich

The historic centre of Lima, like no other place, has witnessed events that have marked and shaped the history of Peru. In the picturesque little squares and evocatively-named streets, inside the golden, gleaming churches, and in the quiet courtyards and cloisters of houses, convents and monasteries; amidst mysterious balconies, elegant domes and resounding bell towers; at the foot of Cerro San Cristóbal and on the banks of the River Rímac lie our memory, our identity, our legacy and even our future.

Time has passed and the city has changed, but its beating, authentic spirit lives on. It is this quality and the exceptional universal value of its historic centre that led to its designation as a UNESCO world heritage site in 1991. Three years later, the city council launched a programme to recover the tangible and intangible integrity of the historic centre of Lima, and those efforts continue to this day.

The historic centre of Lima, founded by the Extremaduran conqueror Francisco Pizarro on 18 January 1535 as the Ciudad de los Reyes ('City of Kings'), covers an area of 1,033 hectares and contains 678 buildings officially designated by the government as historic monuments, 1,292 buildings with monumental value, 25 buildings with modern monumental value, 64 urban-monumental ensembles, and around a hundred public sculptures also designated as cultural heritage. It is the Peruvian historic centre with the largest number of listed monuments, churches, convents, monasteries, museums and movable cultural assets. In addition, it is home to the national archives as well as 10 intangible cultural assets with heritage status. In short, it is the most important heritage site in Peru and, without exaggeration, one of the most notable in the whole of Latin America.

Such monuments a physical testament to our history. How are we to understand our past without Lima's Baroque churches, or our present without the bustling Plaza San Martín, scene of countless political demonstrations? How to understand our curious temperament without the

Courtesy of Pinacoteca Municipal Ignacio Merino. MML

Panorama of Lima, 1871 (Guillermo Tasset)

'Lima is the dream homeland for Americans.
Which 20-year-old born in America never dreamed of Lima?
Lima is the aspiration for everyone; for very few, the reality…
Something intimate, tender and painful stirs in me as soon as
I hear its name.'   N. Avellaneda

latticework balcony of the Torre Tagle or the Rococo setbacks of the Huérfanos church? How to understand our festive spirit without the Plaza de Acho? How to understand the earthquakes that rock us now and again, and our inventiveness, without the technology that enabled us to build castles with reeds and mud? How to understand our ambitions without the murals on the walls of the Franciscan monumental complex? How to understand ourselves today? The answer to all these questions lies in our architecture.

Every page in the great book of the historic centre captures our unique character. With its interwoven causes and consequences, our architecture represents the most authentic reflection of who we are. A conscientious study of our old masonries offers the most effective way to understand our society, without the typical Lima veils.

Thirty years have passed since the historic centre was included on the UNESCO World Heritage List, but despite the progress made since then, many battles remain to be won in terms of ensuring a true appreciation of the need to preserve the cultural values of old Lima with integrity and authenticity. Our efforts in this respect are not the first. The initial work was undertaken by the National Council of Historic Monument Conservation, created by various eminent figures and with Rubén Vargas Ugarte at the helm. It was the days of the 1940 earthquake and the regrettable expansions of streets which led to the first massive destructions in the historic centre in pursuit of a misconceived progress.

At the time, Raúl Porras Barrenechea spoke for many when he called for a halt to such interventions: 'Leave us, the elderly of Lima, at least the babbling river of the Yungas, the stone bridge of Montesclaros and the romantics, the alameda of Micaela Villegas,' he wrote. 'And let the monks in their threatened cloisters add to their morning prayers this supplication on behalf of the city: Spare us, Lord, from mayors, earthquakes and urban developers.'

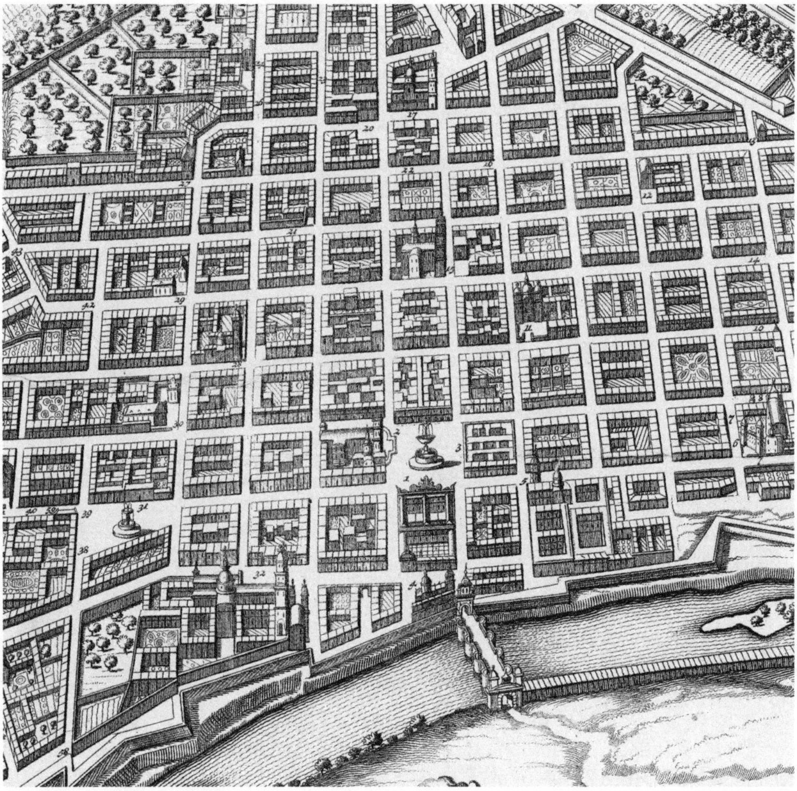

The 'City of Kings,' 1685

After various thwarted attempts to seek protection for Lima's urban heritage, in 1961, during the mandate of Mayor Héctor García Ribeyro, the Junta Deliberante Metropolitana de Monumentos Históricos, Artísticos y Lugares Arqueológicos was created with the primary mission of identifying and listing buildings and urban ensembles with monumental value.

Prominent among the members of the board were the architects Rafael Marquina y Bueno, Héctor Velarde, José García Bryce, Víctor Pimentel Gurmendi and Luis Miró Quesada. Unfortunately, then as now, pressure and private interests in conflict with the conservation of Lima's cultural heritage put an end to existence of the board which, had it survived as an entity with executive powers, would have guaranteed a legacy with a more uniform urban landscape. The board was dissolved in 1964 and no similar municipal body existed until the creation of the Programa para la Recuperación del Centro Histórico de Lima (PROLIMA) in 1994. The efforts of this group of architects, historians and urban planners laid the foundations for the designation and demarcation of the historic centre of Lima as cultural heritage of the nation in 1972.

The defenders of Lima left a deep trail. If we revisit their legacy, it is clear that they were constantly battling between light and darkness, with those who, out of ignorance or malice, championed the denaturalisation or destruction of Lima. Just three years ago, the approval of a Master Plan for the historic centre of Lima up to 2029 ushered in a new era, this time with a firm management framework to steer the comprehensive recovery of the centre in the coming years. While this may seem like a Herculean task, it inspires considerable hope – especially judging from the number of improvements already made and the ones expected in the next few years and beyond.

This splendid guide not only reflects the architectural and urbanistic excellence of old Lima but offers a fine instrument for discovering and appreciating it, and for renewing our commitment to its protection and recovery in the future.

Luringancho

Sto Cristoval

los Amancaes

Geronymo

Co Tablas

Torres

Monton de Trigo

Boca Negra

Almacen de Polvora

Cerro de S. Bartolome

Cerro del Pino

LIMA

Acequias para riego de los sembrados

Miraflores

Sta Beatriz

S. Isidro

Cerro Orvanta

Orvanta

Furreyna

Malalechuz

Arsona

Colorada

Exercicios

Ovague

Goto

Magdalena

Camino de los empedrados

Paulo

S. Miguel

El Balconillo

Huaca de las vacas

Candelaria

Tendano

Pan de Azucar

La Legua

Maranga

Rio Rimac

Bellavista

La Horadada

Ac.a

A F

A t.

A t.

A t.

Castillo del Callao

A t.

I.a del Fronton

P.ta Boqueron

A t.

Isla de S.n Lorenzo

Los Palominos

Map of the anchorage of Callao, 1811

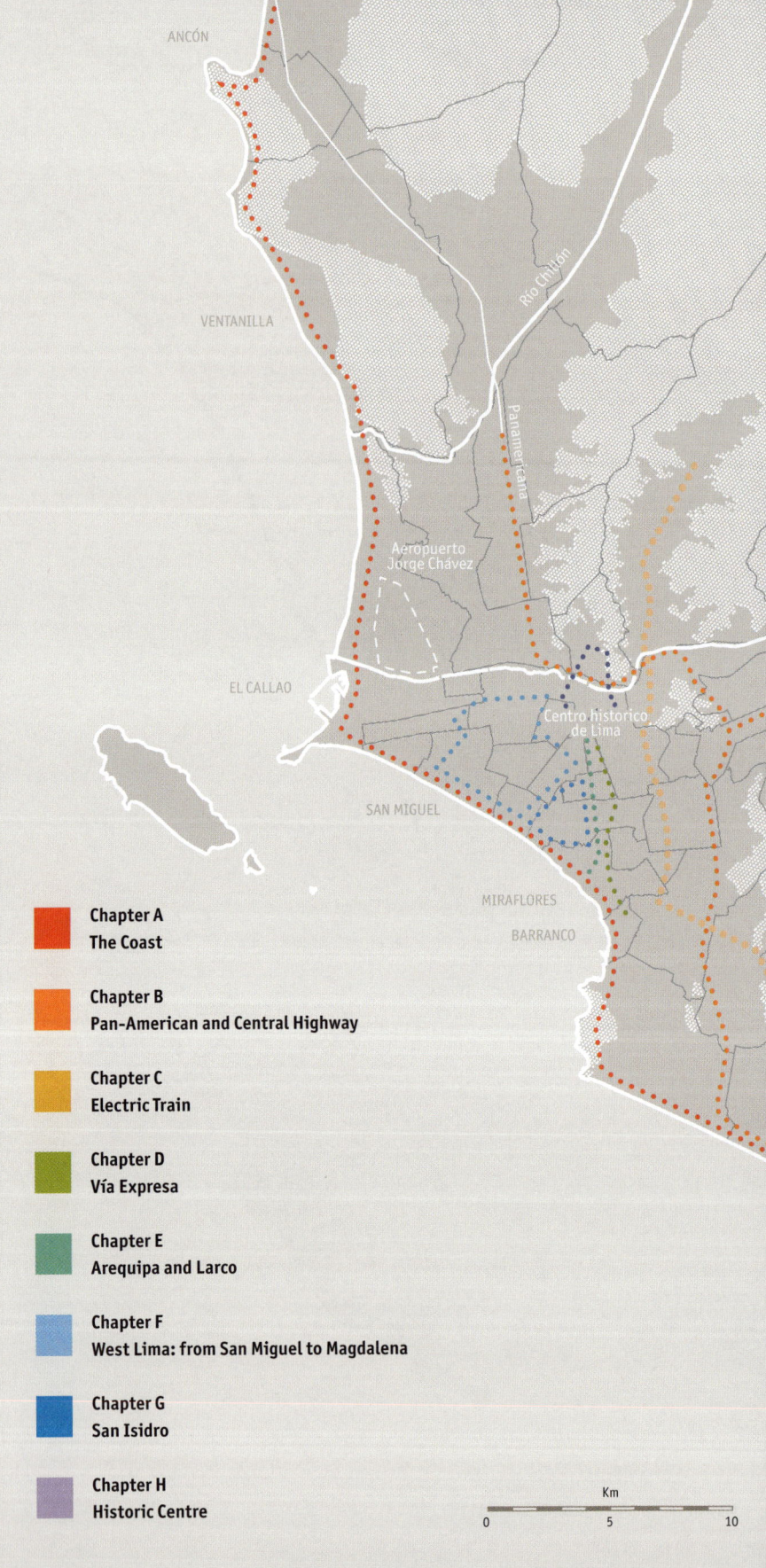

ANCÓN

VENTANILLA

Río Chillón

Panamericana

Aeropuerto
Jorge Chávez

EL CALLAO

Centro histórico
de Lima

SAN MIGUEL

MIRAFLORES

BARRANCO

Chapter A
The Coast

Chapter B
Pan-American and Central Highway

Chapter C
Electric Train

Chapter D
Vía Expresa

Chapter E
Arequipa and Larco

Chapter F
West Lima: from San Miguel to Magdalena

Chapter G
San Isidro

Chapter H
Historic Centre

Km

0   5   10

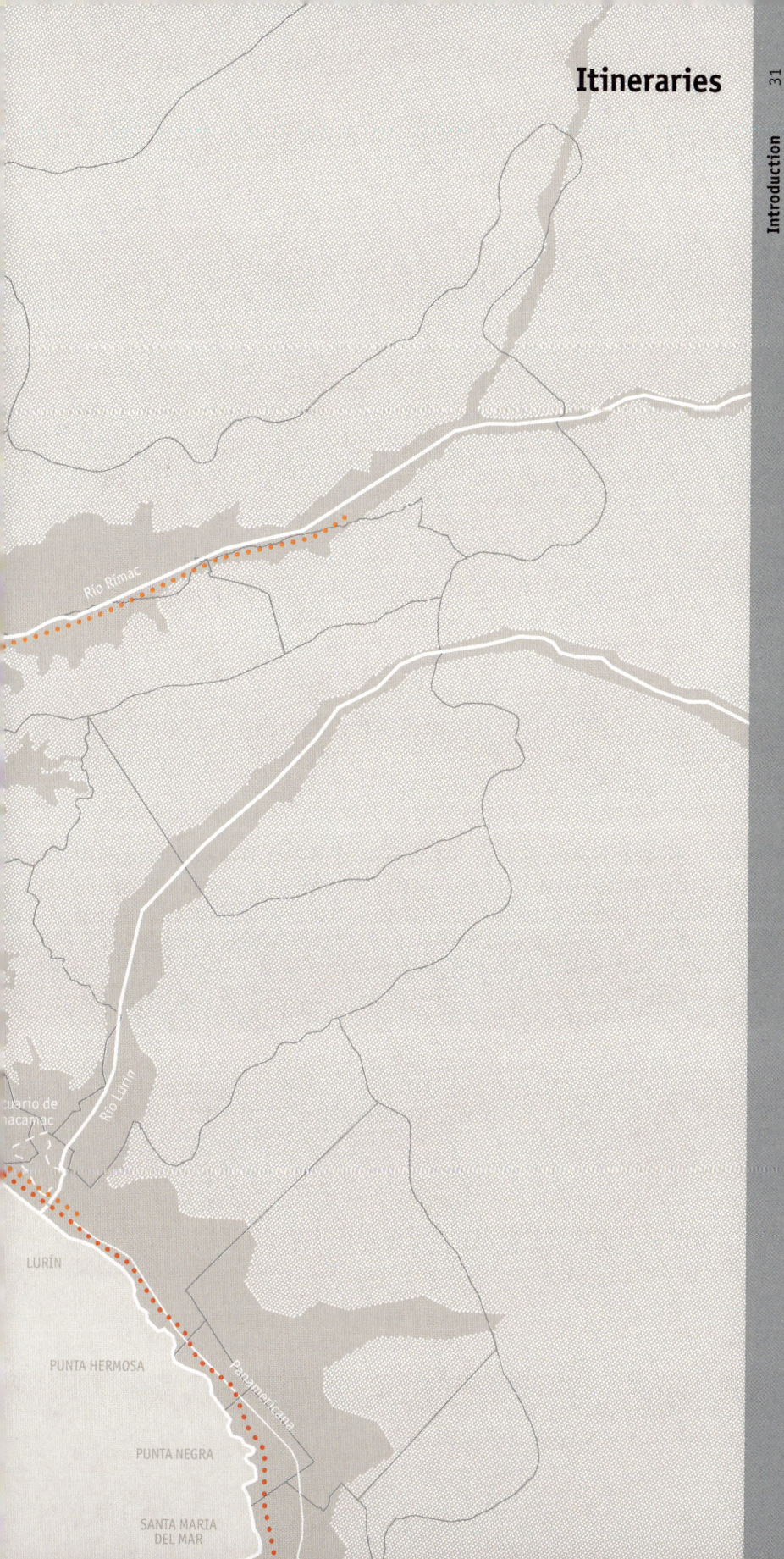

Río Rímac

Río Lurín

...uario de ...acamac

LURÍN

PUNTA HERMOSA

Panamericana

PUNTA NEGRA

SANTA MARIA
DEL MAR

The Coast

A

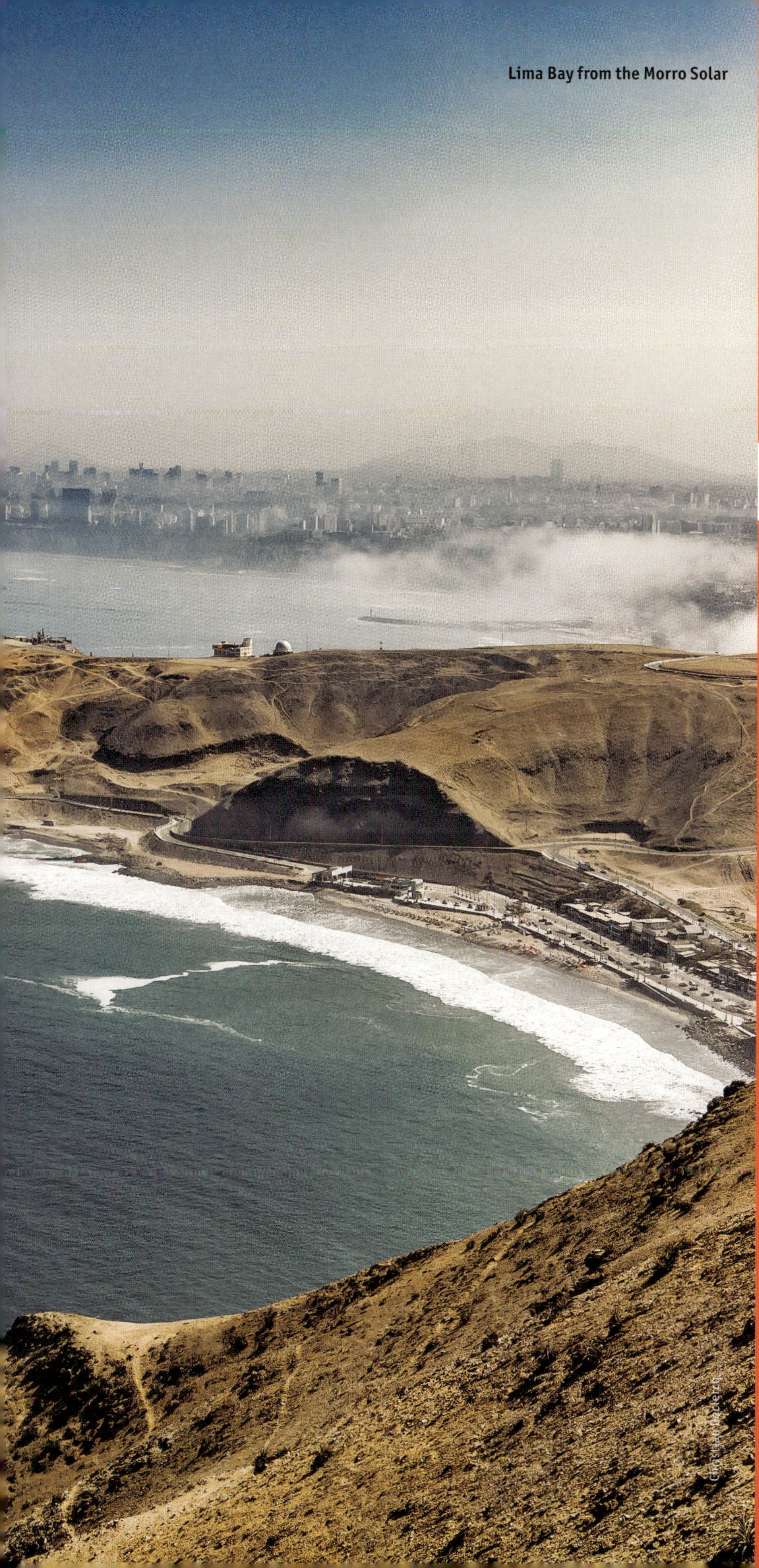

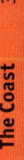

A

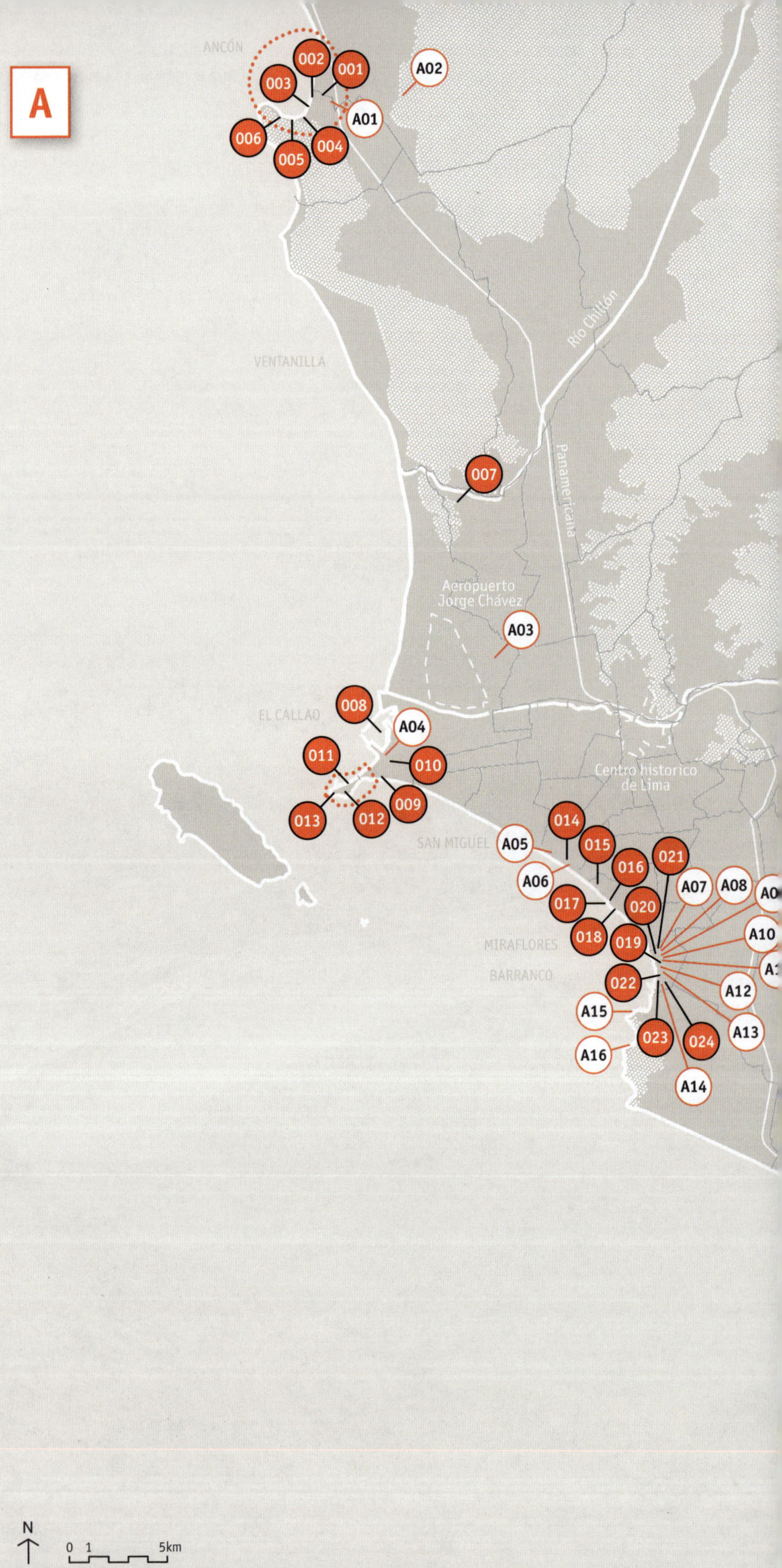

ANCÓN

002 001
003 **A02**
A01
006 004
005

VENTANILLA

Río Chillón

007

Panamericana

Aeropuerto
Jorge Chávez

A03

EL CALLAO
008
A04
011 010
013 012 009

Centro histórico
de Lima

SAN MIGUEL

014
015 **A05**
016 021
A06 017 **A07** **A08** A0
020
018 019 **A10**
MIRAFLORES **A1**
BARRANCO 022 **A12**
A15 **A13**
A16 023 024
A14

N

0 1   5km

A

Bay of Ancón from the Edificio Balcones (Ruth Alvarado, Óscar Borasino)

Balneario de Ancón

As the northernmost district of Metropolitan Lima, Ancón has been a place of settlement since antiquity due to its position as a natural port. The first archaeological sites were discovered during the construction of the railway, inaugurated in 1870, that connected the district to the city of Lima. Since then, remains of the Chavín, Huaura, Chancay and Inca cultures have been found in the area. It was with a view to exhibit these pre-Columbian artefacts that the journalist and architect Alejandro Miró Quesada created a board of trustees for the site museum, which opened to the public in 1993. Guillermo Málaga designed a small building (001) accessed by a series of stepped platforms paved with cobbles and natural stone, on which various volumes house a modest exhibition programme and public terraces covered by simple awnings, perfect for the desert climate. On a plastic level, the work connects well with the surrounding landscape, both for its volumetry and colour, although its condition has somewhat deteriorated.

The place is located on the edge of what is now known as 'Old Ancón,' the small town that grew up around the railway, built between 1870 and 1920, based on an urban plan that has always precluded the entry of vehicles. The monumental area has had national cultural heritage status since 1989 and comprises the so-called 'ranches' (002), single- or two-storey houses fronted by wooden porches that sometimes unite different

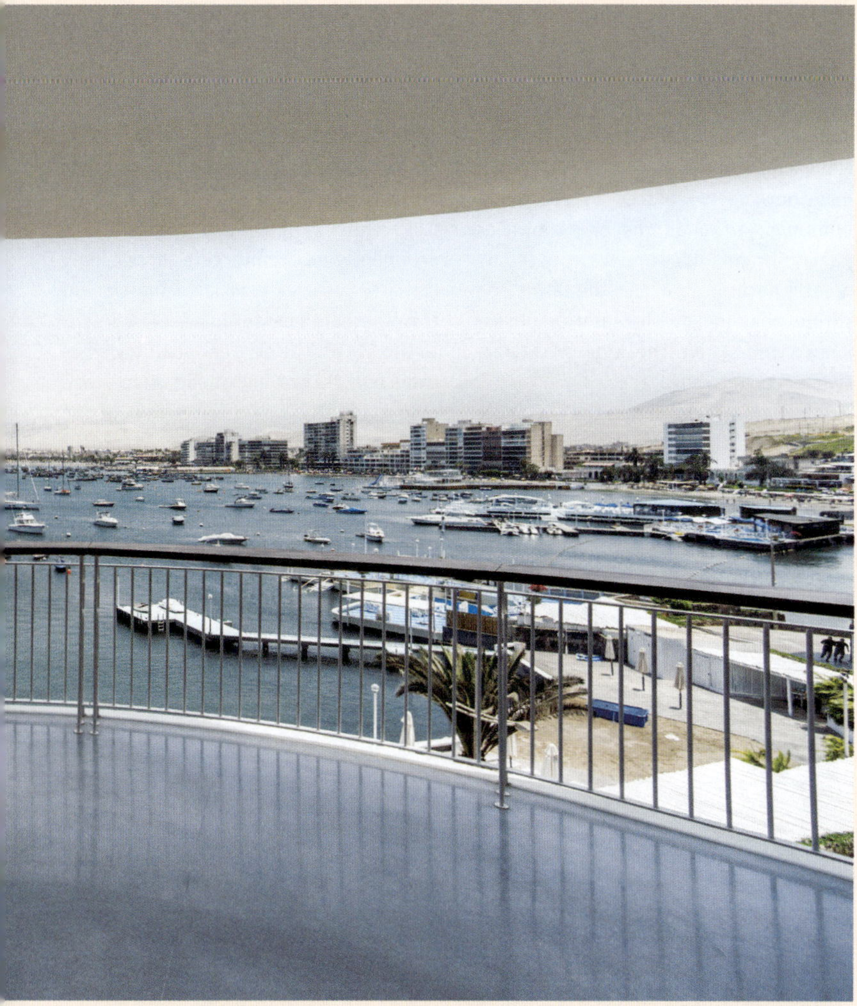

Museo de Sitio de Ancón
Calle Loreto 546, Ancón
Guillermo Málaga
1994

001 A

properties and with eclectic ornaments forming garlands, arches and balustrades. The floor plan of this typology is composed by concatenated spaces, devoid of corridors and transitional areas. Many of the houses on the waterfront have now been replaced by apartment buildings, although the one known as Rancho Grande has survived. Others are greatly deteriorated, but the lawns and shrubs that invade the interior pedestrian streets give the area an attractive, decadent appearance.

The local church two blocks away, near the Parque Central, was designed by Enrique Seoane and opened in 1944. Composed of a nave with auxiliary facilities, it has a thoroughly modern floor plan but incorporates simplified neocolonial ornaments at the entrance and on the bell tower. This abstract interpretation of the style, which appears on the entrances of many houses in Lima built in the first half of the twentieth century, enabled the architects of the day to camouflage an underlying architecture increasingly stripped of the classicist inertias of the nineteenth century.

In the 1940s, the original small town became one of Lima's most exclusive beach resorts. Built along a waterfront whose paving recalls Burle Marx's design for Copacabana, it can only be explored on foot or on one of the popular *anconetas*

Ranchos de Ancón

Malecón Ferreyros, Calles Balta, 2 de Mayo and Abtao, Ancón
1870–1920

IPMIL. Universidad Nacional de Ingeniería

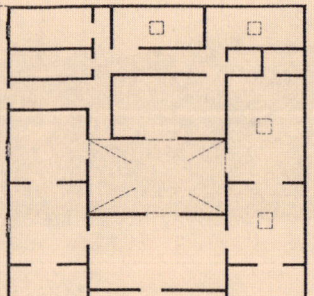

Ranch house on Jirón Abtao 290

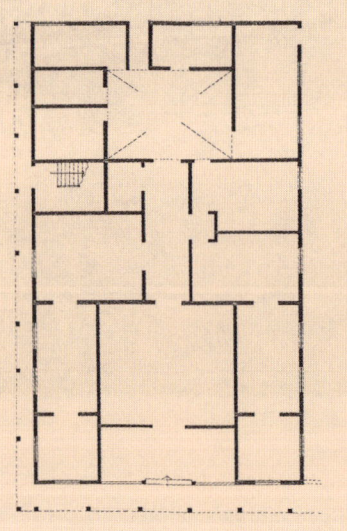

Ranch house on Malecón Ferreyros 960

Rancho Grande

Casino de Ancón

Malecón Ferreyros, Ancón
Hector Velarde
1946

(four-wheel bikes). The route takes in works designed by some of the finest Peruvian architects of both the modern and contemporary periods.

From north to south, the first to appear is Héctor Velarde's Casino (003), a four-storey building adapted to the topography with a cane-shaped floor plan and large stepped terraces. Glazed envelopes and superior awnings contribute to the overall light appearance of this construction, designed with meticulous attention to climate comfort.

A little further along the waterfront, opposite the Parque San Martín, is a multi-family building with a singular structure in which the central core, with cruciform piers, supports the entire cantilever perimeter. Concrete horizontal parapets anchored by tensile piers form the main façade. The modulation of the glass, the brick finishes, certain ventilation details and the entrance steps in natural stone generate a discreet but skilfully executed work.

Located on the other side of this small beach is a wide-span structure on a narrow plot, perpendicular to the sea, with apartments beginning on the third floor. The façade is made of white-painted concrete, exposed brick and smoked glass, enriched by overhanging eaves and vertical slats. The rooftop has a series of sculptural volumes and is connected by a walkway to a car park at the rear, accessed from Avenida Las Colinas.

Renzo Rebagliati

Malecón paving

The amoeba-shaped floor plan of the Edificio Balcones (004) by Óscar Borasino and Ruth Alvarado hugs a bend in the road with a series of undulating terraces. Next, we find a row of adjoining rationalist buildings, the first by architect Germán Costa and the second by Ernesto Aramburú, the future mayor of Miraflores and driving force behind the Costa Verde project, formed by a series of refined cantilevers that project over a rock covered by a natural vertical garden. This feature serves as a cave-like entrance to the project.

Edificio Balcones
Malecón Ferreyros, Ancón
Ruth Alvarado, Óscar Borasino
2016

004 A

Renzo Rebagliati. Courtesy of OB+RA Arquitectos.

On the opposite side of the road, overlooking the ocean, Enrique Seoane designed three single-storey houses (005), each with their own jetty, that project over the water by means of concrete beams with variable sections. The project contains a certain degree of structural exhibitionism, with setbacks on the roof and oblique beams echoing the architecture that Walter Weberhofer – a former employee at Seoane's studio – was practising in Santa María del Mar, the upmarket resort in the south that was then beginning to compete with Ancón.

Tres viviendas
Malecón San Martín, Ancón
Enrique Seoane
1962

005 A

Renzo Rebagliati

Beyond the headland, on an irregular trapezoidal plot, stands the Edificio Neptuno (006), a light and somewhat fanciful construction that won the Chavín Prize in 1958. Its elliptical floor plan reflects the author's desire to maximise the views in this privileged location and create a singular work that would stand out from the nearby buildings. The result is an expressionist display in which nothing is rational. The structure is formed by 11 pilotis, of which only four – on the side facing the ocean – have a circular section. The lobby is separated from a boat house by a wavy wall that hugs an oval staircase and the lift. The building is raised slightly from the ground but integrated into the waterfront by means of a flight of steps on one side and a small garden on the other, which has been altered to facilitate access. The apartments are organised around a corridor that provides access to the rooms, arranged radially on the perimeter, and ends at the kitchen area, which is protected on the façade by vertical fibre cement sunshades. The lounge has floor-to-ceiling sliding windows with aluminium frames, ultra-modern features at the time. The balcony is a tensioned frame of the desert landscape and the ocean views. The edges of the floor slabs are finished with blue ceramic tiles laid in a slightly oblique upright position, imitating the angle of the railings.

A little further along, on the Malecón Bardelli, stands La Genoa (2014), designed by the studio 51-1 Arquitectos. On Playa Hermosa, near Plaza Gaviotas, we find apartments designed by Gabriel Tizón in 1960 with a symmetrical floor plan and refined elevations, still in good condition today. The two streets immediately behind the waterfront are lined with single-family houses, including one by Theodor Cron, recently refurbished by Adrián Novoa. Following the coastline, beyond the Playa de San Francisco Grande, we come to the only part of the resort that unfortunately has no public access: the Marina Lancheros condominium, with three interesting houses by Barclay & Crousse, 51-1 and Giovanni Schettini.

Edificio Neptuno
Malecón San Martín 684, Ancón
Alberto Menacho
1958

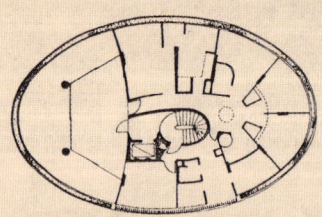

006 A

Typical floor plan

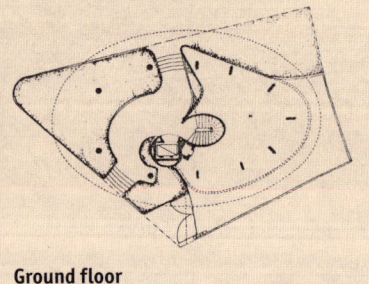

Ground floor

IPMIL, Universidad Nacional de Ingeniería

Enrique Jara

A

Huaca El Paraíso

San Martín de Porres
2500 BCE

007 A

What makes Lima such a unique city is the presence in its metropolitan area of ruins from settlements dating back thousands of years. Scattered across the urban fabric and occasionally accompanied by pockets of desert, the different sites shed light on the habitat of these earlier settlers, their isolation in an endless world, their harsh living conditions and their vulnerability. The constructions also reflect the ambitions of these cultures and contain all the hallmarks of civilisation: the search for stability to withstand both earthquakes and the passage of time by means of stepped stone and clay walls, sometimes as thick as a metre; the protection from adverse weather conditions and the search for a certain degree of comfort by means of shaded, covered and ventilated spaces; the distribution of the spaces to separate tasks, in this case administrative and ceremonial, like the Temple of Fire; and the attention paid to finishes – layers of clay painted red, white, black or ochre, all now lost, convey an idea of the beauty of these places and their aesthetic relationship with nature, very different from the

camouflage we see today. Ultimately, it is the Vitruvian triad of *firmitas, utilitas* and *venustas* that we find in these ruins from more than 4,000 years ago, located in the Chillón Valley inside a larger complex of residential precincts. Discovered by Louis Stumer in 1950, they were published for the first time in 1964 by Thomas C. Patterson and Edward P. Lanning, who dated them to the Preceramic period. The research continued in 1965 with Frederic Engel and in 1982 with Jeffrey Quilter, but it was not until 2008 that the Ministry of Culture designated the site an intangible cultural asset, in a country that is one of the five cradles of civilisation.

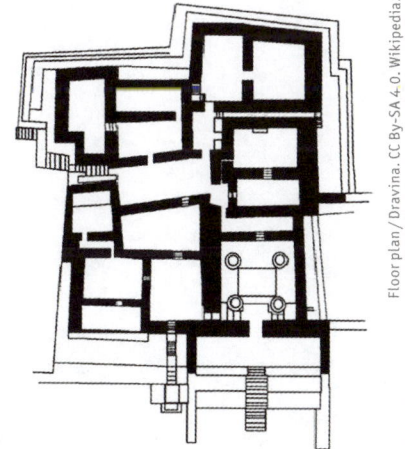

Floor plan / Dravina. CC By-SA 4.0. Wikipedia.

Evelyn Merino Reyna

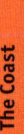

A

Puerto del Callao
Avenida Atalaya,
Jirón Manco Capac, El Callao
Since 16th century

008 A

Sheltered by Lima Bay, between the mouth of the River Rímac and the La Punta peninsula, Callao was founded in the sixteenth century and is the most important port on the Pacific coast of South America. It comprises the Peruvian navy docks and three commercial terminals. The port handles over 50 million tonnes of cargo per year and more than 80 per cent of the county's maritime exports, which in turn represent more than 70 per cent of all exports from Peru. In economic figures, every year more than 25 billion US dollars worth of cargo leaves the port, of which nearly 60 per cent is metal, mainly copper and gold. In the past the port was a target for pirates and witnessed some of the most important battles in the history of America. The urban impact of this infrastructure is best understood by crossing the industrial park that flanks both sides of Avenida República Argentina: military installations, petrochemical plants, foundries and steel plants, logistics centres, food processing plants, textile companies, car parks, service areas and the largest retail store for building materials, Las Malvinas. In fact, this hub of production and services, which begins at Plaza Garibaldi next to the Callao Maritime Customs Office and ends practically at Plaza de Armas in the Cercado de Lima district, represents the economic map of the country as home to all the medium-sized and large business groups.

División Naval Francesa. Biblioteca Nacional de España

Port of Callao, 1876

Autoridad Portuaria del Perú

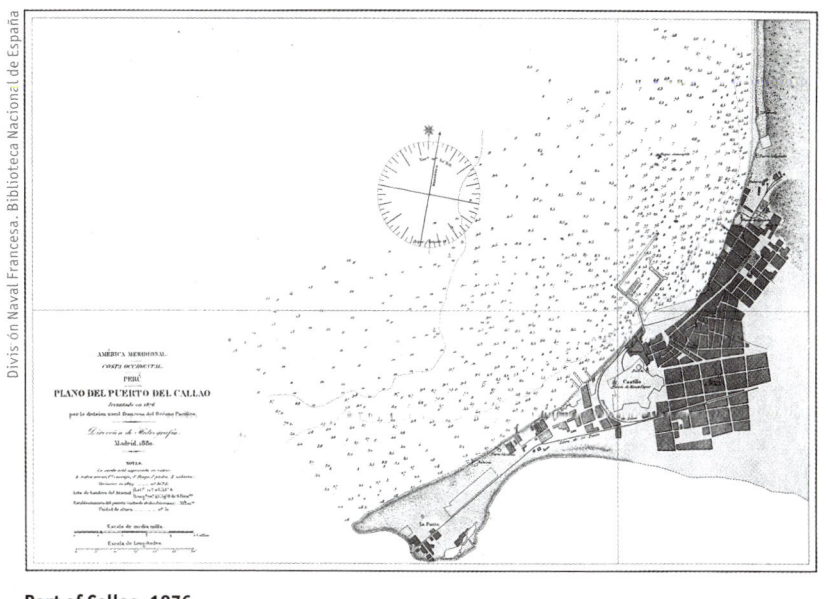

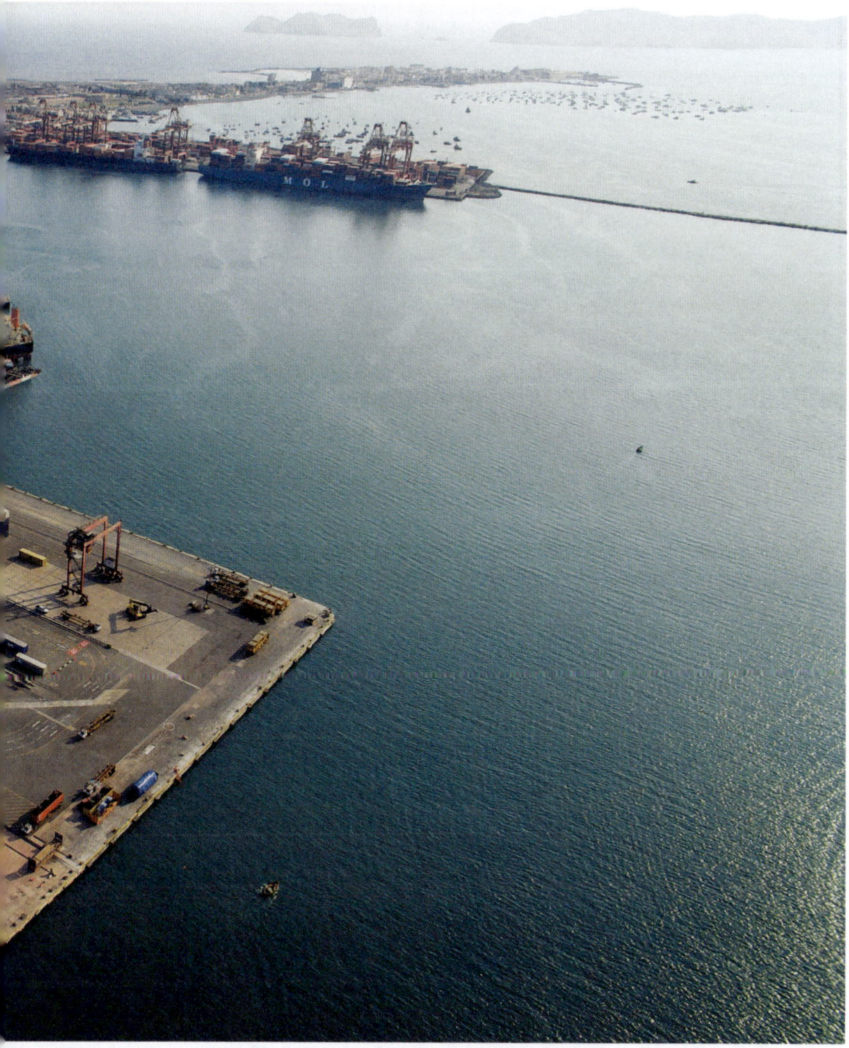

Explicacion.

1. Punto de Habitacion del Comandante en la Ciudad, con Vigia.
2. Vigia en la Huaca de Puyana.
3. Ydem en el Morro Solar.
4. Ydem en la Huaca de la Legua.
5. Ydem en el Arsenal.
6. Plaza del Callao.
7. Vigia en la Isla de S.ᵗ Lorenzo.
8. Surgidero de las Embarcaciones.
9. Isla del Fronton.
10. La Peña Horadada.
11. Camino del Callao.

Location of the Fortaleza Real Felipe and other coastal surveillance points, 1801

Fortaleza Real Felipe

009 A

Plaza Independencia, El Callao
*Luis Godin, José Amich,
Juan Francisco Rossa*
1774

Located in a strategic position in the bay, between La Punta and the Port of Callao docks, this Vauban-style military fortification was built in the eighteenth century at a time when colonial Peru was undergoing a civilising process through engineering and urban practices. The abundant cartography from the period clearly demonstrates the different stages of modernisation in the city. At the time, Callao was a small town protected by a flimsy wall; it was also a target for pirates and corsairs because ships set sail for Spain from this bay. The wall acted as a tax control barrier but lacked the necessary defensive characteristics. After its destruction in the 1746 earthquake, Viceroy José Antonio Manso de Velasco embarked on the construction of what became the most ambitious project in Lima during the viceregal period and the most costly ever undertaken by

PLANO

de la Situacion Local y Respectiva de las
Vigias de Mar entablecidas en la Capital
del Apostadero del Callao de Lima, por
su primer Comandante propietario el
Brigadier de la Real Armada D.º To-
mas de Ugarte y Liaño.

Escala de Tres Millas.

Lima 8 de Octubre de 1803.
José de Moraleda

A

the Spanish in America. It was inaugurated during the mandate of Viceroy
Manuel de Amat y Junyent in 1774,
together with the San Miguel Fort
and the San Rafael Battery, two small
constructions – now lost – built soon after
to cover the fortress flanks. Together,
they formed a defensive system known
as the 'Castles of Callao,' which became
the scene of battles and sieges during
the Independence and Pacific wars. The
fortress occupies seven hectares, including the pebble-paved parade ground. The
walls are built with blocks of sandstone
brought from the islands of San Lorenzo
and El Frontón, with a brick course along
the top. The fortress is shaped like an
irregular pentagon, with a perimeter
moat and five pentagonal bastions at the
corners, each equipped with either 16 or
20 gun ports and accessed by a ramp. Two
turrets – both later additions – crown
the bastions facing the bay. Known as
'The King' and 'The Queen,' on clear days
they afford magnificent views of the
coast and the monumental area of Callao,
where a few mansions from the republican
era can still be found.

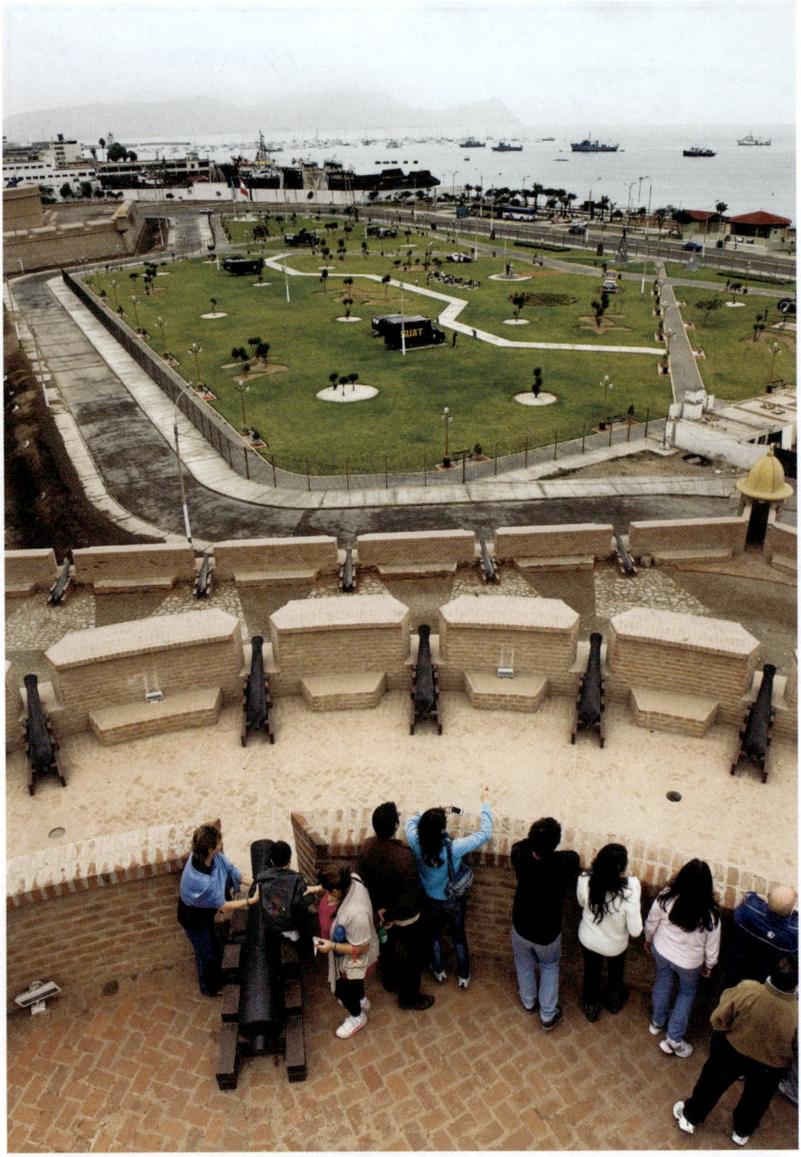

Gonzalo Cáceres

View of the port from the Fortaleza Real Felipe

Gonzalo Cáceres

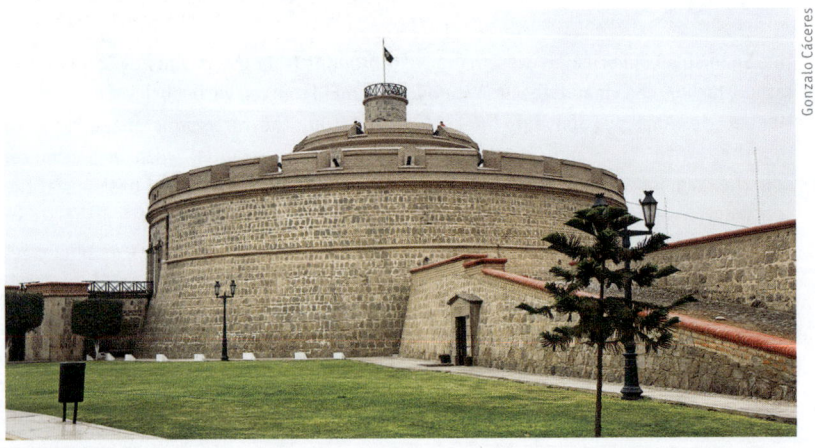

The King's turret

Edificio Ronald

Calle Constitución 250, El Callao
Engineer Bunting
1929

A

The irregular layout of Callao's historic centre is home to numerous interesting buildings, including this remarkable one developed by a well-known industrialist of British descent who was keen to establish European architectural tastes in his city. The Edificio Ronald is a six-storey symmetrical construction in the academicist style. The main entrance is through a double-height passage with a stained-glass ceiling that crosses the building from front to back like an internal street, clearly influenced by the commercial arcades of the late nineteenth century. The top floor is crowned by a dome on each façade and includes generous open spaces from which to enjoy the views. The classicist ornamentation features busts of famous figures on corbels, Ionic chapiters on ornate columns and marble claddings. This was also the first building in Callao to be fitted with lifts. Neglected for years and occupied by more than a hundred families living in crowded conditions, it was restored in 2011 and hosted a well-known interior design fair to mark its grand reopening. Nowadays, it comprises exhibition spaces, artists' studios, shops and restaurants, forming part of a strategy to regenerate the area through art. However, the initiative has aroused controversy because, as has happened in the historic centres of many European cities, this may result in the displacement of the local population and an increase in property prices.

La Punta

The quiet district of La Punta occupies a narrow peninsula between the bays of Miraflores and Callao in the Pacific Ocean. Its earliest dwellers were native fishermen known as Pitipiti, who settled on the isthmus. Located west of the port, La Punta was never incorporated into the commercial and economic axis that emerged in the direction of Lima during the colonial period.

The nineteenth century was well under way when the first signs of urbanisation appeared. In 1868, the opening of the Hotel Internacional paved the way for the development of La Punta as a resort for the upper-middle class, which gained a further boost when a new railway connected the peninsula to the capital. The characteristic ranch houses (012) emerged at this time, many of which were built by Europeans who had been drawn to the country by the economic boom prompted by the guano trade. The typology proliferated in many holiday resorts during this period. Heirs to the colonial house, the ranches were built with wood, adobe and *quincha* (a mixture of clay and reeds). They had a front porch and occupied the entire plot, forming rows of houses. The floor plan is composed of a sequence of concatenated spaces. La Punta is home to several fine examples, including the houses at numbers 300 and 382 on Avenida Grau and on the second block of Calle Medina.

From 1910 onwards, the ranches gradually gave way to eclectic-style garden villas and an incipient use of concrete. One example of this typology is the Peruvian Yacht Club at Avenida Bolognesi 781, a grand construction with a large double-height central hall with a gallery around the top floor and a rectangular lantern on the roof. Another, somewhat extravagant, example is the Moorish-style Casa Rospigliosi located at the

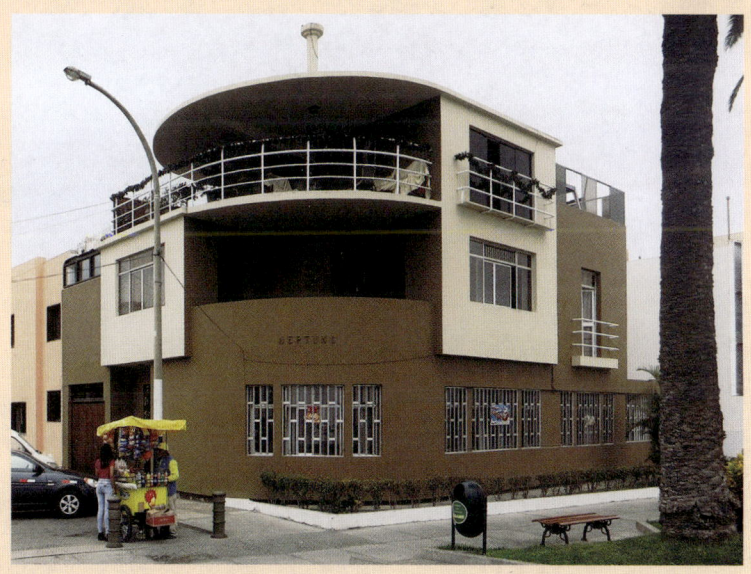

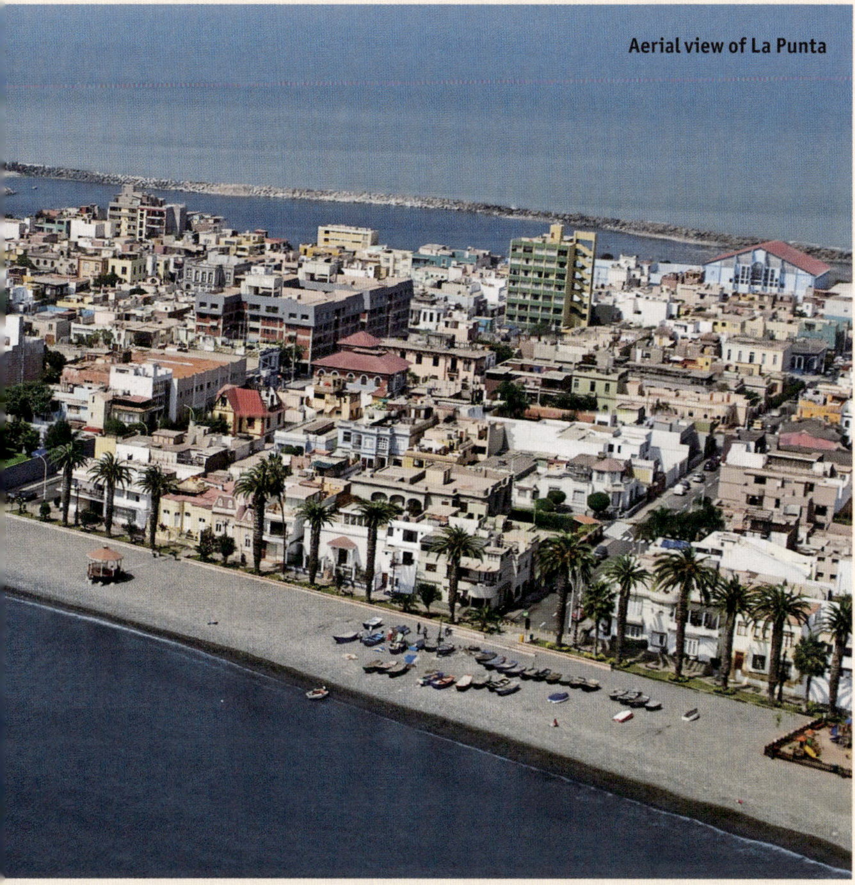
Aerial view of La Punta
Evelyn Merino Reyna

Casa Ulloa

011 A

Calle Elías Aguirre 495, La Punta
Héctor Velarde
1936

Colin Post. *Lima City of Kings*

Aerial view of La Punta

A

Evelyn Merino Reyna

Ranchos republicanos
Avenida Grau 3, Calle Medina 2, La Punta
1890–1910

Avenida Miguel Grau 300

Colin Post. Lima City of Kings

intersection of the Pardo waterfront and Avenida Bolognesi. Also located in this area are interesting examples of *quintas*, clusters of single-family houses grouped around a communal street or courtyard, such as those found at Calle Palacios 331–351 and at the corner of Calle Tarapacá and Calle García y García.

During the 1920s, the creation of wide boulevards by the Leguía administration led to the expansion of the city towards the summer resorts, which were gradually absorbed into the capital as districts. La Punta was formally integrated into

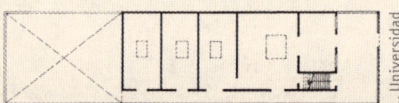

First floor of a ranch house on Calle Medina 257

IPMIL. Universidad Nacional de Ingeniería

the metropolis in the 1940s, coinciding with the appearance of the first modernist constructions on the peninsula. For example, Héctor Velarde built the Casa Ulloa (011) at Calle Elías Aguirre 495 in 1936, incorporating balconies, tubular

Calle Medina 393

Colin Post. Lima City of Kings

Edificio de oficiales y administración de la Escuela Naval del Perú

Calle Medina 5, La Punta
Adolfo Córdova, Carlos Williams
1962

IPMIL. Universidad Nacicnal de Ingeniería

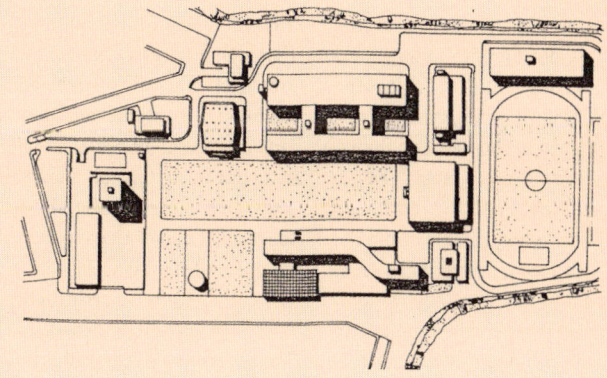

Colin Post. Lima City of Kings

railings and porthole windows in the Streamline Moderne style. In 1942, he used the same language for the Club de Regatas La Unión in Plaza José Gálvez, which is characterised by its refined façades and regular grid structure.

A fine example of a modernist work is the Edificio de oficiales y administración de la Escuela Naval del Perú (013) by Adolfo Córdova and Carlos Williams, which won the Tecnoquímica Prize in 1963. A large platform serves as the base for the two elements that form the composition: a long single-storey prism that accommodates the offices, protected from excessive sunlight by the cantilevered roof, and a square tower that rises from the basement through a sunken courtyard and houses the residential area.

Today, La Punta is a district of permanent rather than summer vacation homes, in which detached houses sit side by side with multi-family buildings. However, and even though it is not far away from dangerous areas, it has preserved its scale and quiet atmosphere, so it is still a delight to stroll along the pleasant streets and waterfronts and gaze across the bay at the island of San Lorenzo from the viewpoint.

Sede corporativa de Los Portales

014 A

Calle Ugarte y Moscoso 991,
Magdalena del Mar
Ruth Alvarado, Óscar Borasino
2012

This 12-storey office building is located on the Avenida del Ejército, which runs parallel to the Costa Verde and crosses the Magdalena del Mar district. Rising from the inverted plinth of the first two floors, the building forms an almost perfect cube, supported by a grid of reinforced concrete pillars slightly set back from the perimeter, with four bays on each side. The envelope is modulated by window frames visible on the outside, renouncing the curtain wall in favour of a repetitive rhythm of shadows that lends quality and character to the volume. The vertical frames have a different finish on the lateral faces, producing subtle effects of colour depending on the direction from which they are viewed. The reflection of the glass varies slightly according to the position of the blinds and the inclusion every three modules of panels that open, a rare feature in corporate buildings but ideal for ventilation purposes. All of this generates richness within a highly controlled framework, producing an architecture of variation and repetition that demonstrates the maturity of two architects who rely on geometrical order, rationalist construction and a certain musical rhythm to achieve the desired result. In the context of Lima, this is a discreet and rare type of architecture, akin to rationalist practices found in northern Europe and similar to what Rem Koolhaas has called 'generic architecture,' a concept crystallised in works such as the Embassy of The Netherlands in Berlin. The result is a 'sponge' building, where what matters is not so much the forms but the activities they contain. It is a civic and necessary building in the sense that it aspires to improve the fabric into which it is inserted.

Renzo Rebagliati

Lugar de la Memoria

Bajada San Martín 151, Miraflores

Sandra Barclay, Jean Pierre Crousse

2013

015 A

A

Awarded the Hexágono de Oro in 2014 and the Oscar Niemeyer Prize in 2016, the Lugar de la Memoria, or 'Place of Remembrance,' is the result of a competition launched in 2010 to provide the city with a documentation centre in memory of the victims of the armed conflict that plagued the country during the 1980s and 1990s. The winning proposal is inserted into the Costa Verde cliffs in an attempt to reproduce the original dimensions of one of the natural descents that link the two levels, which had been severely impacted when the area was opened to vehicular traffic. The building manages to stand aloof from the surrounding hustle and bustle and simultaneously establishes a dialogue with the topography and landscape, creating an interesting atmosphere for quiet reflection. The project is conceived as an ascending itinerary that begins at the access road and the large public esplanade generated by the meticulous terracing of the terrain, from

Cristóbal Palma. Courtesy of Barclay & Crousse

Cristóbal Palma. Courtesy of Barclay & Crousse

which the building emerges with its powerful materiality. The ascent continues inside the building through a series of ramps that rise to the different levels and exhibition spaces. The itinerary ends at a large roof deck where the stepped flooring invites a progressive rediscovery of the landscape around the bay, providing another space for reflection and a transition between the exhibition and the journey back to the city.

Cristóbal Palma. Courtesy of Barclay & Crousse

Restaurante El Mercado

Avenida Hipólito Unanue 203,
Miraflores
Jaime Ortiz de Zevallos
2010

016 A

Chef Rafael Osterling's restaurant is located on a triangular plot skilfully resolved with a Cartesian floor plan. The kitchen area occupies the vertex and the dining room the longest side, covered only by the first-floor volume cantilevered over the car park on the street. The service areas and staircases are located parallel to the interior walls, while the first floor is given over to the chef's kitchen, staff facilities and offices. The building harmoniously combines practically every possible material: a black-painted steel structure, party walls finished in rustic brick and concrete envelopes. The horizontality of the forms recalls the modernist Californian houses of the second half of the twentieth century, while the wooden strips and stretcher frames of the perimeter are reminiscent of the fishermen's huts on the north Peruvian coast, from whose culture the restaurant borrows some of its recipes. Above all, the place is defined by meticulous attention to detail, from the furniture and lighting to the graphic design of the menus and coasters, creating a cheerful and sophisticated atmosphere that has made it one of the most charming restaurants in Lima. This is also true of the chef's first establishment, a mansion on the Calle San Martín in Miraflores, whose walls are decorated with a magnificent collection of contemporary art.

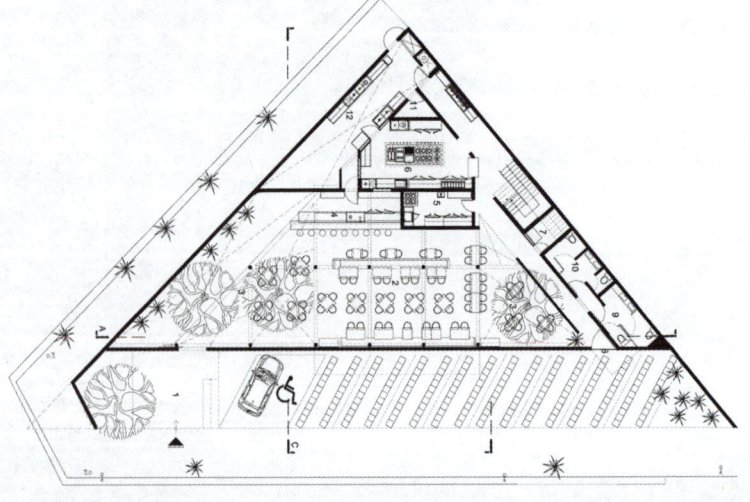

A

Renzo Rebagliati

Malecón de Miraflores

Malecones de la Marina,
Cisneros y de la Reserva,
Miraflores
Municipalidad de Miraflores
Since 1990s

017 A

From San Miguel to Chorrillos, the Lima districts located along the high coastline of the Costa Verde cliffs have responded to their privileged position by creating different promenades or waterfronts at the edge of the sheer drop to the ocean below. The Malecón de Miraflores is probably the finest one. In fact, such is its importance that it has transcended the district scale and become a metropolitan park, visited daily by people from all parts of the city. Its origin dates back to the 1950s, when the Parque Alfredo Salazar first opened. Today, it covers approximately 4 kilometres of the coastline, parallel to the highway, and is articulated by a variety of parks and recreational and sports facilities. A balcony over the ocean, it establishes a constant dialogue with the characteristic topography of the cliffs, narrowing and expanding according to the available space, taking advantage of existing flat areas such as the Parque María Reiche, hugging the precipices and even spilling down the slopes to a certain extent, as in the case of the Parque Itzhak Rabin. In a somewhat less fortunate way, the Villena Bridge closes the gap over the Balta descent. High-rise buildings line the waterfront. Most of them are apartment blocks for high-income families, like the Malecón Yoo by French architect Philippe Starck. These buildings and the cliffs on which they stand form the city's most iconic skyline. In 2021, the 'Friendship Bridge' over the San Martín descent opened, linking the Malecón de Miraflores and Malecón de San Isidro in an awkwardly articulated intervention. Further south, there has been talk of building a footbridge to Barranco over the Armendáriz descent, but it has yet to materialise.

Playas de la Costa Verde

Circuito de playas
(Pedestrian descent via Malecón
28 de Julio 585, Miraflores)

018 A

The paradox of Lima is that while it occupies a privileged location on the edge of the Pacific, it has always turned its back on the ocean. The first important settlements were located far away from the coast in search of safe, fertile areas. The Spanish connected the colonial city to the ocean through the Port of Callao, some 13 kilometres from the centre. In the mid-eighteenth century, European doctors made health resorts fashionable. Chorrillos emerged alongside the Playa de Agua Dulce in 1850, and a few years later the Hotel Internacional in La Punta welcomed the first holidaymakers. At the beginning of the twentieth century, a new resort grew up in Barranco and, in 1935, the baths opened in Miraflores in a building designed by Héctor Velarde, now lost, where the first generations of Peruvian surfers learned their craft. With the exception of La Punta, which is situated at sea level, these resorts were developed on the existing natural descents that span the 60 metres or more that separate the city from the ocean below. Little by little, the city expanded and changed its relationship with the coast. In the 1960s, the architect and future mayor of Miraflores, Ernesto Aramburú, instigated the construction of the Vía Expresa, also known as El Zanjón ('The Gorge'), and promoted the use of the earth removed by civil engineering works to reclaim land from the ocean. A system of breakwaters was built to temper the currents, generating a series of beaches connected by a highway whose name, the Circuito de Playas de la Costa Verde ('Costa Verde Beach Circuit'), stems from plans to cover the cliff slopes with vegetation. Today, the highway includes a boulevard connected to the waterfront

Christian Declercq

Gonzalo Cáceres

A

by flashy pedestrian platforms. Few urban centres of this size offer the chance to bathe and surf practically all year round, and this contact with nature changes the perception of the city. It is advisable to check the degree of difficulty of the breakers before going into the water. Barranquito and Makaha are quiet beaches with instructors and equipment for hire for beginners. Redondo, Los Yuyos, La Pampilla and Punta Roquitas are recommended for experienced surfers, while experts can head to the other side of the Morro Solar headland to La Herradura, where Daniel Arana's magnificent Edificio Las Gaviotas awaits what seems like inevitable ruin. Beyond Paso de la Araña lies Playa La Chira, a spectacular desert area unfortunately affected by a sewage outlet pipe, preventing its use. The critic Reyner Banham once talked about surfing as a generator of urban culture and the attendant combination of sport and modernity. Looking at postcards of Malibu from the 1950s, with its rocky cliffs and desert landscape, it is impossible not to think of Lima and the potential offered by its relationship with the ocean. The Costa Verde now requires an ambitious project that prioritises pedestrians and improves access, vegetation and the beach infrastructure. It is the city's great challenge on the horizon, complicated by the fact that each district has authority over its own stretch of the coastline. Fast vehicular traffic is incompatible with what should be the Lima's finest public space.

Gonzalo Cáceres

View of Playa La Herradura

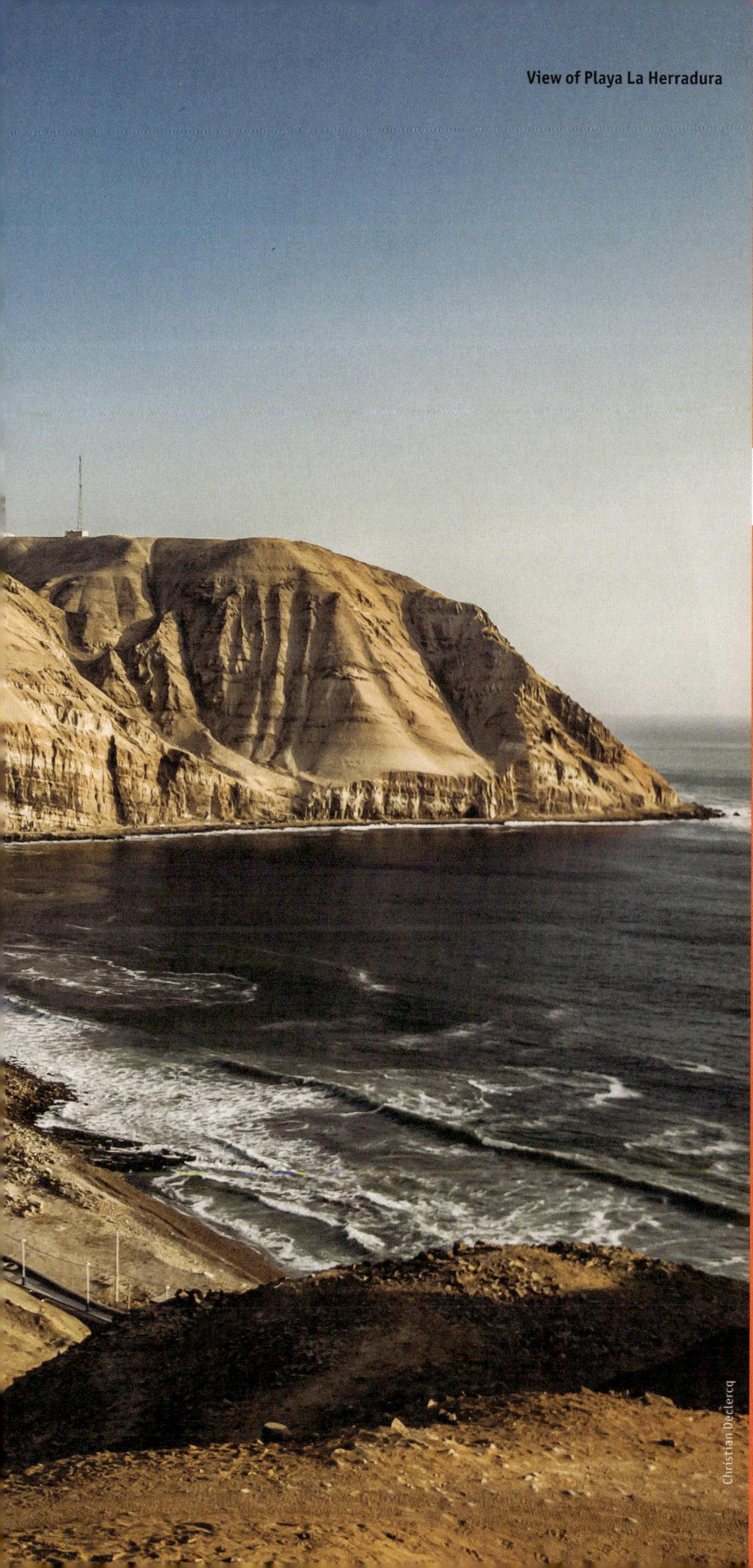

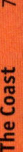

Christian Declercq

A

Renzo Rebagliati

Bajada de baños
Barranco
Early 20th century

019 A

The cliffs along the Costa Verde – the natural boundary between the city and the ocean – contain a series of ravines that span the 60-metre drop and which for centuries have provided the residents with access to the shore. As the virtues of sun and sea began to be extolled in the nineteenth century, resorts grew up around some of these ravines, which soon came to be known as *bajadas de baños*, or 'bathing descents.' The one in Miraflores, now called Bajada Balta, has become an important artery for vehicular traffic. In 1934, Héctor Velarde built changing rooms and toilet facilities at the foot of the *bajada*, and although now lost, the building was a forerunner of the Peruvian modernist movement. The resort that emerged around the Chorrillos 'bathing descent' had a distinct English style, with handsome constructions and an elegant waterfront. Destroyed in 1881 during the Chilean invasion, it was reconstructed but disappeared for good as a result of the 1940 earthquake. Unlike the previous descents, the Barranco *bajada de baños* has preserved the human scale and pedestrian nature of its origins. Stone-paved and surrounded by colourful vegetation, the start of the descent on Jirón Domeyer is easily missed. After crossing the Avenida Grau, it opens onto an area of green terraces crowned by the dilapidated silhouette of the church of La Ermita. Beyond the Puente de los Suspiros that has spanned the gorge since the nineteenth century, the path narrows and becomes steeper in its descent to the ocean. Terraces, viewpoints and secondary access steps flank both sides, as well as old constructions made of wood and *quincha*. Most notable among these are the rows of narrow republican ranch houses with porches and balustrades. Initially used by fishermen to reach the ocean, the ravine experienced its heyday in the 1920s when it connected the village of Barranco to the bathing facilities located at its foot. Today, it offers one of the most iconic images of this bohemian district.

Instituto Francés de Estudios Andinos

Jirón Batalla de Junín 314, Barranco
José Bauer, Augusto Román, Enrique Santillana
2022

020 A

Of all the historical typologies of architecture in Lima, the ranches and mansions from the republican period, found in Ancón, La Punta, El Cercado, Pueblo Libre, Barranco and Chorrillos, perhaps have the closest connection to contemporary architecture. The reason these houses have survived in such good condition is their earthquake resistance, since timber frames have a high tolerance to movement. Their structural and decorative elements adopt a vernacular industrial modulation, resulting in buildings with a marked lightweight appearance. They also adapt admirably to the city's humidity and mild temperatures, with courtyards, galleries, latticework and *teatina* skylights regulating the exposure to sunlight and creating cross ventilation to generate comfortable, luminous and very attractive spaces. All of these elements, in their updated versions, are present in this work, the headquarters of a French cooperation institution that has hosted research fellows and scientific activities for more than 70 years. The complex is composed of a monumental mansion, refurbished to accommodate administrative offices, a bookshop and a café, and a new two-storey pavilion that

All photos: Juan Solado. Courtesy of Roman Bauer Arquitectos houses a library and research offices, erected behind a courtyard on a very narrow plot. The new building is formed by a concrete base on which the wooden structure rests, post-tensioned with steel cables. This structure supports a series of stretcher frames filled with *quincha*, a local traditional building system based on reeds and clay that provides good thermal insulation and is applied here in a refined manner rather than reproducing the rustic imperfection of the old building methods. One of the standout features is the double-height reading room with overhead lighting, designed to capture the best hours of sunlight but also to reset the building every night as the breeze from the ocean, situated just a few metres away, closes the passive cooling circle.

A

Taller de cerámica

Calle Manco Capac 269,
Barranco
Michelle Llona, Rafael Zamora
2015

This small building in Barranco accommodates a production and sales programme for handmade pottery. It includes a kiln, a workshop, a display area, a storeroom and offices spread across a concrete porticoed structure with two storeys and a basement, on a plot 30 metres deep and just 6 metres wide. The envelope has subtle nods to the architecture of the republican ranch houses in the district: the 1.2-metre-deep balconies on the façade, the wooden shutters behind the window frames, and the longitudinal *teatina* skylight that illuminates and ventilates the main space, which is double-height and spanned by a steel walkway suspended from the ceiling on circular-section braces. The interior finishes, such as the white terrazzo floor tiles with black flecks, exposed concrete walls (sometimes painted over in white), steel and wooden rails and light, modular furniture, harmonise beautifully with the ceramics on display. An aesthetic world associated with the desert culture has dominated Peruvian architecture in the last two decades, with works of indisputable quality that embrace a minimalist, abstract and monochromatic materiality that manages to be both brutalist and refined at the same time. It is this aesthetic that we see here, enriched in line with the interior design practised by the latest generation of Lima architects, more attuned to the colours and textures of the mountains and rainforest. The result is more Baroque yet more contemporary.

Michelle Llona

Michelle Llona

Billy Hare. Courtesy of Mario Lara Arquitectos

Edificio de viviendas

022 A

Calle Bresciani 100,
Barranco
Mario Lara
1990

In recent decades, Mario Lara
has produced architecture with
a distinctly recognisable style, combining simplified classical ornaments
with brightly-coloured façades. This
composition, combined with the skilful
distribution of the apartments in line with
local uses and meticulous landscaping
and lighting, recreates the same atmosphere of nineteenth-century architecture that he has reproduced to great
acclaim in Lima's wealthier districts.
The Avenida Pedro de Osma, a tree-lined
boulevard that begins at the district's
Plaza de Armas, is flanked on the right
by a series of passages that make for
a pleasant stroll perpendicular to the
ocean. At the end of the Calle Bresciani,
overlooking the Pacific, we find Lara's
most published and perhaps finest

work. A volume over 60 metres wide is divided into four units with different forms, finishes and accesses, creating the visual effect of small independent buildings. The construction is simple but the geometry is complex, with setbacks and terraces that culminate in a turret adorned with chapiters and a bevelled-edge cornice, steel rails, façade appliques, tropical vegetation and classical furniture that evokes the feel of a belvedere. A cheerful yet nostalgic building, it contains all the hallmarks of this prolific architect whose unique style chimes with the tastes of well-to-do society. The layout of vintage paving, the use of bright colours for window frames and, above all, a brilliant command of the *atrezzo* – awnings, pergolas, upholstery, garlands, sculptures, crests, urns, potted plants and fountains – all create a unique atmosphere, attracting the subconscious gaze and echoing a recognisable bygone era.

Billy Hare. Courtesy of Mario Lara Arquitectos

Blue façade of the building

Edi Hirose, courtesy of Rafael Freyre

A

Restaurante Central

Avenida Pedro de Osma 301,
Barranco
Rafael Freyre
2018

 023 A

Peruvian cuisine is a fusion of two worlds. On one hand, it is characterised by a strong emphasis on fish and seafood, of coastal origin and Japanese influence, often prepared by chefs trained at international schools and restaurants; on the other, it draws on the agricultural world of the provinces, with fruit and vegetables grown in the deserts, mountains and rainforests of a country which, to quote Ferran Adrià, is the closest thing to paradise on earth. These ingredients have given rise to world-class restaurants in Lima, including the fine example of Central, a veritable ecosystem in itself where everything blends to perfection – so much so that one cannot help but wonder if Virgilio Martínez is only a chef. In any case, his restaurant has won more awards than any other in the city. His kitchen is a laboratory and his work a meticulous study of food and nature, but above all, of beauty. The colours and harmony of his compositions are so rich and the identification with the country's textures so immediate that it seems fair to describe his menu as the ultimate aesthetic version of Peru. His dishes are like

César del Rio. Courtesy of Central Restaurante

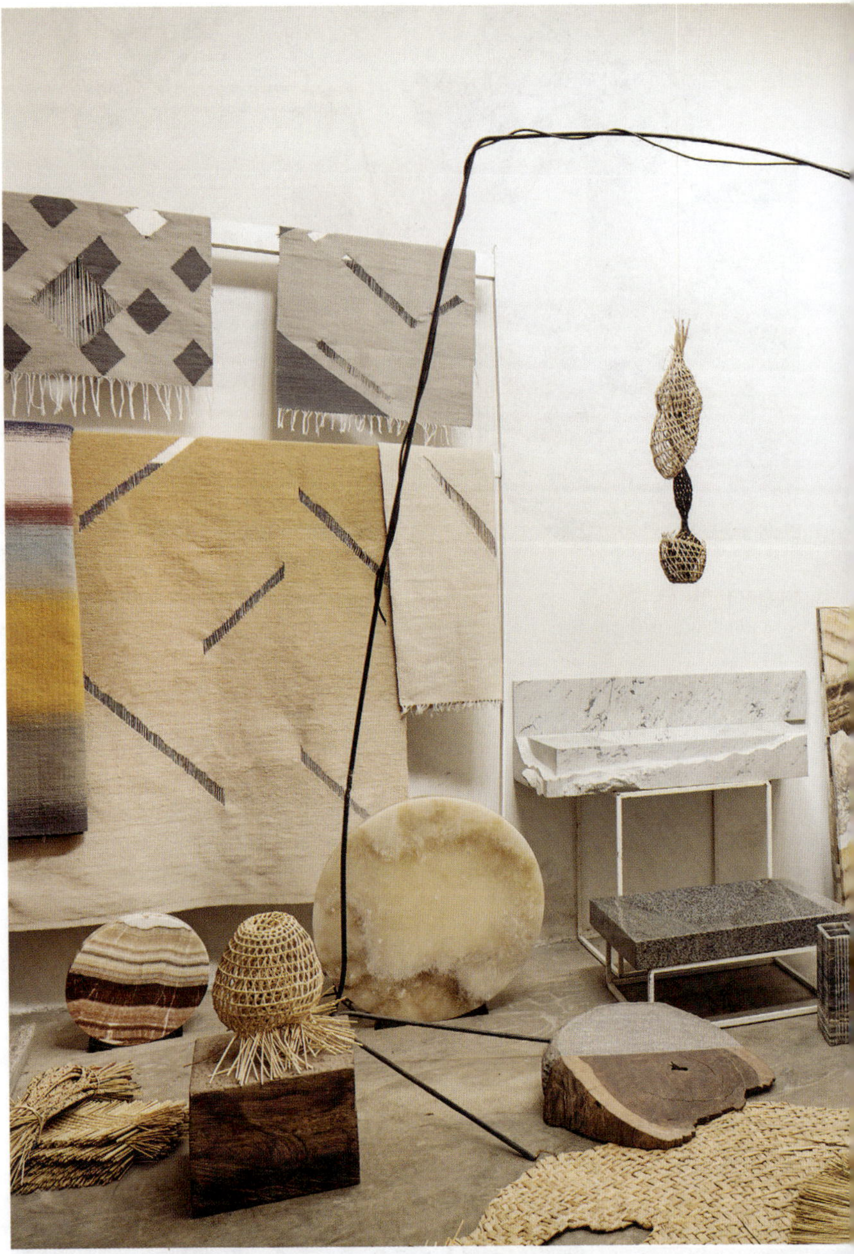

Rafael Freyre's workshop

Furniture

Juan Pablo Murrugarra. Courtesy of Rafael Freyre

the still lifes of Francisco de Zurbarán splashed with the colours of Hieronymus Bosch. Constructed from organic products grown in their own vegetable garden and inorganic materials from the surrounding landscape, they represent the cornucopia of Peru, filled with fruits of paradise, gnarled mushrooms, slippery molluscs and root tubers with traces of straw and soil. Rafael Freyre – architect, actor and designer – and artist Ana Teresa Barboza have framed these compositions with hand-crafted materials. Working together with stonemasons, blacksmiths, potters and weavers, they help elevate traditional handicraft to another level. In 2018, Central relocated to the premises formerly occupied by the Asociación Cultural Túpac Amaru in the Barranco district. The project preserved the existing three-storey structure but reinforced it to withstand the loads of an intensive programme in which the dining areas are but a small fraction of the overall floor space. Pavilions were added in the garden, which includes parking areas

Interior view of the restaurant

and, as one would expect, picturesque winding paths. The interior is a succession of 'servant' and 'served' spaces, separated by glass walls that offer diners a glimpse of the activity in the kitchens, pantries and laboratories. The building is a showcase of natural materials: Arequipan volcanic stone, Andean travertine, onyx from Ayacucho and Huaraz, clay-rich adobe, copper and bronze metalwork, tropical wood from Madre de Dios and animal-fibre textiles. These not only appear on the façade but also in the furniture, tableware and cutlery, integral parts of a design project that encompasses every scale. But the building itself is only the public face of a much larger project that comprises three restaurants in Lima (Central, Kjolle and Mayoy) and one in Cusco (Mil Centro), run by Virgilio and Pía León. In addition, the Mater Iniciativa organisation, led by Malena Martínez, brings together a team of archaeologists, anthropologists, geographers, biologists, nutritionists, engineers, designers and artists who conduct expeditions in the rainforest and produce exquisite nature publications that recall the curiosity and ambition of Alexander von Humbolt.

Palacete de Osma

Avenida Pedro de Osma 421,
Barranco
Santiago Basurco
1908

A

The Palacete de Osma was built in 1906 as the summer residence of the Osma family. At the time, republican ranch houses – light, adjoining structures with a front porch and a floor plan composed of concatenated spaces – were giving way to constructions surrounded by gardens, with load-bearing walls and ornate façades. In 1948, the owner started exhibiting his collection of viceregal art to visitors by appointment, an activity which the family's heirs continued intermittently until the mansion officially opened as a museum in 1987. The building had already been declared a national monument in 1980 and refurbished by the firm Cooper Graña Nicolini Arquitectos in 1983, leading to the removal of some secondary constructions and the consolidation of the current layout. Since then, it has become a cherished work of Barranco architecture, perhaps because of its eclecticism but also undoubtedly because of its pavilion-style quality, with the main volume set back from the street and another building at the rear that was used as a banqueting or events hall. Both volumes are raised half a storey above the gardens that are planted with exuberant tropical vegetation. The floor plan is organised around an axis of symmetry, with the main block accommodating two symmetrical corridors leading to a series of awkwardly articulated spaces. The rear volume, which has a more flexible and modern distribution, is connected to the garden by a double flight of steps and has a more austere decorative programme, with wooden shutters at the arched windows lending lightness to the overall appearance. In 2016, a competition was launched to extend the facilities with a series of cultural spaces and a hotel on the adjacent plot. A team formed by Nómena Arquitectos and Jaime Lecca won the contract with a project that included a series of four-storey buildings with façades modulated by wood and glass. As of the date of publication, construction has not yet commenced.

Museo Nacional

Antigua Panamericana Sur 80,
Lurín
Alexia León, Lucho Marcial
2021

025 A

In 2014, the Ministry of Culture launched a competition to design the building for an institution whose mission was to preserve, restore and exhibit more than 50,000 objects from the nation's historical heritage and serve as the flagship for a national network of state museums. The plot chosen was located in the desert south of Lima near the Temple of the Sun, opposite a wetland with views of the Pacific Ocean and the Pachacamac Islands and at the intersection of Villa El Salvador, Villa María del Triunfo and Lurín, three districts with a combined population of more than a million inhabitants and hardly any cultural facilities. Like all interventions on this scale, it has aroused a certain amount of controversy, not least because of the lack of adequate transport connections: the residents of these nearby districts are only able to reach it by car or will have to wait until the final section of the electric train is built. The challenge which the institution must address is therefore to promote efficiently structured educational and management programmes aimed at encouraging the cultural dynamics that already exist in these emerging communities to ensure the population's appropriation of the infrastructure. The complex has an underground section, located at a lower height than the Temple of the Sun to respect the horizontal perspectives from Villa El Salvador. It is a classical building in terms of its tripartite organisation of the compositional elements: base, peristyle and entablature. A large access plinth connects it to the rocky terrain, resting on foundations that recall those of a medieval castle. Set back from this platform is the square-plan temple with latticework envelopes that echo pre-Columbian architecture while simultaneously generating a highly

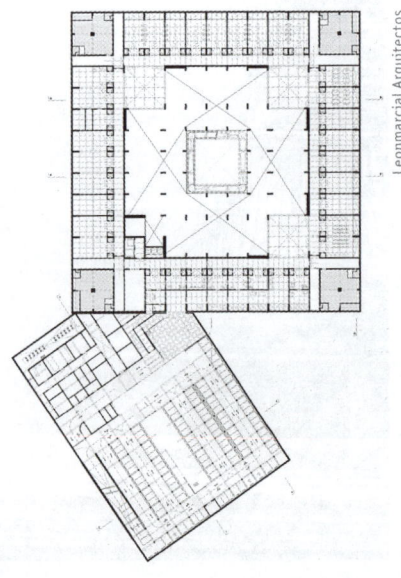

Leonmarcial Arquitectos

All photos: Lucho Marcial

Lucho Marcial

The desert and the Museo Nacional

Lucho Marcial

Façades

Leonmarcial Arquitectos

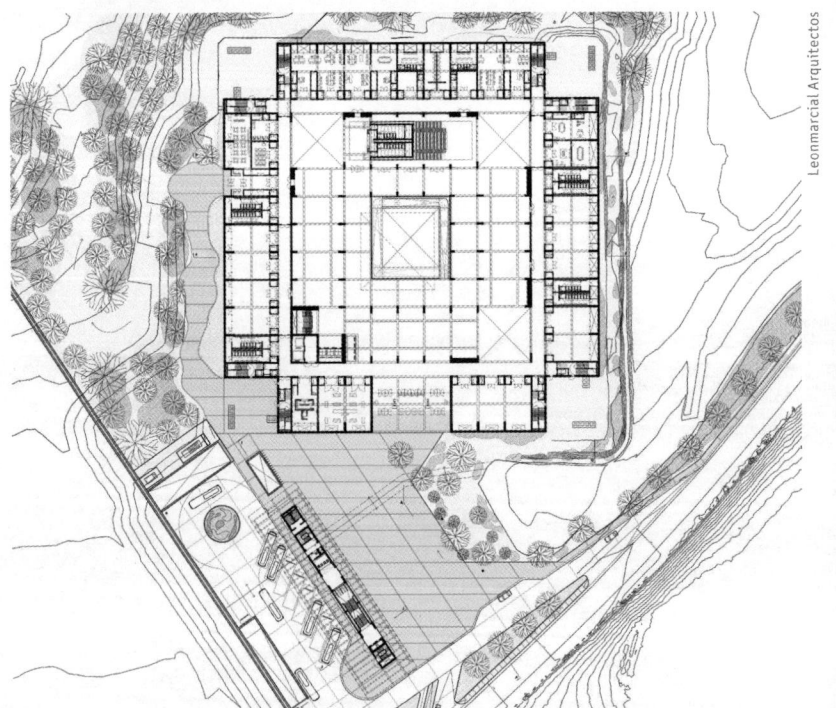

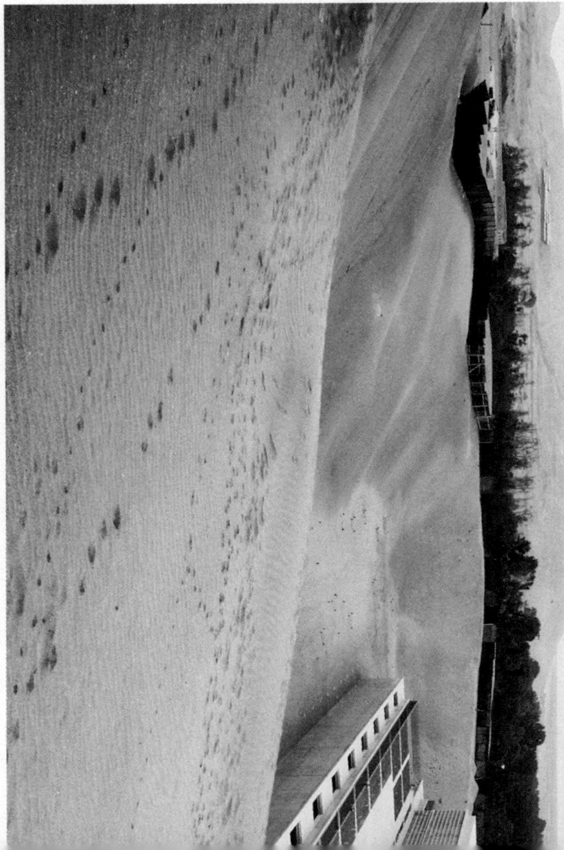

A

The desert, the Museo Nacional and the ocean

contemporary sense of transparency. The finely executed reinforced concrete structure is articulated around a large central space with cathedral-like proportions and overhead lighting modulated by mechanised slats to create penumbral atmospheres for the exhibitions. A long steel ramp climbs around this space to the accessible roof at the end of the itinerary, connecting the museum to the surrounding landscape and highlighting its enormous scale. Also classical is the way in which the floor plan is organised, with symmetry in both directions and four light wells clearly separating the 'servant' and 'served' spaces, which are connected by a corridor that leads seamlessly to the different facilities, freeing the central space from services and evacuation routes. The building is still an infrastructure, but in all likelihood the vegetation designed by Claudia Melgarejo will gradually invade it, humanising the interior courtyards

and the memorable transition spaces between the concrete walls and the rocky desert. The dramatic effect of the light filtering through the latticework and the materiality of the interiors, with red concrete terrazzo floors, subtly coloured rails, wood finishes and glass partitions, form a highly refined base that will undoubtedly be further enriched with museological programmes and new materials and colours, adding layers of complexity to one of the most ambitious buildings ever undertaken in Peru. This is a contemporary temple which, as such, aspires to become a picturesque ruin one day, perhaps discovered by archeologists like the Temple of the Sun. The robust construction will certainly withstand the passage of time beneath the sand, in a dialogue with the future generations to whom these architects have sent a message of order, rationality and beauty.

Museo de Sitio Pachacamac

026 A

Santuario Arqueológico
de Pachacamac, Lurín
Patricia Llosa, Rodolfo Cortegana
2015

Dating back to the fifth century and occupied by different cultures through the ages, the Pachacamac Sanctuary is undoubtedly one of the most important archaeological sites on the Peruvian coast. A museum had been built on the site in the 1960s but soon became obsolete, leading to the launch of a competition to design a new structure. The winning project has been praised in international forums and was a finalist for the 2014/2015 Mies Crown Hall Americas Prize. The new museum, which recounts the sanctuary's important role as a place of pilgrimage in pre-Columbian times, stands on a plot with a gradient of more than 7 metres, covered with long paths adapted to the topography. Streets, ramps and stairways lined by walls converge at a stepped plaza, echoing the elements of pre-Hispanic constructions. The layout includes a pre-existing garden and retaining wall from the old museum. The built programme, divided into a series of exposed concrete volumes, emerges in the interstices in this network of paths, on the different levels dictated by the topography. The systems of ramps used outside the museum continue inside, directing the gaze and framing the views of different points of the sanctuary and the surrounding desert landscape. At the entrance, the building minimises its height and offers practically blind façades, diminishing its presence to avoid competing with the existing constructions. Its full scale is only revealed, and even augmented, when viewed from the stepped plaza at the other end of the plot. The same is true of the slab that forms the esplanade, which almost seems to float over the terrain.

Cristóbal Palma. Courtesy of Llosa Cortegana

Llosa Cortegana

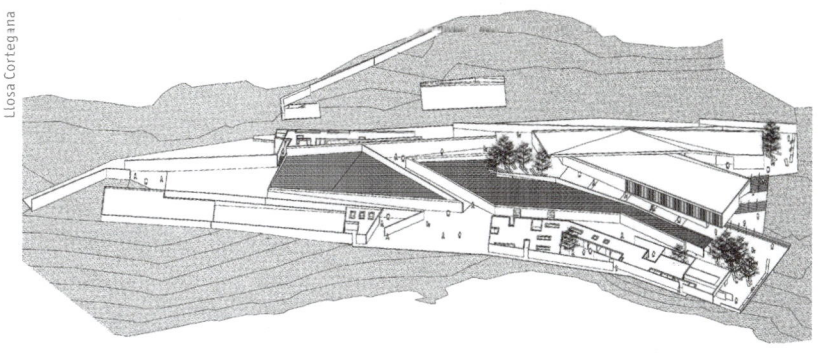

Juan Solano. Courtesy of Llosa Cortegana

Llosa Cortegana

All photos: Museo de Sitio de Pachacamac. Courtesy of Llosa and Cortegana

Santuario Arqueológico de Pachacamac

027 A

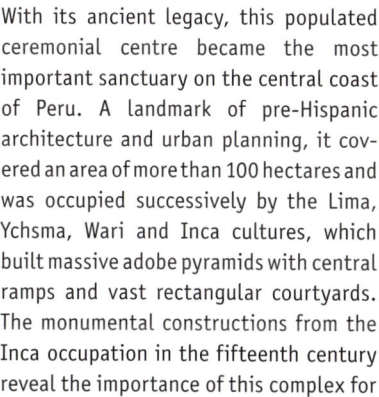

Antigua Carretera Panamericana
Sur Km. 31.5, Lurín
Lima, Ychsma,
Wari and Inca cultures
1st–15th century

With its ancient legacy, this populated ceremonial centre became the most important sanctuary on the central coast of Peru. A landmark of pre-Hispanic architecture and urban planning, it covered an area of more than 100 hectares and was occupied successively by the Lima, Ychsma, Wari and Inca cultures, which built massive adobe pyramids with central ramps and vast rectangular courtyards. The monumental constructions from the Inca occupation in the fifteenth century reveal the importance of this complex for the empire. The most emblematic building is the Temple of the Sun, a centre of worship located in the north-west sector of the site. Raised above the ground and facing the ocean, it is made up of a series of platforms situated at different levels and precisely orientated to worship the solar deity. Other important constructions include the Aqllawasi, where women were trained to serve the nobility, the Tauri Chumbi complex, an elite residence, and the Pilgrim's Plaza, a vast esplanade 320 metres long and 9 metres wide used for public ritual and political activities. An intricate layout of streets and perimeter walls controls the access to these spaces. The Pachacamac idol, a deity related to the earth and earthquakes, once drew pilgrims from all over the Inca Empire; the paths they followed to reach the complex still shape the city today.

A

Casa Ghezzi

Malecón Jahuay, Lote N°5,
Playa Pulpos, Lurín
Juvenal Baracco
1984

028 A

In the 1980s, the exponential growth that Lima had been experiencing started to spread to the beaches south of the city with the developmment of second homes for use in the summer. Juvenal Baracco was put in charge of the urban development of Playa Pulpos and designed some of the houses in the first row that were built on a slope facing the ocean. This one is a meditation on the beachfront holiday home. The main space is a large square terrace where family life, leisure activities and social gatherings take place. A light, permeable roof made of eucalyptus wood and cane protects it from the sun and provides two ceiling heights: 2.1 metres over the circulation area around the perimeter and 5 metres over the central part of the space. The closed programme is located around the terrace, contained in a U-shaped masonry volume that ensures privacy and frames the views. The traditional interior circulation has been eliminated, with the rooms opening directly to the outside. In addition to accommodating a kitchen, a service area, a master bedroom and a living room that doubles up as a guest room, the typological modification continues with a dormitory-style room fitted with bunk beds. Local materials such as reeds and clay were used in the execution, as well as simple building methods. According to the architect, these even included techniques used in shanty towns. All of these aspects, plus the use of colour, the geometry and the volume with autochthonous references, reveal Baracco's interest in architecture with a regional identity. The house was subsequently extended by another similar construction located higher up. More recently, it has undergone alterations that jar with the original *sauvage* spirit, such as the conversion of the sandy slope into an additional access with steps and creeping plants, the incorporation of a small swimming pool and a change of colour. Even so, it remains an iconic work for several generations of Peruvian architects.

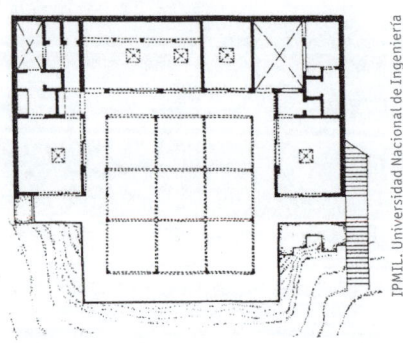

IPMIL. Universidad Nacional de Ingeniería

Casa Santillana

Playa Escondida,
Punta Negra
Enrique Ciriani
1999

029 A

With the development of new holiday home complexes on the coast to the south of Lima, the beach house has become a testing ground for Peruvian architects and the typology most exhibited in international forums. This house, with roots in the modernist movement, became the paradigm for a new architectural type and a benchmark for subsequent projects with similar circumstances. The building is designed as a transparent cube surrounded by a band of concrete that generates different spatial situations in its progression, with open and closed areas, covered and uncovered at different heights, allowing the space to flow horizontally and vertically. As the architect says, the design seeks to 'open the closed spaces and close the open spaces.' The ground level operates as a semi-underground plinth closed to the outside, where the bedroom, service and parking programmes surround an interior courtyard. This void is prolonged vertically and on the next level extends into the transparency of the public areas – living room, dining room, kitchen and porch – which open onto the surrounding landscape. On a third level, floating above the kitchen and dining room, are the master bedroom and the terrace. The meticulous design is replete with details, such as the sliding mirror door in the master bedroom that reflects the ocean, providing an incomparable view from the bed. Such is the delicacy of the project that the house behind it still has a good view of the landscape.

A

Jean-Marie Monthiers. Courtesy of Enrique Ciriani

Jean-Marie Monthiers. Courtesy of Enrique Ciriani

Casa Fernandini

Malecón Santa María,
Santa María del Mar
Walter Weberhofer
1958

Between 1957 and 1960, Walter Weberhofer developed 12 single-family homes at the Santa María beach complex. Some of them have since been demolished but several are still standing. The one he designed for the future mayor of Lima, Ana Fernandini de Naranjo, is undoubtedly the most iconic. Embedded in the hillside of a narrow rocky headland that juts into the ocean, the house is raised several metres above ground level to maximise its views of the bay. It is flanked by two caves that cross the strip of land from one side to the other and through which the waves penetrate, enveloping the construction with the sound of the ocean. A third, higher, hollow connects the back of the house to platforms facing the open sea. The expressive volumetry – symmetrical and star-shaped – is composed of the superimposition of a quadrangular ground level and a triangular top level. The non-alignment of the vertices of the two floor plans generates several terraces with different orientations. The house is accessed by stone steps that wind their way up the rocks to the ground floor, where the large living-dining room with three terraces is located, as well as the kitchen and service areas. On the top floor

are the bedrooms and a fourth terrace. A roof with a striking permeable cantilever forms the crest of this construction, that brings together some of the main features of Weberhofer's architecture, whose plastic expressiveness is based on a profound structural knowledge.

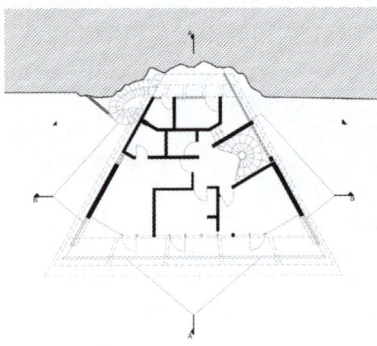

First floor

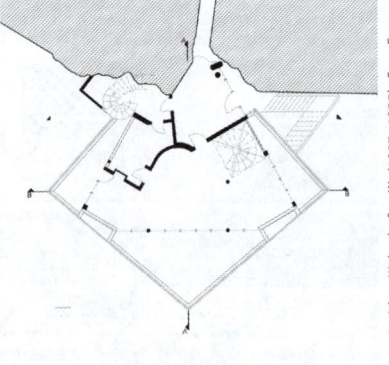

Ground floor

Archive: Weberhofer, W. (1957–1958). Casa Fernandini (Plans). Archive of the Weberhofer family, Lima

A

Club Esmeralda

Avenida Las Sirenas,
Santa María del Mar
Walter Weberhofer
1957

031 A

In his youth, the Peruvian architect Walter Weberhofer worked with Enrique Seoane and was a great admirer of Oscar Niemeyer, whom he once met on a trip. And if the Brazilian architect worked closely with structural engineer Joaquim Cardozo, a fundamental figure in Weberhofer's career was Miguel Bozo. At this sailing club, modernist geometry is dislocated on every scale: pillars, floor slabs, walls, planters and rails are twisted in an expressive display that reveals an extraordinary command of both drawing and building. In order to provide an ocean view, the social area is situated on the highest part of a trapezoidal plot, raised above an entrance that is reached by a ramp. In front of the building, a large salt-water pool opens onto the Pacific Ocean, with a steel-tube awning around the entire perimeter to shade the sun loungers. As well as providing an artificial beach, this area is used for sporting events thanks to a hydraulic system that was quite advanced in its day. Although still in use and in a good state of repair, the building has undergone several alterations, mainly affecting the finishes: some of the paving has been replaced by industrial porcelain tiles, part of the stone cladding has disappeared and the original aluminium carpentry has been replaced by a poorer quality version.

Crist an Santandreu

Casa Lercari

Avenida Las Sirenas Mz. A, Lt. 7,
Santa María del Mar
Walter Weberhofer
1958

032 A

Walter Weberhofer left a series of works in Santa María del Mar that merit some form of comprehensive protection by the public administration. Modernist in style, they have a highly personal expressionistic touch that makes them immediately recognisable. This particular house, still in perfect condition, deserves special attention. Facing the ocean, it is organised around three levels resting on a rock, with a spectacular structure and details such as the steps, aluminium carpentry and finishes that will enthral architecture buffs. On the Calle Miramar, next door to Club Esmeralda, is another building called Las Sirenas, a complex and somewhat deteriorated construction that displays a catalogue of wall solutions, rails and finishes. And on the Santa María waterfront, another outstanding work – Weberhofer's last – is the Edificio Bertolero (2000).

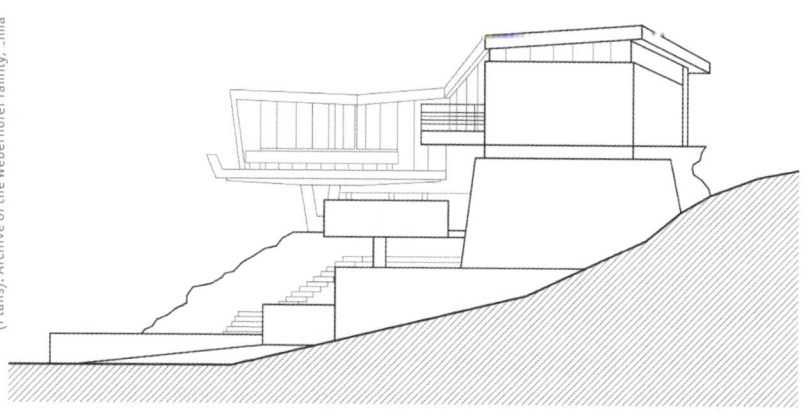

Archive: Weberhofer, W. (1957–1958). Casa Lercari (Plans). Archive of the Weberhofer family, Lima

Leonardo Finotti

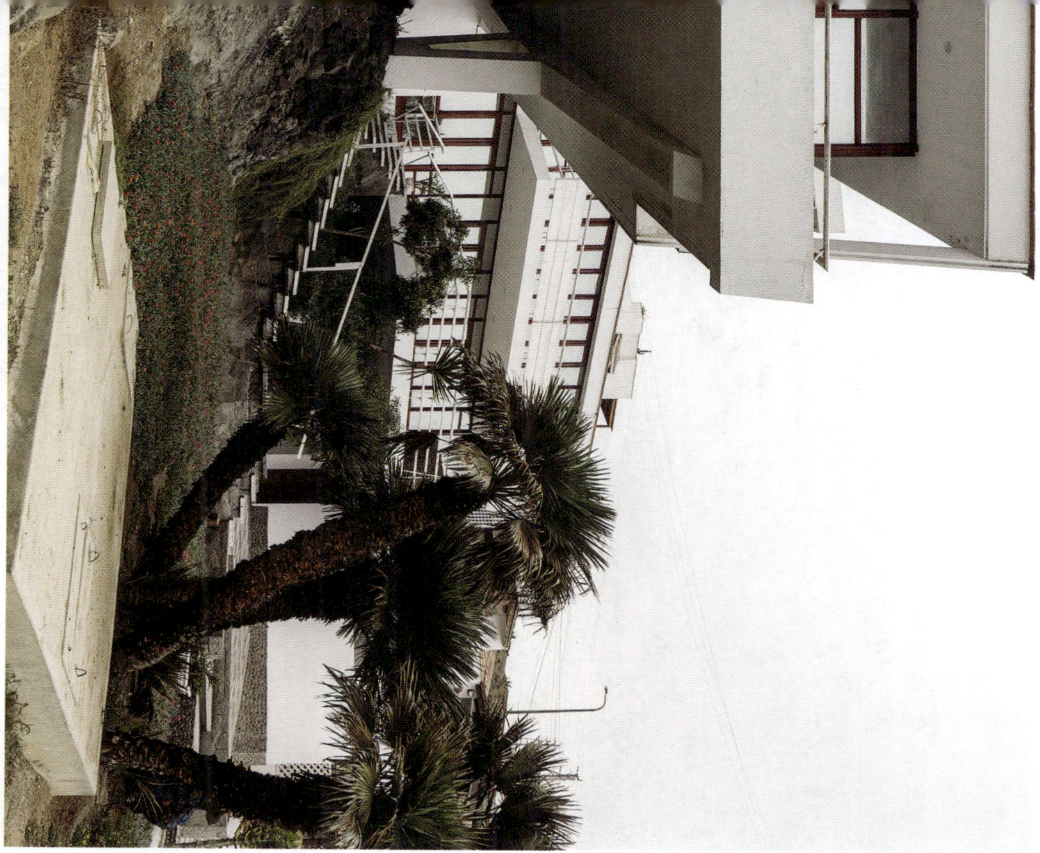

Club de playa La Honda

033 A

Pucusana
Ruth Alvarado, Cynthia Watmough
2004

Scores of beach condominiums have appeared to the south of Lima with the sole aim of achieving maximum occupation of the coast by means of plots for single-family homes without any of the balance between urban planning and landscape that is necessary to add value to this type of development. The building regulations are poorly articulated and have generated typologies such as the beachfront semi-underground, stepped house delimited by retaining walls. The result: visually destroyed coastal landscapes and dark, poorly ventilated homes. However, this coastal condominium has long been a favourite with architects. Like so many other holiday home developments in Peru, it is private with controlled access from the highway. What makes it rare, however, is that it respects the first fringe of the plot, leaving the

coastline intact and placing the buildings at the top of the slope, offering an example in how to inhabit the desert in an attractive way. The old summer houses of the 1950s have given way to multi-family buildings with as many as five storeys in some cases, such as Building H (1996) by Cynthia Watmough and Alfredo Benavides that won the Hexágono de Oro and is formed by stepped volumes that recall the Spanish architecture on the Mediterranean coast, and the La Honda building that Ruth Alvarado designed in 2007, which stands on an irregular plot and has an interior garden. The beach club nestles at the bottom of the slope on the left-hand side of the cove with a series of curved walls that hug the coastline to form a swimming pool, terrace and promenade around one of the dark rocky outcrops that delimit the beach, with bathing platforms that afford some of the most stunning views of the coastal desert. It received an honorary mention at the fourteenth Pan-American Architecture Biennial (2004).

Asia

Panamericana Sur km 92–102
Asia, Cañete
1990s

034 A

Plataforma Urbana

Located in the heart of the coastal desert, in Cañete province, Playa Asia has become a type of summer satellite town for Lima's wealthiest and a paradigm for multiple real estate initiatives. Families had been camping on weekends at the beach, near a bull-breeding ranch, since the 1960s. Some time later, Las Palmas was formed and developments spread from the 1990s onwards. The residential complexes sit side by side for several kilometres along the coast. They are conceived as private clubs with the social ties between the partners playing an important role. Single-family homes and community facilities form an oceanfront ecosystem, hidden away from the hustle and bustle of the city. Each condominium is bounded by walls and gates with entry control, which has been criticised for obstructing the public access to the coast. On the waterfront, a more or less continuous promenade connects the developments and allows the residents to mingle. On the sand, the property is defined by the beach umbrellas, each of which is linked to a house. The architecture follows a constant pattern of white low-rise houses with a rooftop terrace, surrounded by lawns and a system of neat, clearly marked paths. Even so, this has not prevented the construction of some outstanding single-family projects. Asia and other beaches of the south have been the setting for several memorable works of recent Peruvian architecture, such as the house at Playa Bonita (Alexia León, 1996), the Casa Gato (Martín Dulanto, 2014), the house on the golf course (David Mutal, 2020) and the house in Totoritas (Llosa and Cortegana, 2018). A major commercial hub that only operates in summer has grown up alongside the developments, although it does not only serve the holidaymakers. Every season, the vibrant nightlife makes it the place to be, attracting revellers from all over the city and transforming it into a metropolitan centre of gravity.

Juan Carlos Martinat, from the Naturaleza Publicitaria series, 2006

South Pan-American Highway to Asia

Casa Totoritas (Llosa Cortegana)

Juan Solano. Courtesy of Llosa and Cortegana

Casa Gato (Martín Dulanto)

Juan Solano. Courtesy of Martín Dulanto

Casa Equis

Playa La Escondida, Cañete
Sandra Barclay,
Jean Pierre Crousse
2003

035 A

This house is embedded deep within its plot like a ruin discovered by archaeologists. Its walls could easily be mistaken for the remains of one of the pre-Inca civilisations that once populated the coast of Peru. As a concrete dug-out camouflaged with the colours of the hill, it offers a valuable lesson in how to inhabit the desert. The floor plan is organised for outdoor living but it is the section that reveals the real logic behind this building: a platform equipped only with the necessary elements to provide protection from the wind and the sun, beneath which are four bedrooms accessed by lateral stairs and a corridor. Although it has the scale of a refuge, the manner in which it appropriates the views of the landscape makes it seem larger than it actually is. Nothing is superfluous here, which perhaps explains why it seems so comfortable to live in. The interior is just a room with a sofa and a fireplace protected by walls that blend tones of ochre, pink and white in the style of Luis Barragán, extended with shaded spaces covered by taut pieces of simple canvas. It makes no concessions to social conventions, nor does it pretend to be a comfortable beach apartment. Contemplating the house, one wonders whether there is really any need for anything else other than contact with the ocean, rocks and sun. The walls of its swimming pool are painted ocean blue and includes a glass element that has caught the attention of the publishing world thanks to a photograph that echoes Nirvana's classic *Nevermind* album cover: iconoclastic hedonism for what is no less than the most published house in the history of Peru.

A

Other Works of Interest

A01 Iglesia de Ancón
Calle Abtao, Ancón
Enrique Seoane
1944

A02 Camino Inca Costero
Parque Ecológico Nacional Antonio
Raimondi, Panamericana Norte, Ancón
Inca Culture
15th century

A03 Ciudad Satélite Santa Rosa
Avenidas Tomás Valle y Pacasmayo,
El Callao
Diego La Rosa, Oscar Borasino,
Manuel Ferreyra, Juan Gutiérrez,
Reynaldo Ledgard, Hugo Romero
1985

A04 Embarcadero Plaza Miguel Grau
Plaza Miguel Grau, El Callao
1897

A05 Puericultorio Pérez Araníbar
Avenida del Ejército 650,
Magdalena del Mar
Rafael Marquina, Werner Lange
1929

A06 Restaurante Limaná
Avenida del Ejército 2011, San Isidro
Sandra Barclay, Jean Pierre Crousse
2020

A07 Plaza San Francisco
Barranco
1895

A08 Palacete Sousa
Jirón Colón 103, Barranco
Eleuterio Alfoy, Gil Márquez
1917

A09 Rancho Esteban Ríos
Avenida Almirante Miguel Grau 428,
Barranco
Hugo Behr
1916

A10 Chifa Chung Yion
Calle Unión 126, Barranco
1923

A11 Restaurante Siete
Jirón Domeyer 260, Barranco
2019

A12 Restaurante Mérito
Jirón 28 de Julio 206, Barranco
Ghezzi Novak (Arturo Ghezzi, Gustavo
Ghezzi), Blanco (Pamela Remy)
2018

A13 Casa Polón Valdés
Jirón 28 de Julio, 439, Barranco
Óscar Borasino
2015

A14 MATE Museo Mario Testino
Avenida Pedro de Osma 409, Barranco
Mateo Pagano, Augusto de Cossio
1898, 2012

A15 Club Regatas de Lima
Avenida Chachi Dibós 1201,
Chorrillos
Manuel Valega Sayán
1958

A16 Edificio Las Gaviotas
Avenida Presidente Billinghurst,
Playa la Herradura, Chorrillos
Daniel Arana Ríos
1960

A17 Edificio Las Sirenas
Avenida Las Sirenas Mz. A, Lt. 7,
Santa María del Mar
Walter Weberhofer
1955

Right: Restaurante Mérito (Ghezzi Novak + Blanco)

Iva - Salinero. Courtesy of Ghezzi Novak

A

Pan-American and Central Highway

B

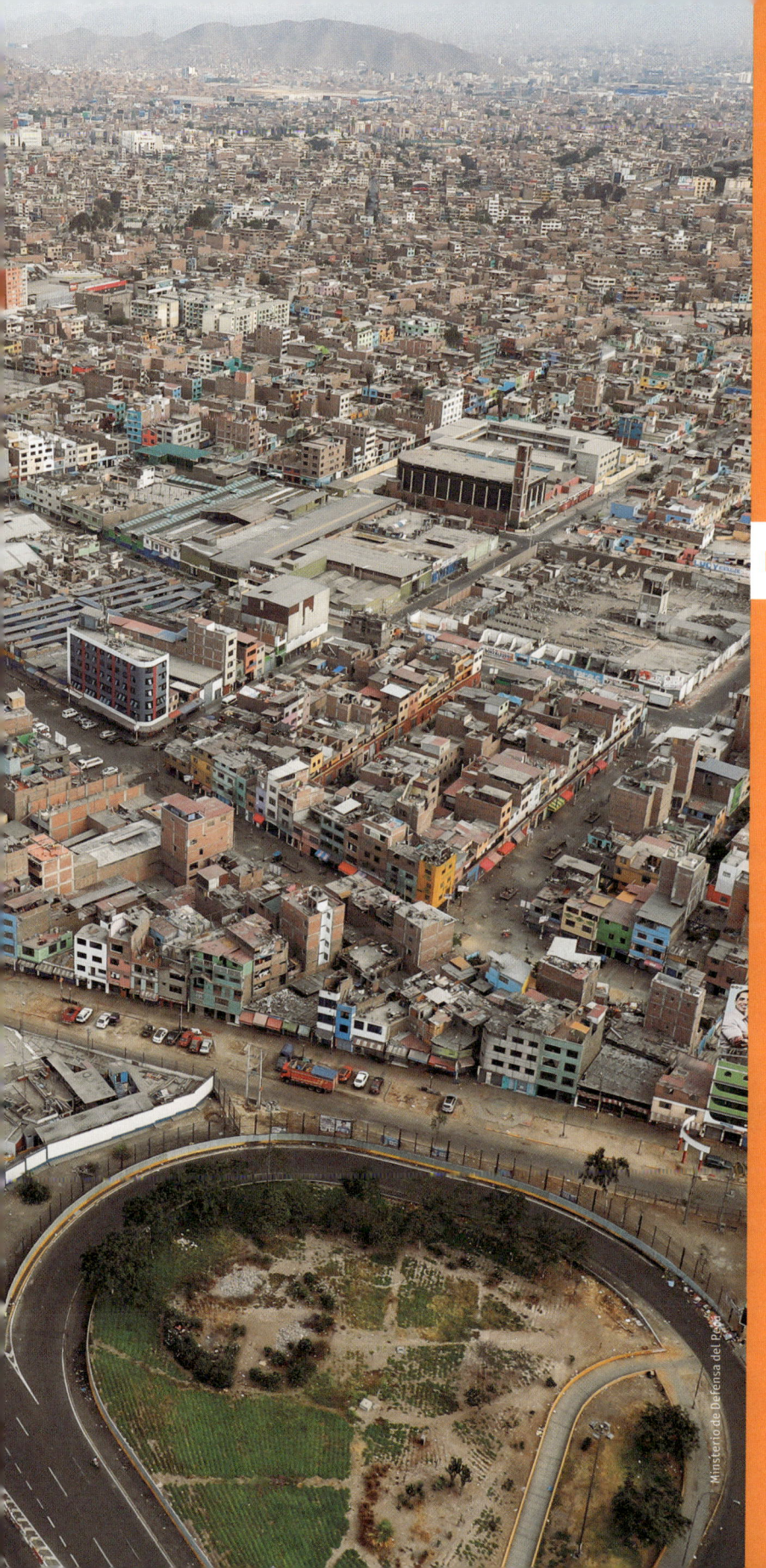

B

Ministerio de Defensa del Perú

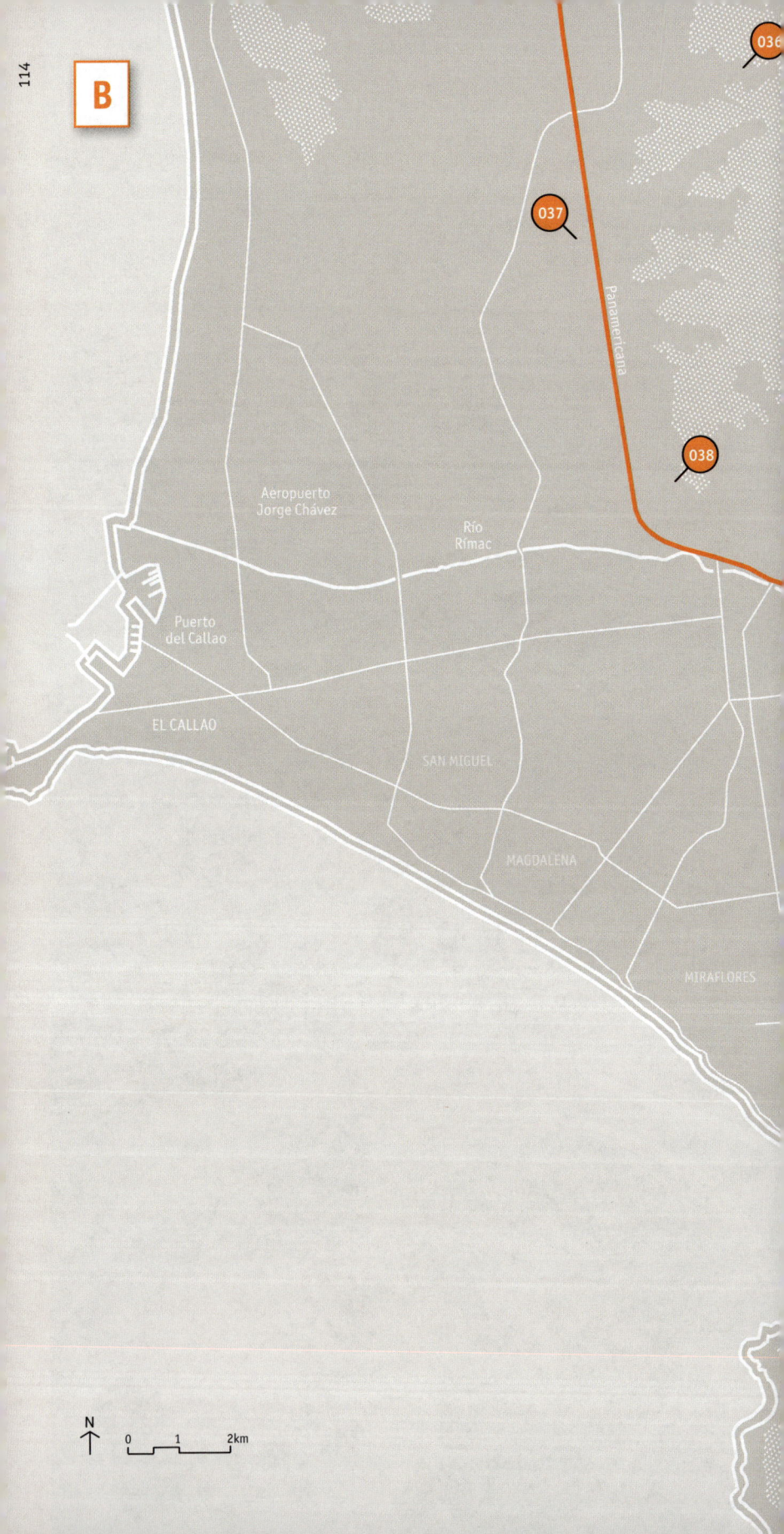

B

036

037

038

Panamericana

Aeropuerto
Jorge Chávez

Río
Rímac

Puerto
del Callao

EL CALLAO

SAN MIGUEL

MAGDALENA

MIRAFLORES

N

0   1   2km

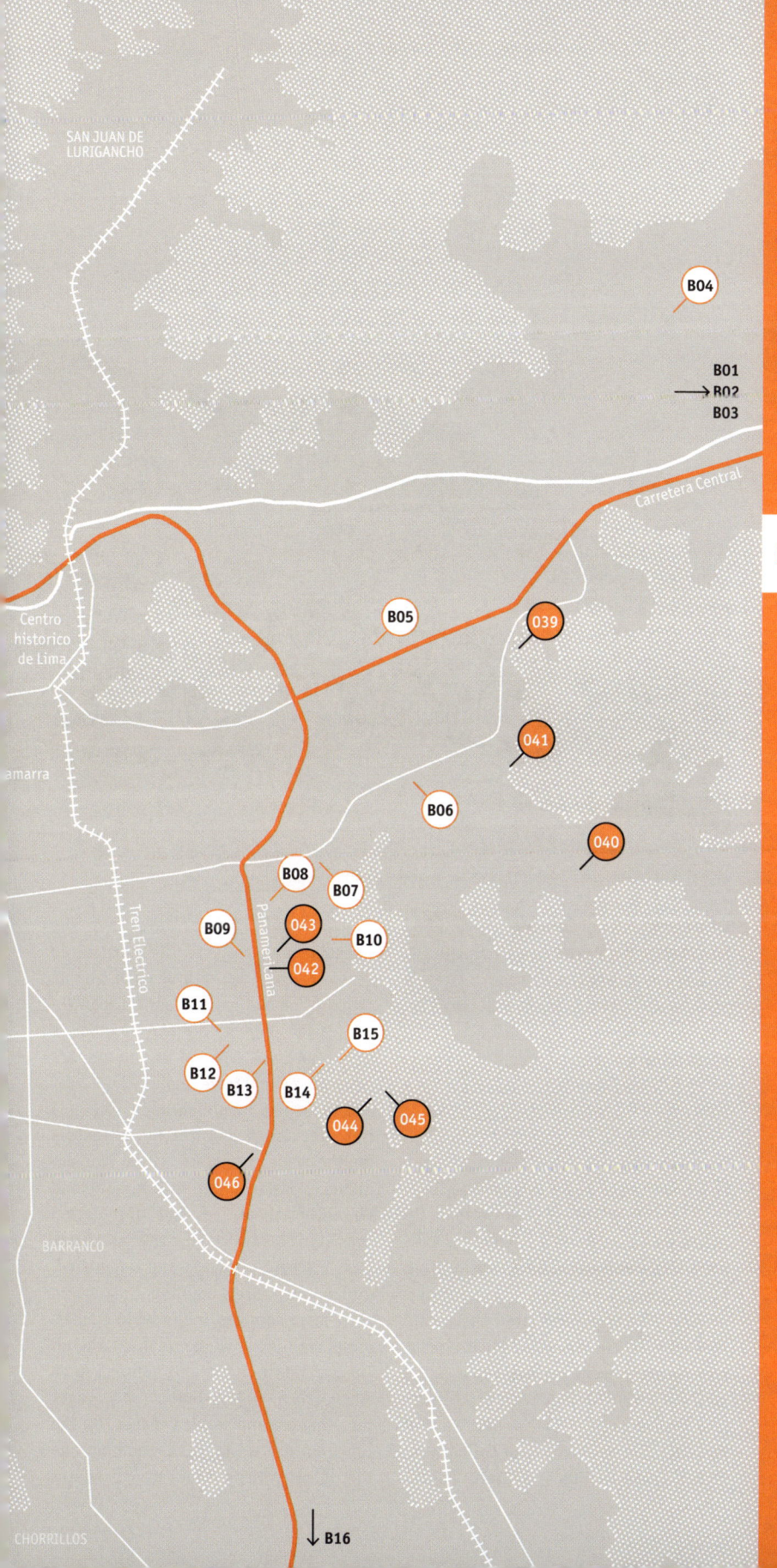

SAN JUAN DE
LURIGANCHO

B04

B01
B02
B03

Carretera Central

Centro
historico
de Lima

B05

039

amarra

041

B06

040

B08
B07

Tren Electrico

B09

043

Panamericana

B10

042

B11

B15

B12

B14

B13

044

045

046

BARRANCO

CHORRILLOS

B16

Local comunal del Comedor San Martín del Once

036 B

Parque Tahuantinsuyo, Comas
Javier Vera, Eleazar Cuadros,
Paula Villar, Ezequiel Collantes,
David Fontcuberta,
María Eugenia Lacarra
2017

Every year since 2002, La Balanza, a neighbourhood at the heart of informal Lima, celebrates the Festival Internacional de Teatro en Calles Abiertas (FITECA), with activities centred around the Parque Tahuantinsuyo. Founded when a group of local artists appropriated the public space due to the lack of adequate infrastructure, the event has emerged as a catalyst for an urban and social regeneration that has attracted the interest and participation of a variety of collectives, including the architects of CITIO (Ciudad Transdisciplinar), who developed the Fitekantropus project. The community centre is the first intervention of this cooperative and experimental urban regeneration project, the aim of which is to extend the awareness of public space generated by FITECA to the whole year and the whole neighbourhood. The idea is to provide a physical infrastructure for the social transformations that are taking place in order to highlight and strengthen them. This first intervention consisted of transforming the San Martín soup kitchen, decaying and underused, into a two-storey building that would offer more services and provide a meeting place for the whole neighbourhood. The ground floor contains a dining room and kitchen, plus a living room, vegetable garden and service spaces. On the top floor are a library, a bedroom and the large volume that accommodates

Eleazar Cuadros

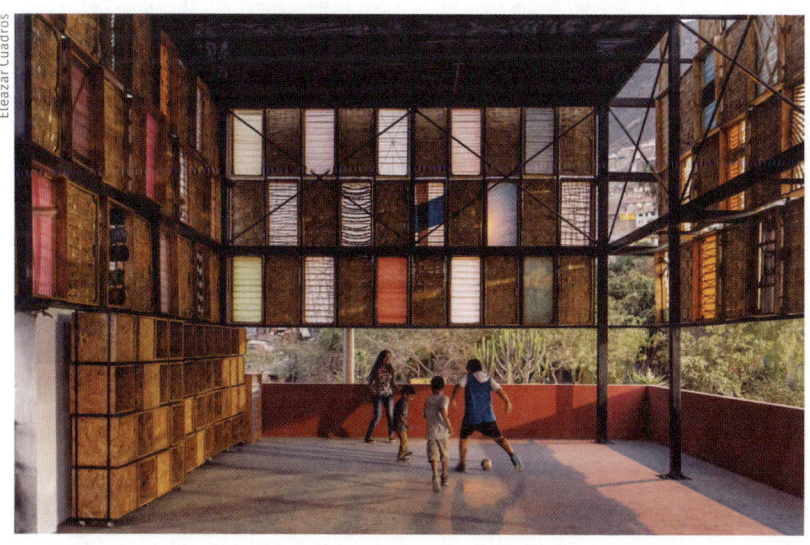

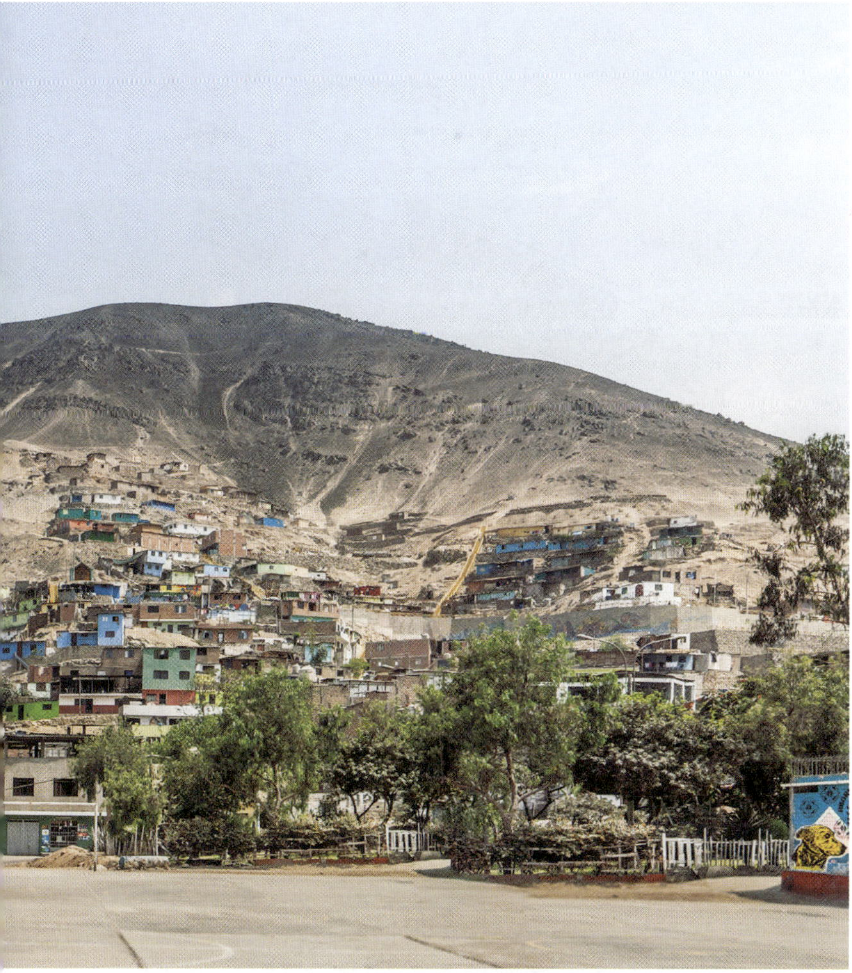

a multipurpose hall, the height of which is dictated by the needs of the theatre workshops. The external wall of this volume – a colourful collage of panels built by local residents after the funding dried up – lends the community centre its characteristic image and makes it the landmark of a new urban centrality.

Eleazar Cuadros

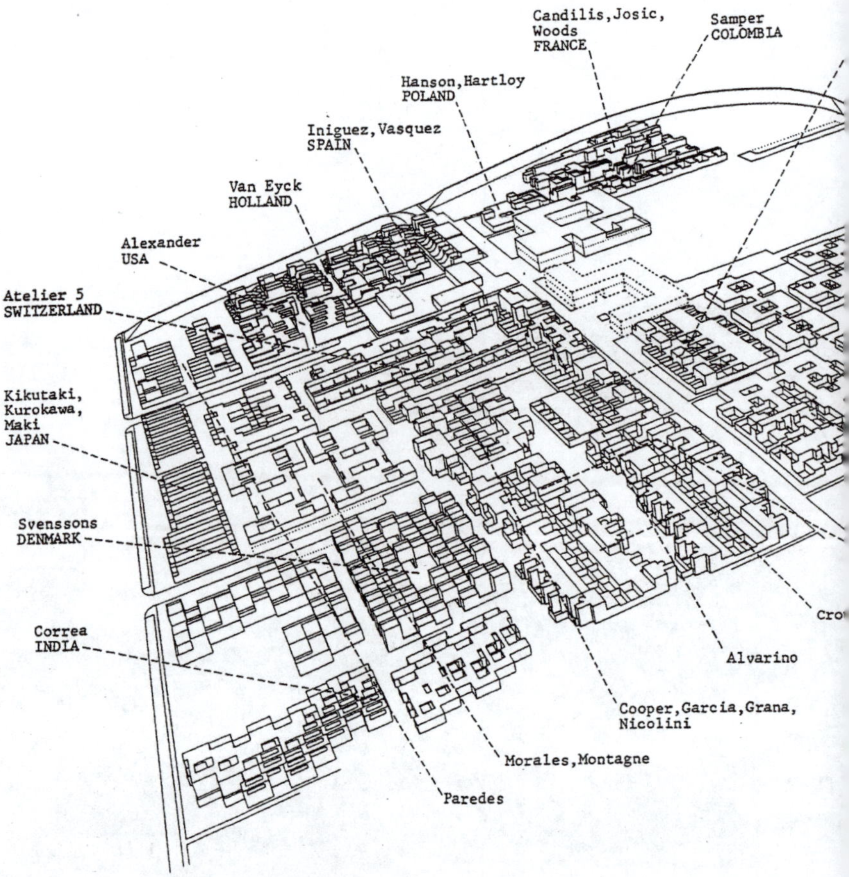

Candilis,Josic,
Woods
FRANCE

Samper
COLOMBIA

Hanson,Hartloy
POLAND

Iniguez,Vasquez
SPAIN

Van Eyck
HOLLAND

Alexander
USA

Atelier 5
SWITZERLAND

Kikutaki,
Kurokawa,
Maki
JAPAN

Svenssons
DENMARK

Correa
INDIA

Cro

Alvarino

Cooper,García,Grana,
Nicolini

Morales,Montagne

Paredes

Proyecto Experimental de Vivienda PREVI

037 B

Panamericana Norte km8,
Los Olivos
Peter Land (Director)
James Stirling; Knud Svensson;
Esguerra, Sáenz, Urdaneta, Samper;
Atelier 5 (Fritz, Gerber, Hesterberg,
Hostettler, Pini); Toivo Corhonen;
Herbert Ohl ; Charles Correa; Maki,
Kikutake, Kurokawa; Vázquez,
Íñiguez; Hansen, Hatloy;
Aldo van Eyck; Candilis, Josic,
Woods; Christoper Alexander; Alvariño,
Guzmán; Ernesto Paredes; Miró Quesada,
Williams, Núñez; Günther, Seminario;
Morales, Montagne; Juan Reiser;
Orrego, González; Vier, Zanelli;
Vella, Bentín, Quiñones, Takahashi;
Llanos, Mazzarri; Cooper, García Bryce,
Graña, Nicolini; Chaparro, Ramírez,
Smirnoff, Wyszkowski;
Crousse, Páez, Pérez León
1966–1978

In his research on this landmark international project, Sharif Kahatt recounts the circumstances in which it came about. In the 1930s, prompted by the rapid growth of Lima's population, the government started developing residential projects for the working class. However, the consensus reached by the mid-1950s was that, while the efforts deployed had been considerable, they were still far too insufficient to address mass migration to the capital and the exponential growth of the shanty towns. As a result, work began on improving these informal settlements through specific programmes to structure them and provide them with basic services such as water, drainage and electricity. This also led to the definition of so-called 'elemental homes,' basic housing units for the owners to complete according to their own needs (a concept revived in recent years by the Chilean architect and Pritzker Prize winner Alejandro Aravena). When the architect Fernando Belaúnde Terry was elected as president of Peru in

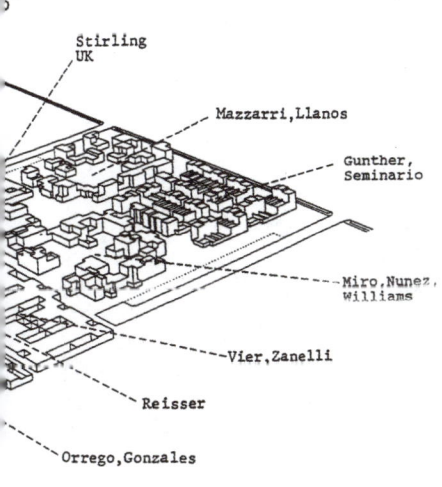

Stirling
UK

Mazzarri,Llanos

Gunther,
Seminario

Miro,Nunez,
Williams

Vier,Zanelli

Reisser

Orrego,Gonzales

parro,Ramirez,Smirnoff,
zkowski

ez,Perez

1963, he revived the neighbourhood unit projects, a concept he had promoted as a deputy. He also decided to explore different mass housing options and, in 1966, he commissioned Peter Land to investigate new housing solutions and building technologies, which led to the establishment of the Pilot Project 1 (PP1), better known by the acronym PREVI (Proyecto Experimental de Vivienda, or 'Experimental Housing Project'). In 1968, an urban planning competition was launched to design 1,500 housing units on a 50-hectare plot in the north of the city. Led by Land and organised in collaboration with the United Nations Development Programme, the competition received 26 entries: 13 from invited international architects (many associated with Team X, as well as representatives of the Japanese Metabolism movement) and 13 from pre-selected Peruvian architects. The brief emphasised the need to work within certain design principles: low-rise, high density; the 'growing house' concept; the innovation, modulation and prefabrication of building systems; flexibility; the optimisation of environmental factors;

Public area

Aldo van Eyck

the importance of public spaces for social inclusion; and the pedestrian scale. The winning projects were submitted by Atelier 5, Maki-Kikutake-Kurokawa, Ohl, Mazzarri-Llanos; Chaparro-Smirnoff-Wyszkowski-Ramírez; and Crousse-Páez-Pérez León. However, the economic and political circumstances following the coup that removed Belaúnde from office and the seizure of power by General Velasco led to a change of direction for the project. An alternative plan for the construction of 2,000 housing units was drawn up. Broken down into

Maki, Kikutake, Kurokawa

James Stirling

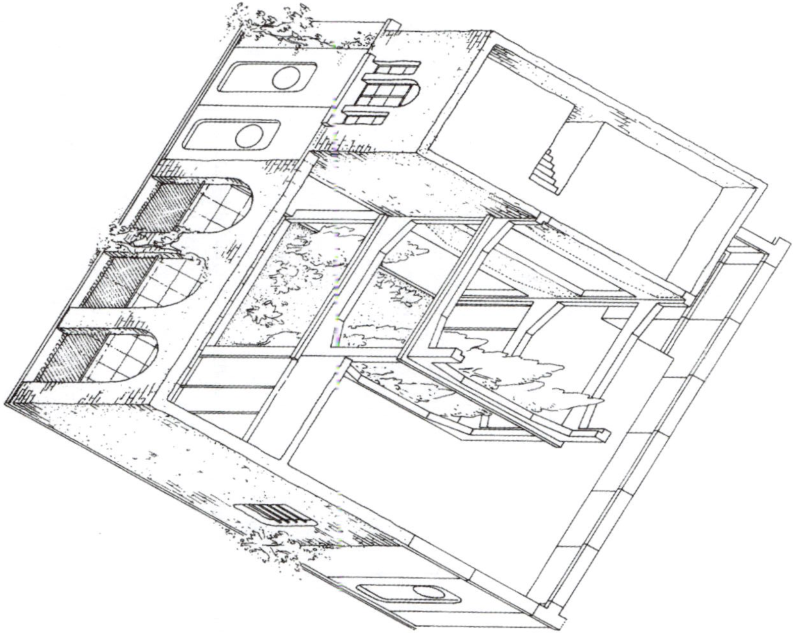

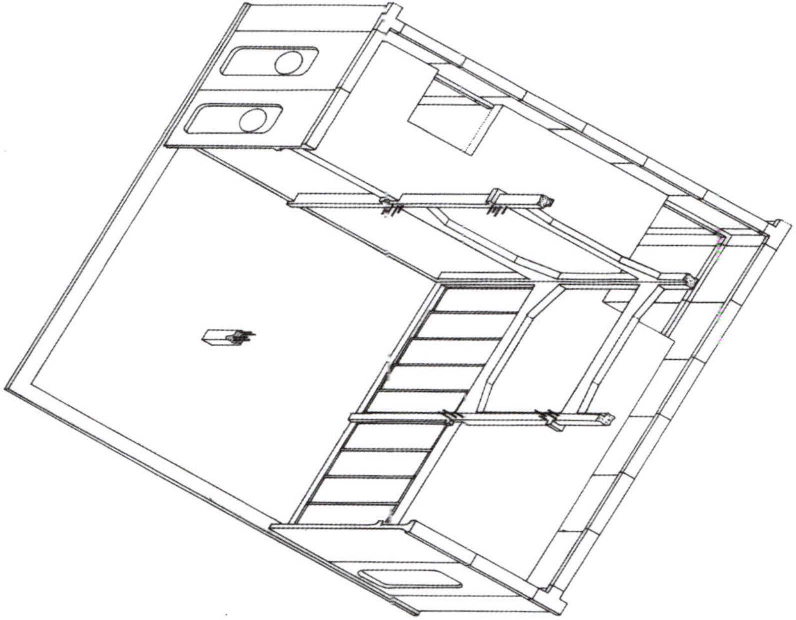

James Sti ling / Michael Wilford fonds. Canadian Centre for Architecture

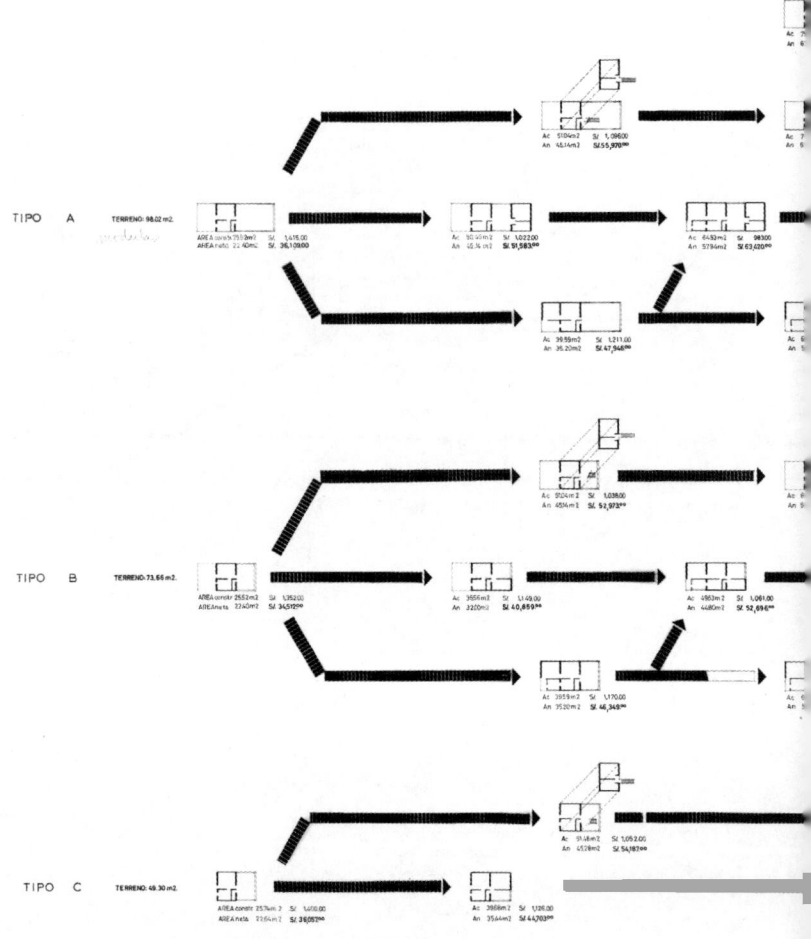

Frederick Cooper, José García Bryce, Antonio Graña, Eugenio Nicolini

four phases, only the first was built. The completed development comprises nearly 500 units and is organised around a central pedestrian axis that connects the different areas. This was meant to be expanded in the three remaining phases. Road traffic is restricted to the exterior with short cul-de-sacs providing access to the interior of the development. A main park articulates the facilities, such as a children's area that still retains some of the original play furniture. The overall layout is dense but alleviated by numerous little squares, gardens and walkways, all of which configure very attractive spatial sequences on an intimate scale. The project is composed of clusters of the different housing types designed in the competition phase and this diversity enriches the overall environment, resulting in a far more interesting ensemble than if it had been awarded to a single winner. To this complexity, it must also be noted that this is a system of single-family houses whose extension designs anticipated by the original architects have not been followed by the inhabitants. As such, the original appearance of the development has changed considerably over time. In fact, visiting the site and attempting to identify the designs of the different architects involved can become something of an archaeological exercise, but that is probably what makes it so radical. The occupants have played a vital role in shaping the final project, which is constantly evolving to this day.

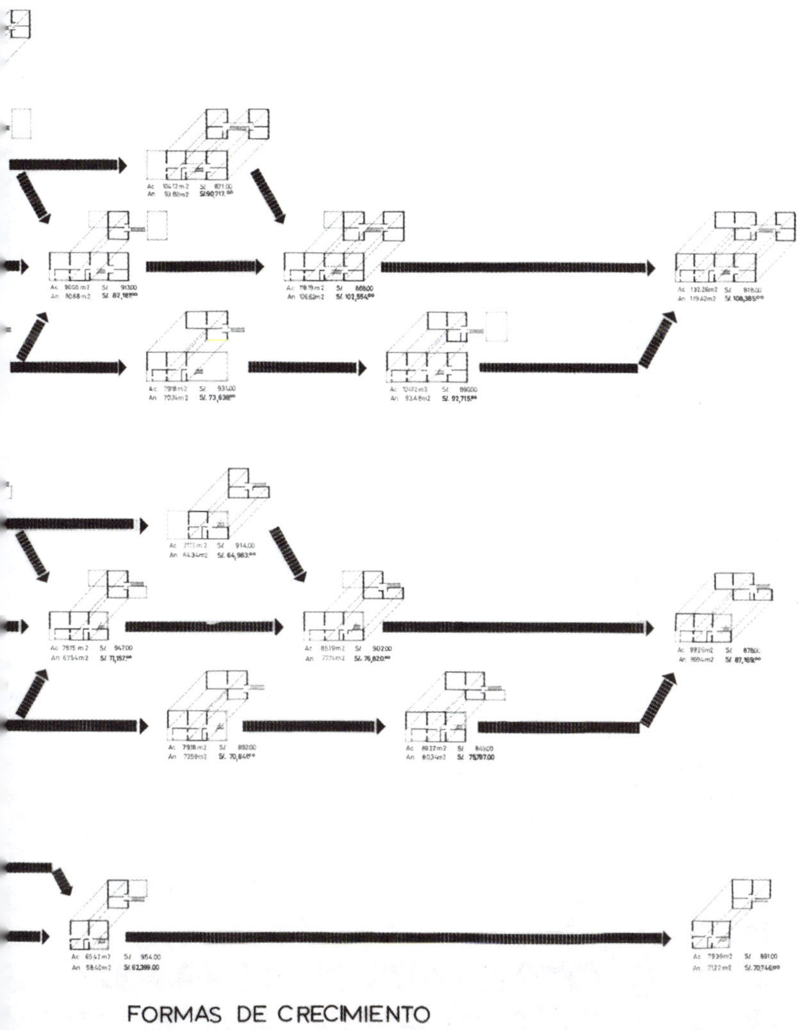

B

FORMAS DE CRECIMIENTO

Knud Svensson

Departamento de Arquitectura 038 B
de la Escuela Nacional
de Ingenieros
Avenida Túpac Amaru 210,
Rímac
Mario Bianco, Juan Benites,
Raúl Morey, Gustavo Tode
1953

The design and construction of what would become Peru's first school of architecture boosted the aims of a profession that had recently been reformed in line with the precepts of the modernist movement. Designated by Fernando Belaúnde Terry in 1951, the Italian architect Mario Bianco and his team took on the challenge of designing a building that would itself represent a lesson in the new architecture. The result is a carefully meditated functional distribution that condenses concepts such as structural rationality, organic forms, spatial fluidity and an open floor plan. The building's volumetry reveals a clear intention: the library, originally situated at the central axis of

Leonardo Finotti

B

symmetry, is suspended on pillars above the main hall in an allegory that puts knowledge at the core of the complex and facilitates a direct connection with the spacious design workshops located in the rear wing. The impact of the sunlight in these interior spaces is controlled by means of overhanging eaves, the depth of which vary according to their orientation, while the large windows establish a visual connection with the gardens. On the ground floor, a pergola with a concrete roof provides pleasant protection for the pedestrian flow of students. The rotunda, where the art classes take place, displays an organic volumetry that recalls the architecture of Frank Lloyd Wright, while the auditorium's intricate brickwork enhances the acoustics. In subsequent years, modifications to the original project have been carried out by outstanding students and members of the faculty – including Luis Miró Quesada, Oswaldo Núñez, Miguel Ángel Llona and José García Bryce – all of whose designs convey their passion for architecture.

Fabio Rodríguez Bernuy

Complejo arqueológico Puruchuco

039 B

Avenida Prolongación
Javier Prado Este 8500, Ate
Ychsma and Inca cultures
12th–16th century

Since its reconstruction by Arturo Jiménez Borja in the 1950s, the Puruchuco archaeological complex has become an endless lesson in ancient Peruvian architecture. Built progressively since the twelfth century by the Ychsma and Inca cultures, this elite residence was strategically located at the foot of a hill and comprises two clearly differentiated zones: a west-facing sector for public activities, organised around a great ceremonial courtyard; and an east-facing sector for the private residential functions of the governor or chief. The architectural composition of the complex is defined by both the material expression of the adobe and the sequence of open and closed spaces intercalated at different levels, which provide optimal light and ventilation to the rooms and afford panoramic views of the Middle Rímac Valley. On a formal level, the double-jamb trapezoidal openings and triangular niches, architectural hallmarks of the Inca period, are indicative of the presence of more important and ceremonial areas. But the importance of Puruchuco transcends its archaeological merits. It was here that the country's first museum was founded in 1960, an institution dedicated to the research and dissemination of studies of the area. Today, the museum continues to organise different cultural events to help preserve the memory of pre-Hispanic ceremonies, such as the Inti Raymi, a ritual celebrated every winter solstice in honour of the sun God.

Section

Courtesy of Pool Porta Architect – AMPA

Fabio Rodríguez Bernuy

Casa D

La Molina
Sandra Barclay, Jean Pierre Crousse
2013

This three-storey single-family house is defined by the austerity of the materials used and its opacity from the street, which provides no hint of the transparency of the interior spaces with respect to the tropical garden. In addition to the main access, a two-section ramp leads to an impeccably executed courtyard with ancient reminiscences, paved with upright placed pebble stones. The floor plan adopts a canonical L-shape with the stairs at the vertex and the bedrooms and social areas along the sides. The black-painted steel window frames and the porcelain flooring in the same colour fit well with the austerity of the structure. It is impossible not to relate Barclay and Crousse's work to the architecture of the pre-Inca civilisations that inhabited Peru's coastal desert, due to the way in which they entrust the resolution of all details to a single material – concrete – built in the way of a rammed earth wall and slightly inclined in this case thanks to the steel reinforcement. The geometry, colours and relationship with the exterior spaces conjure up an image of what those ancient constructions must have been like before they fell into ruin.

Gonzalo Cáceres. Courtesy of Barclay & Crousse

Gonzalo Cáceres. Courtesy of Barclay & Crousse

Banco de Crédito del Perú 041 B

Avenida Centenario 156,
La Molina
*Arquitectónica (Bernardo
Fort Brescia, Laurinda Spear)*
1990

In 1977, Bernardo Fort Brescia and Laurinda Spear, the latter an early collaborator at the Office for Metropolitan Architecture (OMA) in Rotterdam, founded the studio Arquitectonica in Florida. They built The Atlantis, a glass block with a cube cut out to accommodate a whirl pool and palm tree. The building made it onto the front cover of numerous magazines and appeared in television series such as *Miami Vice*, marking the beginning of an international career that allowed them to build across America and Asia. In the late 1980s, they designed the headquarters of the Banco de Crédito del Perú, located in Santiago de Surco. The floor plan adopts the form of a square block, one side of which is open to the sloping terrain, allowing the hill to penetrate the courtyard, almost like a landslide. The building is structured by an orthogonal grid of columns, interspersed by follies that disrupt the frame, creating unstable geometries that recall the early diagrammatic plans of Rem Koolhaas and Elia Zenghelis. Surreal, panoptic spaces alternate with others of a corporate nature that emerge on the façade, creating a Mannerist composition that references both history and modernity, with a somewhat unlikely mixture of styles and materials: the black marble placed diagonally on the façade and intersected by horizontal bands of glass, and the columns with galvanised steel cladding, tangent to the perimeter, which lend greater emphasis to the elevations than the volumetry. With its references to tradition and the avant-garde, this somewhat disconcerting work occupies a fine line between the sublime and the kitsch. Ultimately, however, it is full of surprising details that serve as an aesthetic testament to a bewildering new era: a risky, cheerful and tropical architecture that opened up a new and hitherto little trodden path in Peruvian modernism.

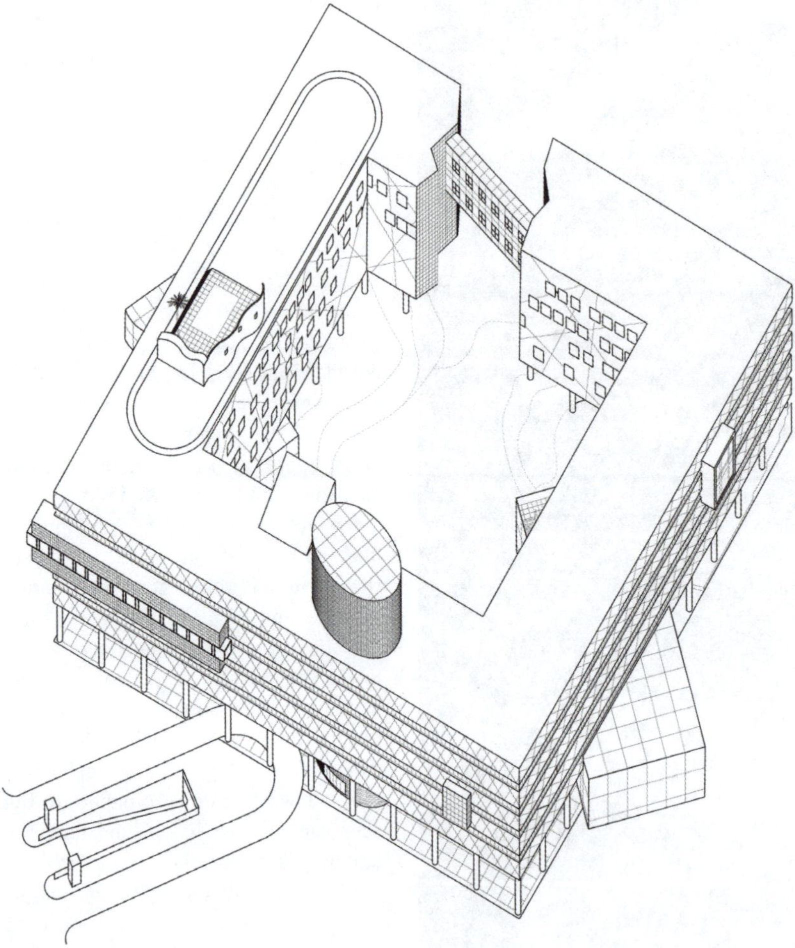

Arquitectonica

Axonometric projection

Daniel Giannoni. Courtesy of Arquitectónica

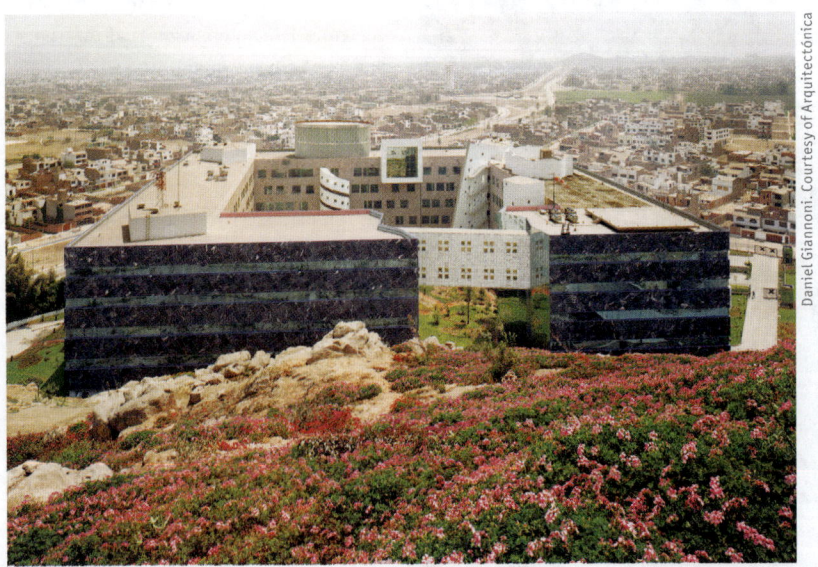

View from the hills

Juan Solano. Courtesy of José Anto io Vallarino

Sede Ferreyros

Jirón Cristóbal de Peralta
Norte 820, Santiago de Surco
José Antonio Vallarino
2007

042 B

Awarded the Hexágono de Oro in 2008, this building serves as the headquarters of one of the country's leading machinery trading companies. It occupies a longitudinal plot adjacent to the Pan-American Highway and comprises two volumes separated by a landscaped space. The main volume is four storeys tall and houses the offices and sales areas. The rear volume contains the caféteria and training areas, which are spread across two floors, while a third level accommodates the cooling equipment, concealed within a curved structure that contrasts with the rigorously straight lines that define the rest of the project. A ceramic cladding with a square modular structure covers the majority of the exterior vertical walls, complimenting the project's refined geometry. By contrast, the south façade of the main volume has a transparent surface composed entirely of large glass panels supported by a steel grid structure. This side accommodates the longitudinal atrium that occupies the entire height of the building, separating the office area from the exterior and incorporating the vertical communications. When viewed from the outside, the atrium also lends the façade a curious sense of depth. The west elevation repeats the same scheme on a smaller scale, ceding prominence to the sales area where the meeting rooms benefit from abundant light and double-height ceilings.

Juan Solano. Courtesy of José Antonio Vallarino

Iglesia del Sagrado Corazón de Jesús

Calle Santorín 258,
Santiago de Surco
Ruth Alvarado, Óscar Borasino,
Alfredo Benavides, Cynthia Watmough
2008

Located in a chaotic area not far from the highway, this project evokes the transition from the mundane to the transcendental, a physical and emotional journey from a visually and acoustically noisy context to an intimate, spiritual place. A long, gentle ramp leads from the corner of the plot to a sunken square protected from the immediate environs, onto which the pastoral facilities open. From the atrium, colossal doors provide access to a vestibule and then a second door leads on to the antechamber, beyond which the main space is visible. The church nave, which has generous dimensions and a sloping elliptical floor plan, is covered by a truncated cone-shaped dome made of reinforced concrete with a thickness of 15 centimetres, eliminating the need for intermediate supports. It envelops the congregation below, inviting quiet reflection. Inspired by the Pantheon of Rome, the dome culminates in a great oculus at a height of 33 metres, drawing the eyes to the sky while bathing the altar in light. The aisles embrace and protect the nave, allowing access without

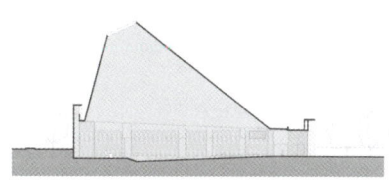

Borasino Arquitectos

Cynthia Wathmoug

interrupting the liturgical services at the front. On one of the aisles, the side chapels overlook a pond and the garden. The other aisle accommodates the confession booths, with soft lighting to create a more intimate atmosphere. Completing the building are the bell tower, baptistery, sacristy, chapel with alabaster stained-glass windows and a volume containing the altar, where a curtain of light illuminates the focal point of the church service. Concrete, stone and wood materialise a building that is not only a local landmark but whose magnificent spatial conception manages to evoke the divine.

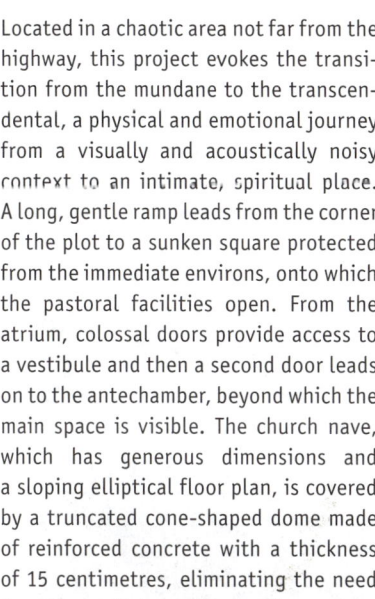

Stella Wathmoug. Courtesy of OB+RA

Casa Plataforma

Jirón Flor de Roca 115,
Urbanización Las Casuarinas,
Santiago de Surco
Alexia León, Lucho Marcial
2013

044 B

Las Casuarinas is a hillside housing development with views of the city and the Pacific Ocean. Most of the houses are built on enormous retaining walls, acquiring additional height and a flat garden area. This house, however, is excavated from the level of the entrance, leaving it free with a platform and an access pavilion surrounded by a garden that has no lawn but nevertheless bursts with colour. This configuration allows pedestrians on Jirón Flora de Roca to see the urban landscape and makes the house invisible from Jirón Los Molles. The building is best interpreted as a section view from top to bottom. The upper floor is composed of a diagonal sequence of concatenated spaces, with bedrooms, living rooms and study areas following one after another. The absence of corridors and the material treatment of the stairs, finished in marble and wood, recall the palaces of the old world. The next floor down opens in a stepped arrangement over a garden with a swimming pool. At the back of the plot, the residual space has been transformed

All photos: Edi Hirose. Courtesy of Leonmarcial Arquitectos

into a charming shaded area, protected by a cantilever and accompanied by a peaceful pond with water lilies, wood chip floors and desert vegetation. The concrete execution is impeccable, but even so, it is surpassed by the design of the rails, fencing and latticework, both outside and inside, which gives the work a colourful atmosphere and a sense of transparency – no minor feat in a city full of walls. This can be appreciated in the grid that delimits the upper perimeter of the plot, especially in the way in which the rails of the terraces are screwed to the edge of the slab, in the green parapet that protects the entrance level and even in the grates for the drains. The

layout recalls the pre-Hispanic architecture of the desert, while the elevations echo those of modern American houses. Although these forms and materials are known, in this house they are placed in a slightly different way: seemingly strange, yet familiar at the same time.

_eonmarcial Arquitectos

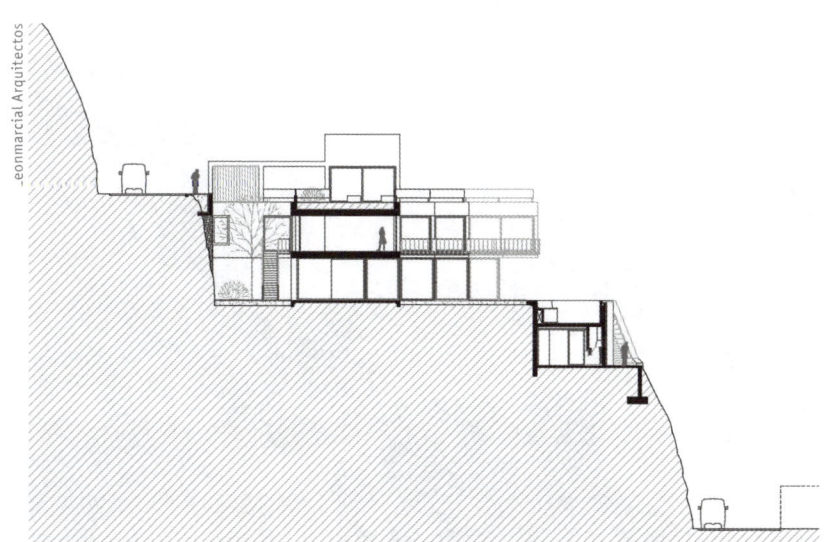

Muro Las Casuarinas - Pamplona Alta

045 B

Santiago de Surco –
San Juan de Miraflores
Since 1985

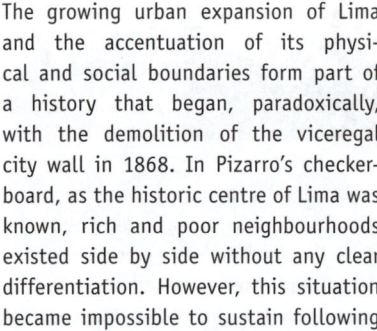

The growing urban expansion of Lima and the accentuation of its physical and social boundaries form part of a history that began, paradoxically, with the demolition of the viceregal city wall in 1868. In Pizarro's checkerboard, as the historic centre of Lima was known, rich and poor neighbourhoods existed side by side without any clear differentiation. However, this situation became impossible to sustain following the population growth at the beginning of the twentieth century. To modernise the city, wide avenues were built on the farm land in the Rímac Valley, leading to a real estate boom. At the same time, in a phenomenon that the government had not foreseen, the first shanty towns emerged in 1913. Despite their improvised construction and lack of access to basic services, these settlements continued to expand, resulting in what Matos Mar has called a 'popular overflow.' By the mid-twentieth century, the two realities of Lima had collided. Founded at the foot of the Cerro San Francisco in 1956, Las Casuarinas became one of the city's most luxurious housing developments.

All photos: Delia Bayona

Meanwhile, on the other side of the hill, shanty towns had been emerging in Pamplona Alta since 1971. In 1985, faced with the threat of land invasions and human trafficking, work began on a three-metre-high concrete wall to separate the districts of Santiago de Surco and San Juan de Miraflores. Today it extends between La Molina and Villa María del Triunfo and is more than 10 kilometres long. Popularly known as the 'wall of shame,' it was partly built by the workers of Pamplona Alta and financed by the wealthy residents of Las Casuarinas. Both sides now live with a wall that symbolises the unequal fragmentation of a city whose unplanned growth is reflected in the segregation of its society; a wall that prevents dialogue, yet says a great deal about contemporary Lima.

B

Las Casuarinas housing development and the Pamplona Alta shanty town

Juvenal Baracco

Aulario en la Universidad Ricardo Palma

046 B

Avenida Alfredo Benavides 5440, Santiago de Surco

Juvenal Baracco, Enrique Bonilla

2011

Located in a low-density residential area of the Surco district, the Universidad Ricardo Palma is part of a civic 'superblock' close to the South Pan-American Highway, on a section with intense traffic all day long. The access lane to the highway from Avenida Benavides cuts diagonally across the plot perimeter, perpendicular to which stand the first constructions that were built, all rationalist designs. The new teaching block connects four of the six buildings (the auditorium and the law, engineering and architecture schools) around three garden courtyards separated from the car park, with a cloister structure well known in educational architecture. The building is classical in terms of its insertion into the urban fabric but complex as regards to its geometric breakdown. Composed of four modules slightly rotated to accommodate the misaligned existing teaching blocks, it is connected to them by means of ball joints with Corbusian geometry, shaped by a glass-brick façade in which the vertical

communication and service cores are located. The façade, with slightly curving lines that interrupt the trapezoidal car park, is perceived in its entirety from the university entrance. A cantilever that serves as a pergola over the entrance leads students to the interior via a long walkway built on a different level from the vehicular traffic, accommodating the topography with ramps and steps. The load-bearing structure, made of exposed steel, is anchored with pairs of V-shaped sloping pillars that reinforce the connections between columns and Boyd beams on the ground floor, counteracting the shear force in the event of an earthquake. On the main façade, the irregular arrangement of sunshades interrupts the elevation profile and lends lightness to the building, which is perceived as a kind of 'work in progress.' This is a building full of erudite references: to classical antiquity in its urban layout, to the modernist movement in the articulation and organisation of the programme, and to avant-garde deconstruction in its structure and envelope. These references demonstrate the torrent of influences handled by its architects – teachers of several generations of architects in Peru – who achieve in this building a pleasing harmony of diverse languages.

Juvenal Baracco and Enrique Bonilla

Juvena Baracco

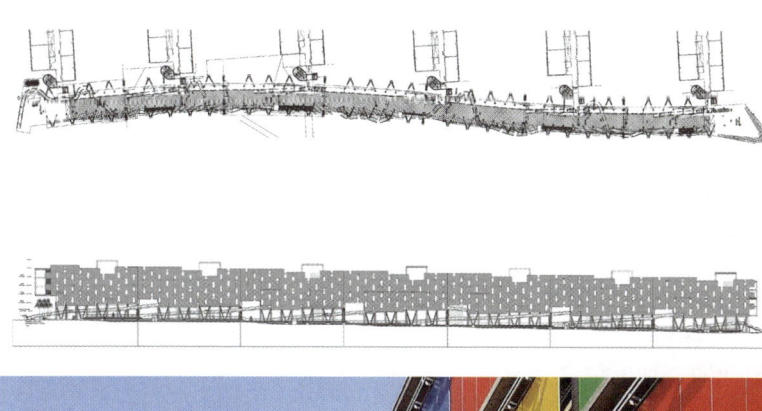

Other Works of Interest

B01 Urbanización Los Cóndores
Carretera Central km27, Chaclacayo
Augusto Benavides Díez-Canseco
1940s

B02 Centro Vacacional Huampaní
Carretera central km26,
Lurigancho-Chosica
Santiago Agurto, Carlos Cárdenas,
José Miguel Flores Estrada,
José Ramos, Luis Vásquez Pancorbo,
Juan Günther
1955

B03 Huaycán de Pariachi
Avenida José Carlos Mariátegui, Ate
Ychsma and Inca cultures
1100–1530 CE

B04 Huaca Cajamarquilla
Lurigancho-Chosica
Lima and Ychsma cultures
600–1450 CE

B05 Laboratorios Montana
Calle Cascanueces, Santa Anita
Michelle Llona, Rafael Zamora
2017

B06 Edificio IBM
Avenida Javier Prado Este 6230,
La Molina
Carlos Arana, Antenor Orrego,
Juan Torres
1978

B07 Universidad de Lima
Avenida Javier Prado Este 4600,
Santiago de Surco
Héctor Velarde
1966

B08 Hipódromo Monterrico
Avenida El Derby,
Santiago de Surco
Alfredo Dammert, Manuel Valega,
Gerardo Lecca
1960

B09 Ministerio de Guerra
Avenida Paseo del Bosque 740, San Borja
Juan Günther Doering
1975

B10 Embajada de Estados Unidos
Avenida La Encalada,
Santiago de Surco
Arquitectónica (Bernardo
Fort-Brescia, Laurinda Spear)
1995

B11 Vivienda unifamiliar
Jirón Monte Flor 693, Urbanización
Chacarilla del Estanque,
Santiago de Surco
Walter Kern
1967

B12 Vivienda unifamiliar
Jirón Monte Flor 270,
Urbanización Chacarilla del
Estanque, Santiago de Surco

B13 Iglesia Luterana
Calle Monte Casino 190,
Santiago de Surco
Óscar Borasino
2015

B14 Casa de Laney Ross
Calle El Cascajal and Jirón Cerro
San Francisco, Urbanización Las
Casuarinas, Santiago de Surco
Walter Weberhofer, Remigio Collantes
1961

B15 Casa Chávez
Jirones Las Laderas and La Cuesta,
Urbanización Las Casuarinas,
Santiago de Surco
Miguel Rodrigo Mazuré
1959

B16 Casa Pachacamac
Lomas de Jatosisa, Pachacamac
Luis Longhi
2009

Right: Gardens of the Urbanización Chacarilla del Estanque

Electric Train

C

The electric train on its way through San Juan de Lurigancho district

C

C

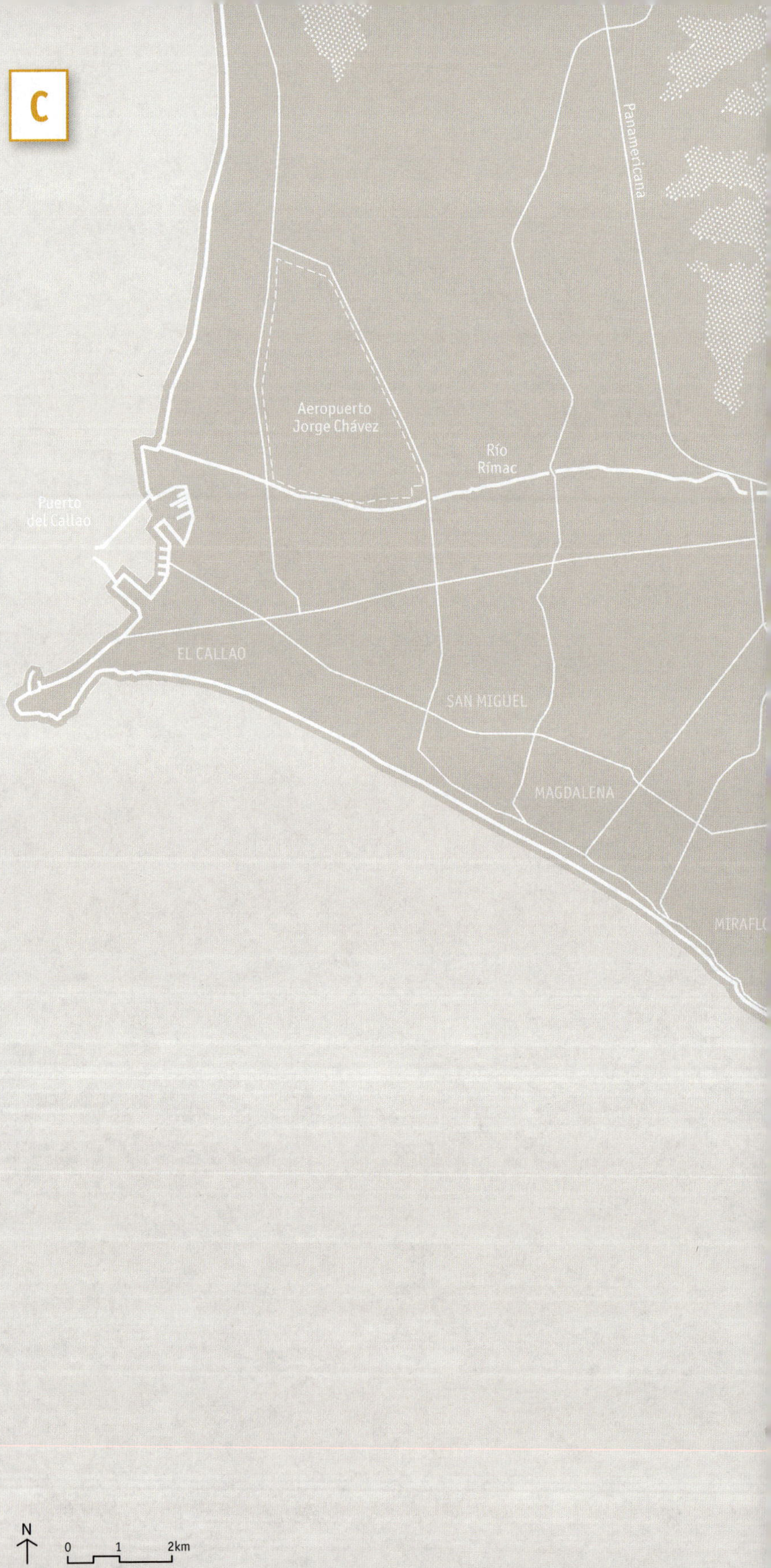

Panamericana

Aeropuerto
Jorge Chávez

Río
Rímac

Puerto
del Callao

EL CALLAO

SAN MIGUEL

MAGDALENA

MIRAFL

N

0   1   2km

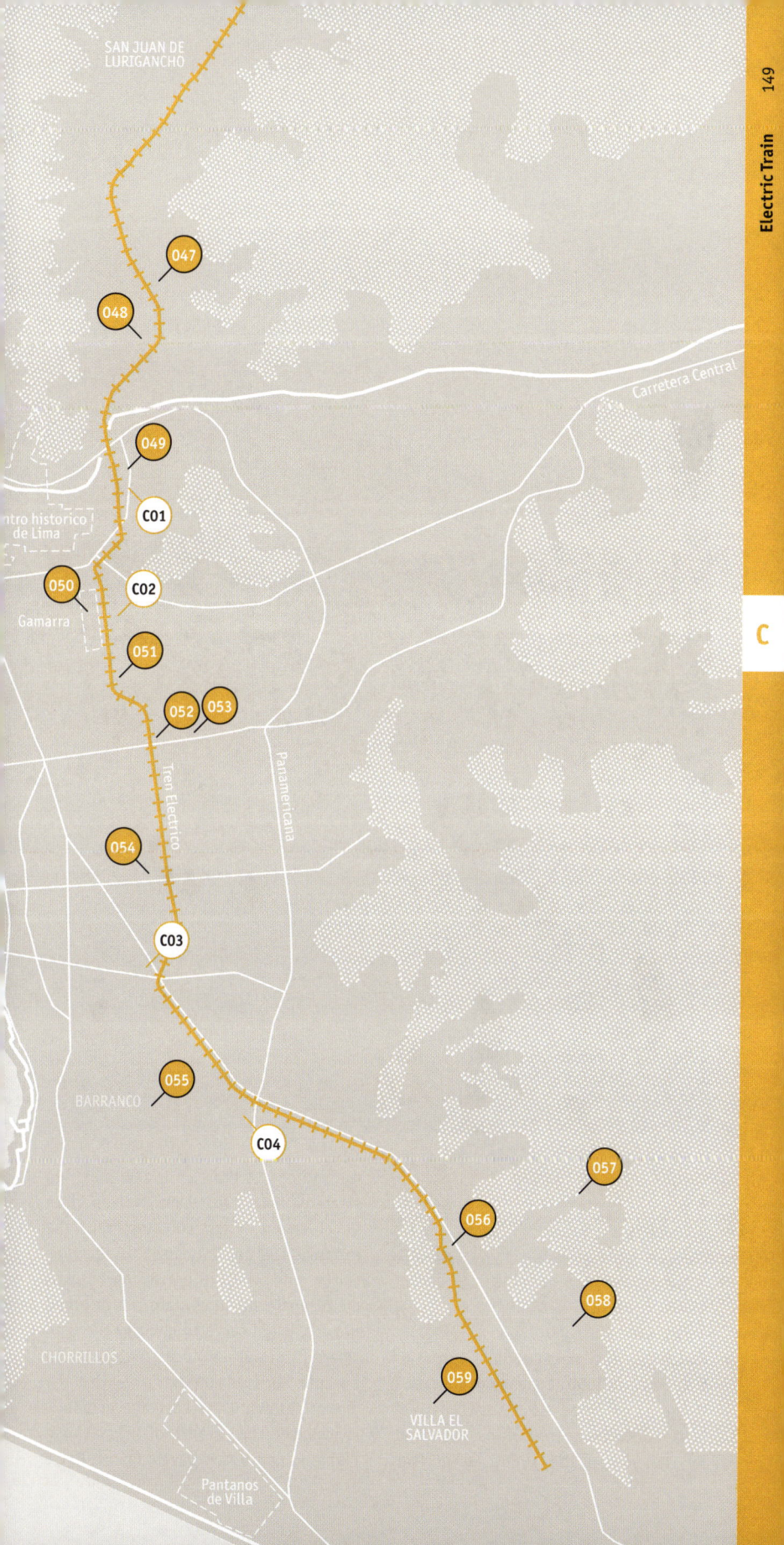

SAN JUAN DE
LURIGANCHO

Carretera Central

047

048

049

C01

Centro historico
de Lima

050

C02

Gamarra

051

052 053

Tren Electrico

Panamericana

054

C03

BARRANCO

055

C04

057

056

058

CHORRILLOS

059

VILLA EL
SALVADOR

Pantanos
de Villa

Parque zonal Huiracocha
Avenida Próceres de la
Independencia 1568,
San Juan de Lurigancho
Patronato de Parques Zonales y Nacionales
1971

047 C

Following the demographic explosion that began in 1950 as a result of migration to the capital, the predictions of the 1949 Lima Pilot Plan were quickly exceeded. By the end of the 1960s, authorities were forced to draw up a new planning strategy. The 1967 Lima Metropolitan Development Plan contemplated the expansion of the city towards the outskirts, and while it proved an insufficient legal tool to contain the informal growth, it did serve to identify the land where future urban infrastructure could be built. In this context, and with the aim of resolving the shortage of public spaces, the Lima branch of the National Planning and Urban Development Office

C

established three different sizes of green areas: four metropolitan parks, three metropolitan-zonal parks and 21 zonal parks, located in consolidated areas as well as expansion zones. The construction of the zonal parks commenced in 1970 but was halted five years later when only 10 of the works had been executed. The Huiracocha zonal park was inaugurated in 1971 and has since become one of the most iconic public spaces in Lima. Its 23.47 hectares serve the district of San Juan de Lurigancho, one of the most populous areas in South America with over a million inhabitants. In 2010, the park was completely remodelled and renamed the Club Zonal Huiracocha, a decision with strong socio-economic connotations whereby the private takes precedence over the public. Today, it boasts a cultural centre with a library, play centre and museum, an artificial lake, sports areas and a 6,000-square-metre swimming pool, the largest in Lima.

Instituto Superior SISE

048 C

Calle Los Líquenes 8,
San Juan de Lurigancho
Patricia Llosa, Rodolfo Cortegana
2018

Although the roots of the San Juan de Lurigancho district can be traced back to the pre-Hispanic period, its size today is the result of mass migration and the consequent growth of Lima since the mid-twentieth century. This expansion, mainly the result of the illegal occupation of land and proliferation of shanty towns, defines the physical appearance of the district and of many other parts of the city, all characterised by a shortage of public space and infrastructure. However, the economic development of these areas and the rise of the so-called 'emerging middle class,' coupled with the trust in education as a catalyst for social mobility, have encouraged several educational institutions to establish facilities in the district. Located near the foundational square of colonial San Juan, the Instituto Superior SISE stands at the vertex of a large corner plot. The five-storey tower (planned to rise to eight in the future) is composed of exposed reddish concrete and has become something of an urban landmark amidst the simple constructions that surround it. The load-bearing structure is composed of a central core, with highly expressive integrated staircases and concrete latticework on the façade that defines the building's external appearance. This volume represents the first stage of a larger project that will include a second tower at the opposite end of the plot, as well as a two-storey base around the perimeter, preserving two large open areas to serve as interior courtyards.

Llosa Cortegana

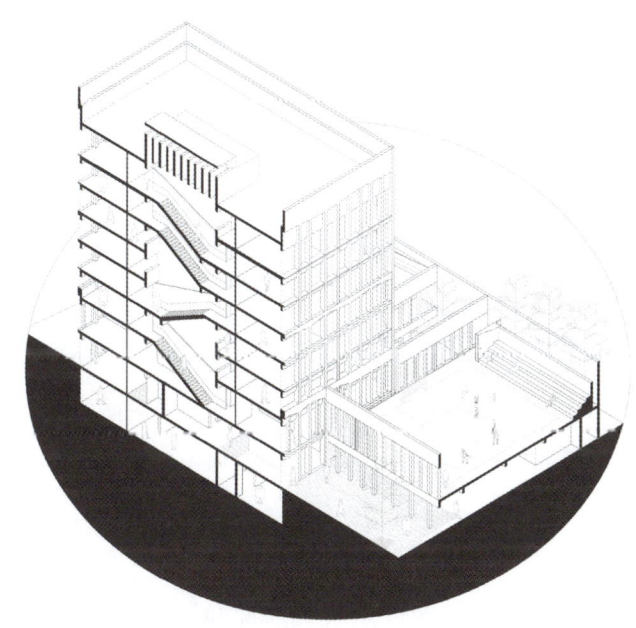

All photos: Juan Solano Courtesy of Llosa Cortegana

Cementerio Presbítero Matías Maestro

049 C

Jirón Ancash 1611,
Cercado de Lima
Matías Maestro
1808

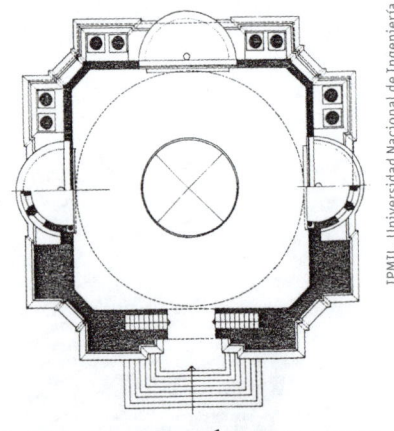

IPMIL. Universidad Nacional de Ingeniería

La Cripta de los Héroes (Émile Robert, 1907)

Conceived as a type of funerary town, the construction of the general cemetery at the beginning of the nineteenth century introduced a new form of urban planning centred on the ideals of the Enlightenment and the neoclassical style. Until then, the population had buried their deceased in underground vaults or catacombs, according to a long-established custom whereby those who were laid to rest near churches were believed to have a shorter path to heaven. However, in view of the epidemics that proliferated within the walled city, a group of doctors asked the Viceroy José Fernando de Abascal for permission to relocate the burial grounds to an east-facing plot outside the city walls. Here, it was thought that the so-called miasma, or foul air, would not harm the population. The presbyter Matías Maestro, a driving force behind the introduction of the neoclassical style in Lima's architecture, was commissioned to undertake this major work.

He designed the symmetrical distribution of orthogonal and diagonal lanes around a central avenue lined with cypress trees, leading to an octagonal chapel that has since been demolished. Over time, this architectural ensemble has been embelished with handsome mausoleums and sculptures that serve as testimony to the various artistic styles and leading figures that have shaped the history of Peru. One of the most outstanding monuments is La Cripta de los Héroes, built in 1908 by the French architect Émile Robert, which contains the mortal remains of the fallen heroes of the War of the Pacific.

iStockphoto. Myriam Borzee

Gamarra

Jirón Hipólito Unanue,
La Victoria
Informal architecture
Since 1970s

050 C

Year after year, the neighbourhood of Gamarra grows: concrete structures and brick façades, without insulation or comfort, benefit from the climate of a city with mild temperatures, low precipitation and tropical humidity. Altogether, they shape a skyline that appears to threaten Lima's financial district, located just two kilometres away. In this neighbourhood, located within the district of La Victoria, the quantity of clothing sold is so great that the square metre price is as high as that of Paris or New York. Each owner has created a high-rise structure of pattern workshops, sewing factories and retail facilities stacked one on top of the other. The result is a mall comprising 17,000 commercial premises housed in buildings that rise to as many as 25 storeys, which together receive over 60,000 visitors a day. Indeed, Gamarra is the most important textile district in South America, both in terms of production and sales. The garments produced here are sold in every province in Peru, as well as in Venezuela, Brazil, Colombia, Chile, Ecuador and Bolivia. The textile production costs are higher than in similar markets in China, but the quality of the cotton is better. The logistics chain is old-fashioned and informal, but there is also much more flexibility. The *jaladores* collect plastic bags of clothes from the factories located on the upper floors of the towers and transport them in carts to the fenced area on the edge of the district, where double- and triple-parked vans wait for the goods. They are dispatched by road to the provinces and by air to the foreign markets. Everything on the 600 metres of Jirón Mariscal Agustín is excessive and colossal: a bustling strip of costumes and colours in a super-dense urban environment that looks like a scene from a video game, with half-finished curtain walls and rows of diabolical 'Shinygirl' mannequins. Unlike every other mall on the planet, there was no grand opening for Gamarra. It emerged next to the city's wholesale market, built in 1945. The vans would stop at La Parada, as the market was then known, laden with fruit from the mountains and then depart empty, until a group known

Gamarra in the 1940s: Parque Cánepa, Mercado de La Parada and the Cerro San Cosme

Gamarra in 2012

Diego Carhuarica

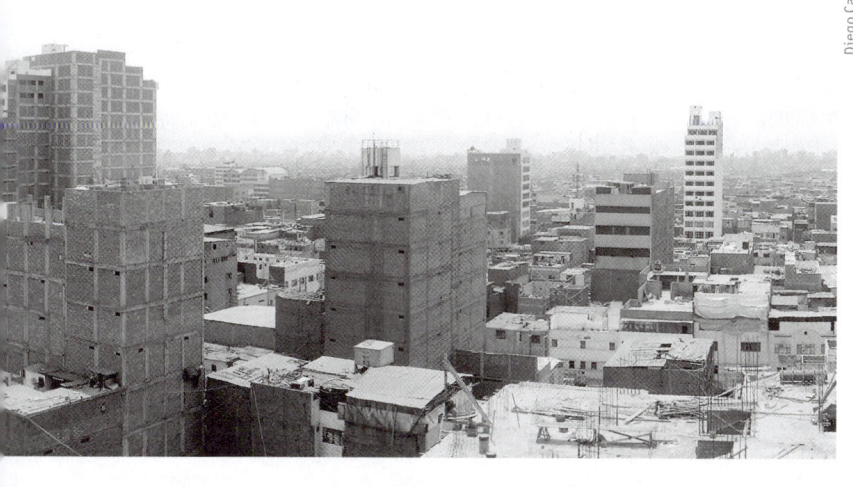

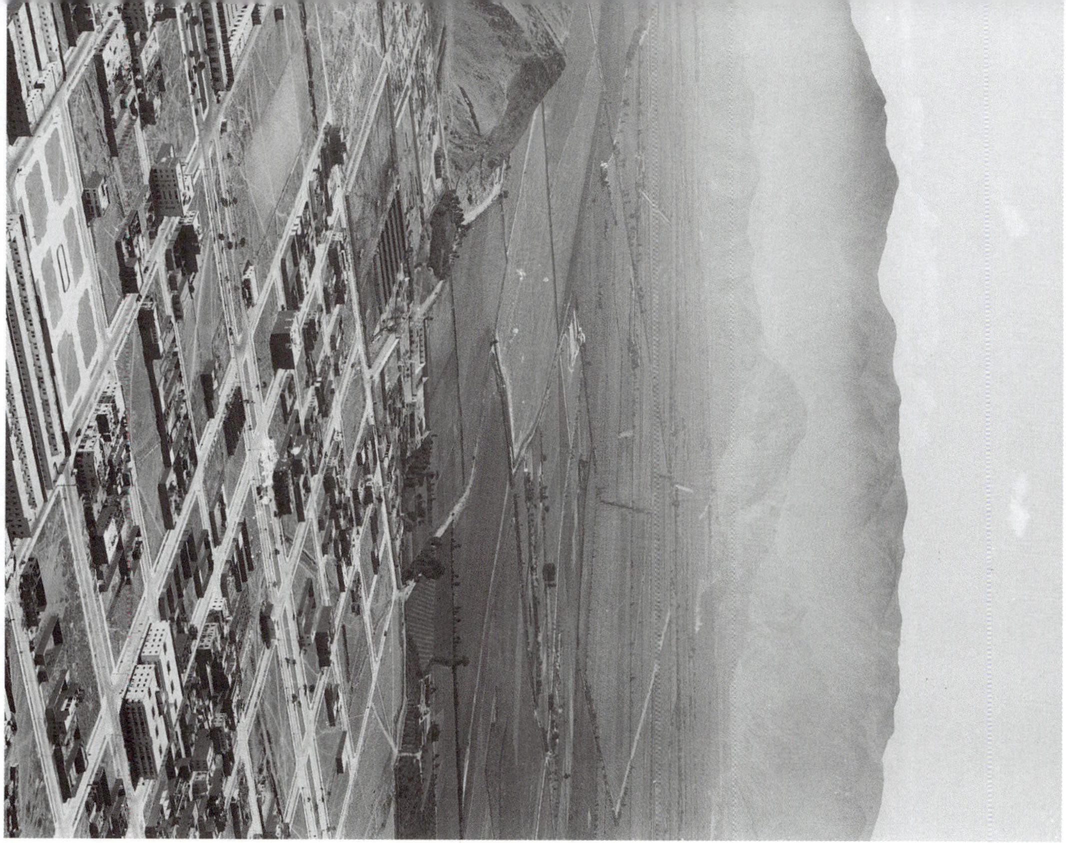

Servicio Aerofotográfico Nacional

View of the Cerro El Pino from Gamarra

as the 'innovators' started filling them with clothes. Fashion was a huge hit, but Gamarra was still a residential rather than commercial neighbourhood, so peddlers and informality emerged. In 1972, the city council reclassified the area, and what followed was a veritable explosion of commerce. The first industrial shopping centres opened, which lobotomised the residential fabric. The street vendors set up small companies, operating rent-free until they made a profit. Soon after, some of them started to expand vertically. The following years saw a gradual increase in demand, to which Gamarra swiftly responded by stepping up production and extending the galleries. The buildings grew upwards, storey by storey, and without demolishing any existing structures or halting production, exploiting every last sol of investment. The result is a now consolidated urban fabric with a commercial skyline. Today, El Damero ('The Grid'), as it is sometimes known, forms a network of regular blocks located within

a fenced zone. It contains over 250 buildings with manufacturing and retail uses. Its defining trait is informality; as such, its appearance is shabby and chaotic. Neither the façades nor the structures obey any established forms or rules. They do not comply with all regulations. Nor is there any institutional representation. Here, elegance is cast aside in favour of convenience. Everything is tailored to commercial activity, the ultimate aim of which is to multiply the exchange of knowledge and capital. Thus, Gamarra has succeeded in producing something that is distinctive and radical, but it has failed to provide the requisite healthiness expected of such an important commercial neighbourhood. The structures are in need of an urgent review to check their earthquake resistance, modernise the evacuation routes and improve safety conditions. In any case, it is a place worth visiting as one the most innovative and outstanding neighbourhoods in Lima, teeming with frenzied vitality.

Inner courtyard of the Galería Yuyi

Capilla de San José
Jirón Teófilo Castillo 2,
La Victoria
José García Bryce
1978

051 C

Prominent amidst the residential urban fabric of the Apolo housing development is the silhouette of this small church that won the Hexágono de Oro at the Peruvian Architecture Biennial of 1981. The building forms part of the Padres Oblatos de San José complex and is located strategically at the axis of the perpendicular street, Jirón Villanueva. The considerable height of this otherwise austere construction and its tall, slender bell tower accentuate its singular character, and the work therefore asserts its role as physical and spiritual beacon of the community. The chapel is situated on the raised part of a multipurpose space currently used as a car park. Access from the atrium is via a three-flight staircase with 45-degree twists that replicate the geometry of the nave's floor plan. The sacristy is located in a separate, pre-existing volume and is connected to the rooms in the seminary that García Bryce built a few years later. The design is defined by a simple rectangular space with chamfered corners, closed almost entirely to invite quiet reflection. Its materiality is expressed through a reinforced concrete structure and exposed brick walls, together with a meticulous study of proportions. The width of the space is equal to its height, while the length is double that dimension. Two intermediate porticoes divide the plan into three identical golden rectangles. The narrow vertical slits on the walls barely allow natural light to penetrate; it therefore enters from above through three skylights that recall the *teatinas*, a local variety of skylight. The largest bathes the altar in light.

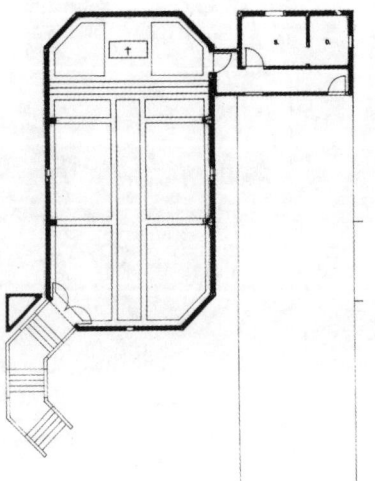

Ministerio de Pesquería

052 C

Avenida Javier Prado Este 2465, San Borja
*Miguel Cruchaga Belaúnde,
Miguel Rodrigo Mazuré,
Emilio Soyer Nash*
1971

The military government that ran the country from 1968 to 1980 created the Ministry of Fisheries and built this headquarters to demonstrate the enormous importance of fishing in the economy of Peru, which had then become one of the leading exporters of fish meal. It is an imposing, brutalist building with exposed concrete surfaces and large panels of smoked glass, arranged in a monumental composition with a distinct sculptural quality. The central section, where the entrance is located, is accompanied by lower but equally robust volumes. This formal deployment is repeated inside. The foyer has cathedral-like proportions and establishes a visual dialogue between the different levels. Various walkways cross the large central void, allowing a horizontal connection between the different wings. The glass panels on the façade and roof allow the penetration of abundant natural light, which is complimented by large cylindrical lamps seamlessly integrated within the ceilings. Although it now houses the Ministry of Culture and a magnificent photography exhibition on the armed conflict of the 1980s and 1990s (*Yuyanapaq*, designed by architect Luis Longhi), it is an oversized and underused

building. Its sheer scale reflects a forceful manifestation of power by the government rather than any real necessity. Even so, its extraordinary expressiveness is undeniable and the building represents one of the most impressive constructions of its time. A genuine spectacle.

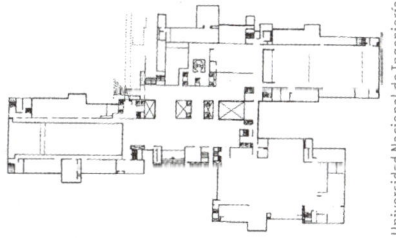

IPMIL. Universidad Nacional de Ingeniería

Candy Torres

Aitor Ortiz. Courtesy of IDOM

Lima Centro de Convenciones 053 C

Avenida La Arquelogía,
San Borja
*IDOM (Tono Fernández Usón,
César Azcárate, Javier Álvarez de Tomás)*
2016

The meeting of the World Bank Board of Governors and International Monetary Fund in 2015 was the inaugural event at this building destined to become a catalyst for the urban transformation of an area that is home to several important infrastructures. Adjoining Lima's tallest tower, this work boasts a considerable scale itself. Its 86,000 square metres accommodate 18 conference halls, all with a flexible structure and different dimensions, as well as interesting open spaces, service areas and a four-level parking lot. The double-height base contains two of the largest halls, one of which has a folding wall and can therefore open directly onto the street outside, generating a large covered square. A perforated five-storey prism rises from the base to accommodate the remainder of the programme. The play between the volumes generates voids with enormous plasticity and outdoor spaces in which the architecture frames the views. The construction culminates in a transparent volume that contains a large hall with a capacity for 3,500 people. Visible behind the glass is the triangulated structure that frees the interior of pillars.

Aitor Ortiz. Courtesy of IDOM

Conjunto habitacional Limatambo

054 C

Plaza Marquina, San Borja
Diego La Rosa, Óscar Borasino, Manuel Ferreyra, Juan Gutiérrez, Reynaldo Ledgard, Hugo Romero
1980

The Limatambo housing estate was designed in 1980 as the government's response to the shortage of homes and a limited market primarily focused on the wealthier sectors of society. The president of the Republic, the architect Fernando Belaúnde Terry, had returned to Peru after a teaching career in the United States and embarked on an ambitious programme to construct housing estates across the whole country. Limatambo is the most representative one. It consists of a network of streets divided by a diagonal axis with apartment blocks ranging from four to seven storeys high. It also includes public spaces, gardens and two 18-storey towers, built in the 1990s, with a cruciform floor plan and a concrete structure, braced on the top with Saint Andrew's crosses. The apartments, most of which have three bedrooms, were built with reinforced brickwork anchored with thin slabs of concrete. The austere finishes are camouflaged by an attractive movement on the façades, not entirely orthogonal, which generates pleasant landscaped spaces in front of the blocks. The façades are decorated with striking colours, differentiating the load-bearing structures from the brick walls, latticework and picture windows that echo elements of European postmodern architecture. The project included the most advanced electricity supply and water regulation systems, manifested most notably by the concrete tank that reflects the aspiration to make the estate self-sufficient at a difficult time when supplies were not always guaranteed. Expressive in its forms and kind to the human scale, the estate fits in reasonably well with the adjacent urban fabrics.

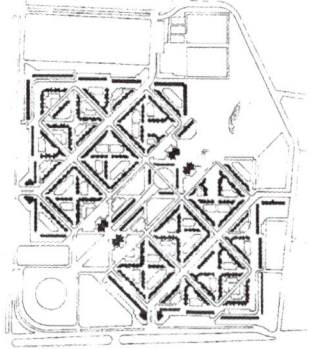

IPMIL, Universidad Nacional de Ingeniería

C

Samuel Povis

Martin Fabbri

Escuela de oficiales de la Fuerza Aérea del Perú

055 C

Base aérea Las Palmas,
Avenida Jorge Chávez
Santiago de Surco
Juvenal Baracco
1984

Situated at the Las Palmas air base, next to the Peruvian Air Force landing strip, the master plan for this complex might easily be that of a large Baroque *palazzo*, with the buildings arranged around a *piazza* in the shape of a Roman circus, with an entrance volume, conceived as a foyer, which was never executed. The dormitory building for the cadets is built with concrete screens parallel to the façade, so light that they create the effect of a piece of origami. The stepped volumetry and smoked glass windows devoid of frames blur the scale, creating an abstract language with references to the pre-Columbian architecture of the desert. The service building has a rectangular floor plan formed by repeated modules, differentiating between 'servant' and 'served' spaces. It

Martin Fabbri

is structured with perpendicular porticoes that create geometries at the points where they intersect, such as the dining room lit from above through cracks. The complex focuses attention on the scenography of the different volumes, using exterior walkways and interior corridors to connect the entrance hall to the other buildings and the auditorium, which is situated underground. The project originally included modular ornamentation on the walls, patterned paving in the square and a baldachin, which had they been built would have formed an improbable scenography, midway between Superestudio and Charles Moore. But even without these elements, it is difficult to capture the torrent of erudite references that resonate in this complex, whose designer makes himself present in each and every corner, resulting in a strange yet familiar work.

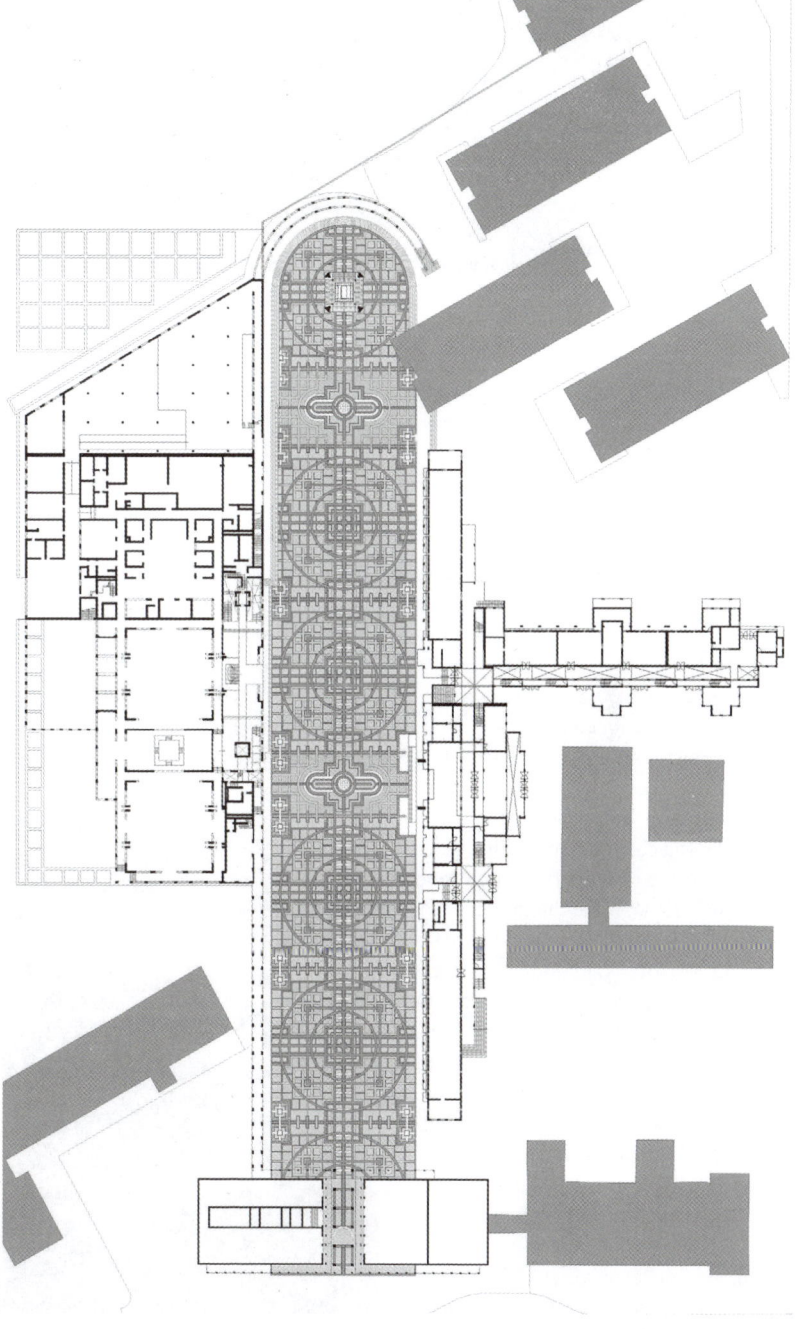

Octavio Montestruque

Terminal Pesquero Villa María del Triunfo   056 C

Avenida Pachacútec 2901,
Villa María del Triunfo
Architect unknown
1990s

The star dish of the gastronomic boom that Lima has experienced in recent years is ceviche, a dish with a history dating back to pre-Columbian times. Such is its importance that the country boasts no less than 35,000 *cevicherías*, nearly half of which are located in the capital. In fact, Peru is one of the largest fish consumers in Latin America. To meet this demand, species from all along the coast, bathed by the cold Humboldt Current, as well as from the rivers in the Amazon and the mountains, arrive in the capital every day for distribution from the two whole-sale fish markets. Ventanilla, in Callao, supplies species for popular consumption in vast quantities and at low prices. The other market, known as the Terminal Pesquero de Villa María del Triunfo, handled 70,000 tonnes of marine products in 2015. Its varied range of fish and seafood supplies the city's restaurants and supermarkets. The building is a simple industrial construction with a gross floor area of 10,000 square metres. Two consecutive vaults with different heights, made from reinforced concrete and covered with fibre cement, define the main space where the commercial activity takes place and which is also accessed by the refrigerated trucks, lined up behind the stalls. Inside, a three-storey volume with a porticoed structure accommodates offices and service areas whose balconies look down on the hustle and bustle that starts at three in the morning when the merchandise, on its bed of crushed ice, is carried in brightly coloured crates from the industrial vehicles to the stalls, filleting area, restaurants and customers.

Cementerio Nueva Esperanza   057 C
Calle Virgen de Lourdes,
Villa María del Triunfo
Informal architecture
1961

C

The origin of the district of Villa María del Triunfo dates back to the 1960s when mass migration from the interior of the country to the capital led to a demographic explosion in Lima. This new, low-income population mainly settled on the outskirts of the city, taking over the free areas. The 'Good Hope' cemetery, which initially operated clandestinely, emerged to meet the needs of this new population, which had largely arrived from villages in the Andes. It occupies an area of approximately 63 hectares, extending across several bare hills and turning the monochrome landscape into a picturesque, multi-coloured spectacle. Various dirt roads and numerous winding footpaths plough through the hill slopes to the graves. Most of these have been excavated directly in the ground, although the cemetery also boasts numerous mausoleums and niche constructions. Few places in Lima capture the city's diversity as succinctly as this cemetery. It is particularly interesting on 1 November, the Feast of All Saints, when thousands of people flock to the graveyard. On that day, the traditions, rituals, music and dances from different regions – not to mention copious amounts of food and considerable drink – transform the cemetery into a colourful festival celebrating both Christian and Andean forms of worship.

C

Eleazar Cuadros

Parque zonal
Flor de Amancaes

058 C

Avenidas 27 de Diciembre
and Los Incas,
Villa María del Triunfo
Aldo Facho Dede,
Ana Ábalos, Pablo Llopis
2015

Despite the growing demand for recreational areas after the disorderly urban expansion of Lima, the construction of zonal parks begun in 1970 ground to a halt in 1975. Over the next four decades, these spaces fell into an increasing state of neglect, but in 2010 a comprehensive remodelling programme was launched and different architectural competitions were announced for the design and installation of more infrastructures of this type on the fringes of the city. In 2012 the submission from the architect Aldo Facho Dede and the studio Abalosllopis

Arquitectos won the competition to build the new Flor de Amancaes zonal park in the Villa María del Triunfo district. Located on a 9.16-hectare plot, the project contemplated a multifunctional programme including outdoor and indoor sports facilities, a bike park, a swimming pool and a garden centre. The new zonal park finally opened in 2016. It is defined by the organic distribution of the built volumes, which maximises the topography of the terrain while generating fluid connections with the existing urban fabric through the public squares that provide access to the park. The design of the park therefore opens the space up to the city, with adapted programmes to the appropriate urban scales: Plaza de las Culturas is a metropolitan public space connected to the CREA cultural centre, and Plaza de los Niños serves the neighbourhood's children and gives access to the play centre.

Eleazar Cuadros

Villa El Salvador

Lima
Miguel Eugenio Romero Sotelo
(Junta Nacional de la Vivienda)
1971

At midnight on 30 April 1971, scores of families armed with sticks and straw mats seized possession of Pamplona, a private plot adjacent to the Colegio de la Inmaculada. The context was the uncontrolled expansion of the city by means of the invasions that sociologist Matos Mar describes as a 'popular overflow.' In the confrontations that ensued with the security forces, the activist Edilberto Ramos was killed, leading to great social unrest. The Jesuit Luis Bambarén, bishop of the so-called 'young towns,' held a celebratory mass to welcome the founders of the new Lima, for which he was arrested and sent to prison. Meanwhile, the Inter-American Development Bank (IDB) was due to hold its summit in Lima on 5 May and the military government was hoping to use the occasion to request support for its investment plans. With the security forces busy preparing the assembly, General Velasco Alvarado decided to sack the interior minister, release the priest and initiate a negotiation that would culminate in the government's concession of a 2,500-hectare plot of land known as Las Pampas de Tablada de Lurín, owned by the Air Force

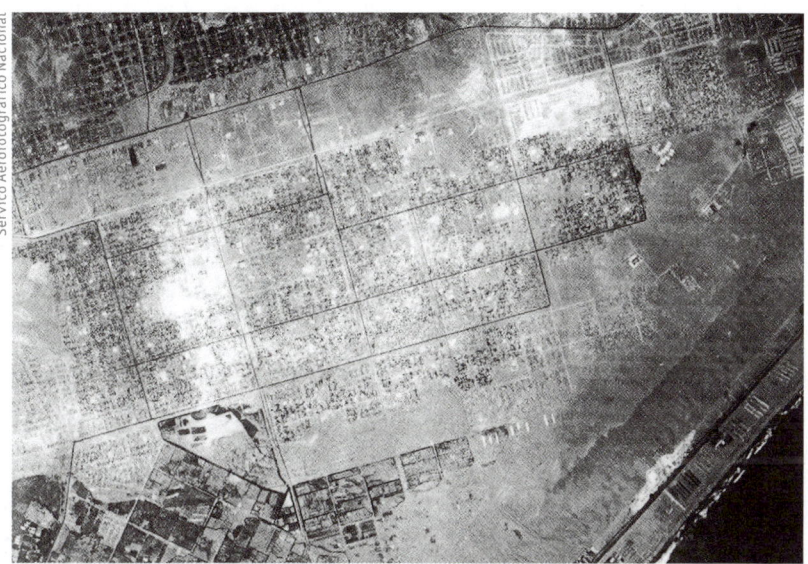

Servico Aerofotográfico Nacional

Asociación Amigos de Villa

Pamplona invasion, 1971

C

and lacking water and electricity supplies at the time. The government assigned the task of urban planning to a team of Junta Nacional de la Vivienda ('National Housing Board') technicians led by Miguel Romero, who designed an urban fabric divided into four zones: residential, agricultural, recreational and industrial (now home to one the city's largest woodwork factories). Each zone had its own neighbourhoods, formed by the repetition of a standard block organised around a service yard. The average residents were couples between the ages of 18 and 33 with several children, mainly from the provinces in the mountains, who were given plots ranging from 108 to 140 square metres on the condition that they erected a fence along the front and rear boundaries within a week. The families occupied their plot initially with a folded straw mat and then with a shack made out of four mats, where they lived for a time until they acquired the deeds to the property. Ownership gave them the right to build a basic home, following a standard model designed to grow over time. As for management, Villa El Salvador emerged at the height of liberation theology with the ambition to become an example for other young towns. The town's self-managed urban community established lines of action – healthcare, production and markets – managed by groups of settlers under the principle that common law was municipal law. The Spaniard Michel Azcueta was the first mayor. The success of Villa El Salvador and the fact that it was a peaceful, popular

Evelyn Merino Reyna

Aerial view of Villa El Salvador

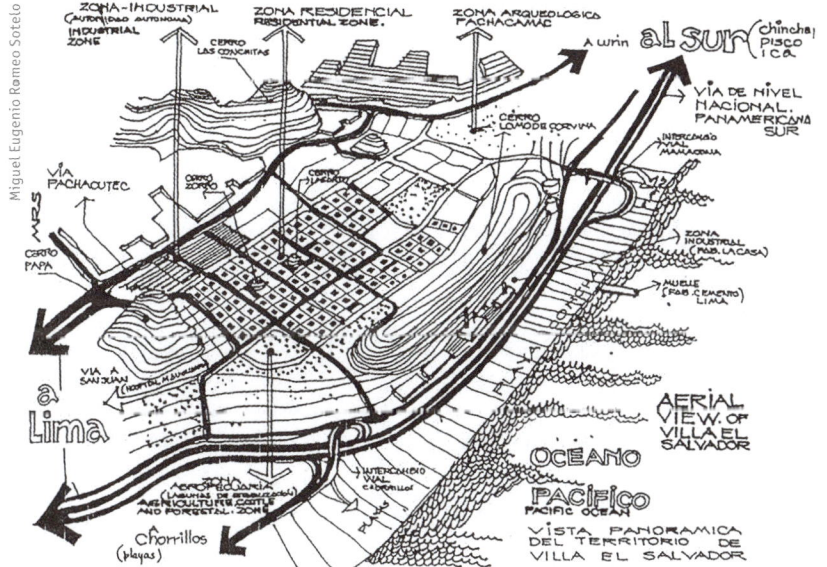

ZONA-INDUSTRIAL (AUTORIDAD AUTONOMA) INDUSTRIAL ZONE · ZONA RESIDENCIAL RESIDENTIAL ZONE · ZONA ARQUEOLOGICA PACHACAMAC · A lurin · al sur (chincha pisco ica) · VIA DE NIVEL NACIONAL. PANAMERICANA SUR · CERRO LAS CONCHITAS · CERRO LOMO DE CORVINA · INTERCAMBIO VIAL MAMACONA · VIA PACHACUTEC · CERRO ZORRO · ZONA INDUSTRIAL (FAB. LA CASA) · MUELLE (FAB. CEMENTO LIMA) · CERRO PAPA · a Lima · VIA A SAN JUAN (HOSPITAL M. MOYANO) · AERIAL VIEW OF VILLA EL SALVADOR · OCEANO PACIFICO PACIFIC OCEAN · Chorrillos (playas) · INTERCAMBIO VIAL CONCHAN · AGROPECUARIA (LAGUNAS DE ESTABILIZACION) AGRICULTURE, CATTLE AND FORESTAL ZONE · VISTA PANORAMICA DEL TERRITORIO DE VILLA EL SALVADOR

Miguel Eugenio Romeo Sotelo

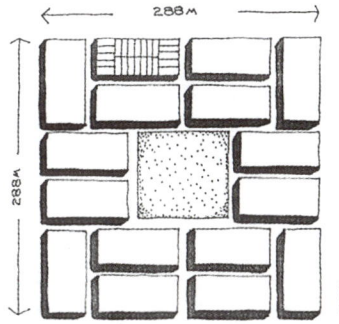

MODULO URBANO
GRUPO RESIDENCIAL

288 M

288 M

MRS

Miguel Eugenio Romeo Sotelo

movement made it an uncomfortable example for Shining Path and in 1992 members of this revolutionary organisation killed María Elena Moyano, the charismatic leader, feminist and deputy mayor. Pope John Paul II visited Villa El Salvador in 1985 and the town has received two important distinctions: the Prince of Asturias Award for Concord in 1987 and the title of United Nations Messenger of Peace in 2007. It has been the scene and battle field of nearly every political and social movement of recent decades in Peru. Today, it is a proud city with a population of nearly 400,000 and a thriving economy. Delimited by the Pachacamac sanctuary, the Pantanos de la Villa wildlife refuge, the Parque Zonal Huayna Cápac and the Atocongo cement plant, it is connected to the rest of Lima by the South Pan-American Highway and the electric train.

Other Works of Interest

C01   **Cementerio El Ángel**
Jirón Ancash, Cercado de Lima
Luis Miró Quesada,
Simón Ortiz Vega
1959

C02   **Mercado Minorista**
Avenida Aviación, La Victoria
1945

C03   **Colegio Alexander Von Humboldt**
Avenida Alfredo Benavides 3081,
Santiago de Surco
Paul Linder
1961

C04   **Conjunto habitacional Los Próceres**
Alameda Manuel Pérez de Tudela,
Santiago de Surco
José Bentín Díez Canseco,
Víctor Hupiú, Alfredo Montagne
1973

Vía Expresa

D

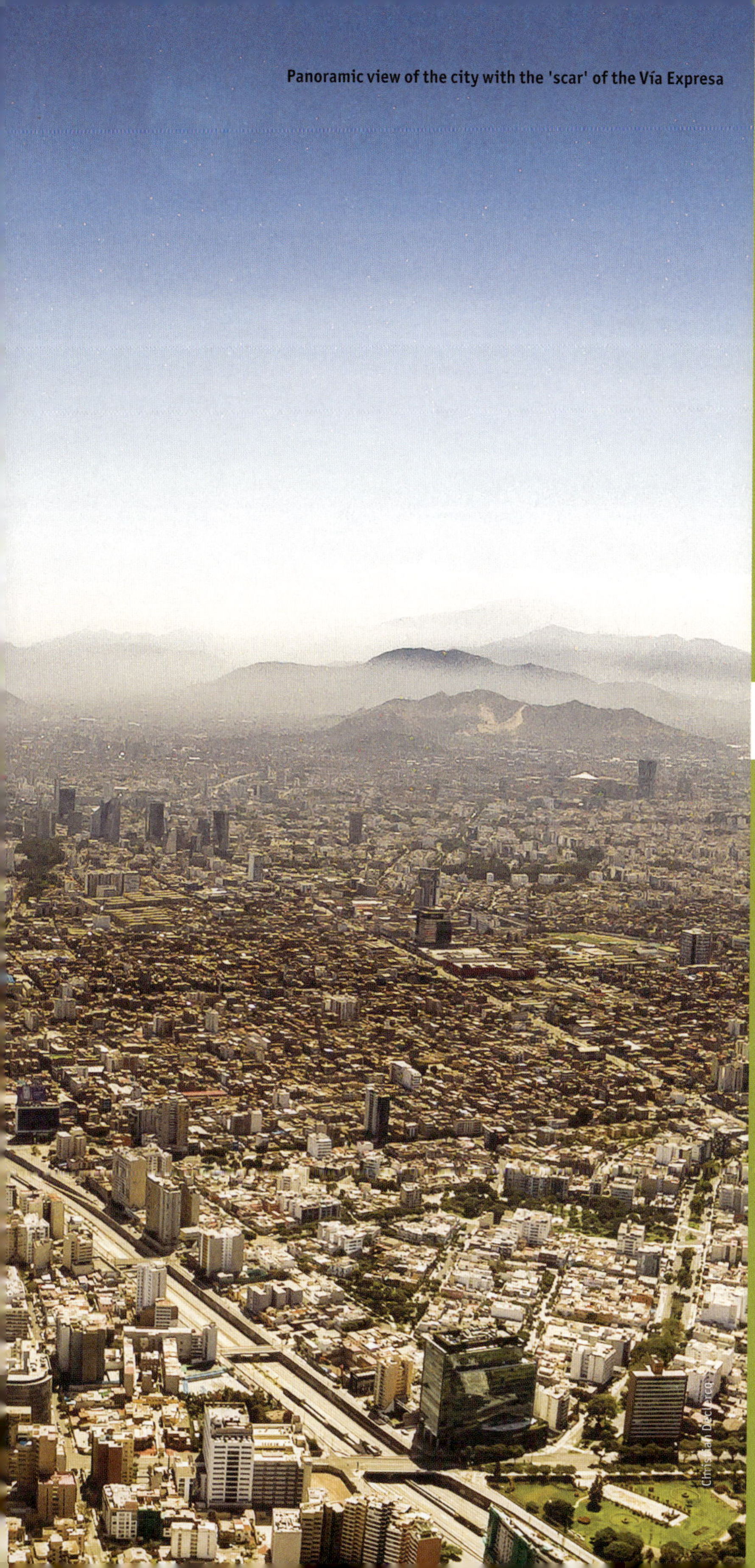

Panoramic view of the city with the 'scar' of the Vía Expresa

D

060
061
D01
D
062
D0
063
D04
D05

N

0   0.5   1km

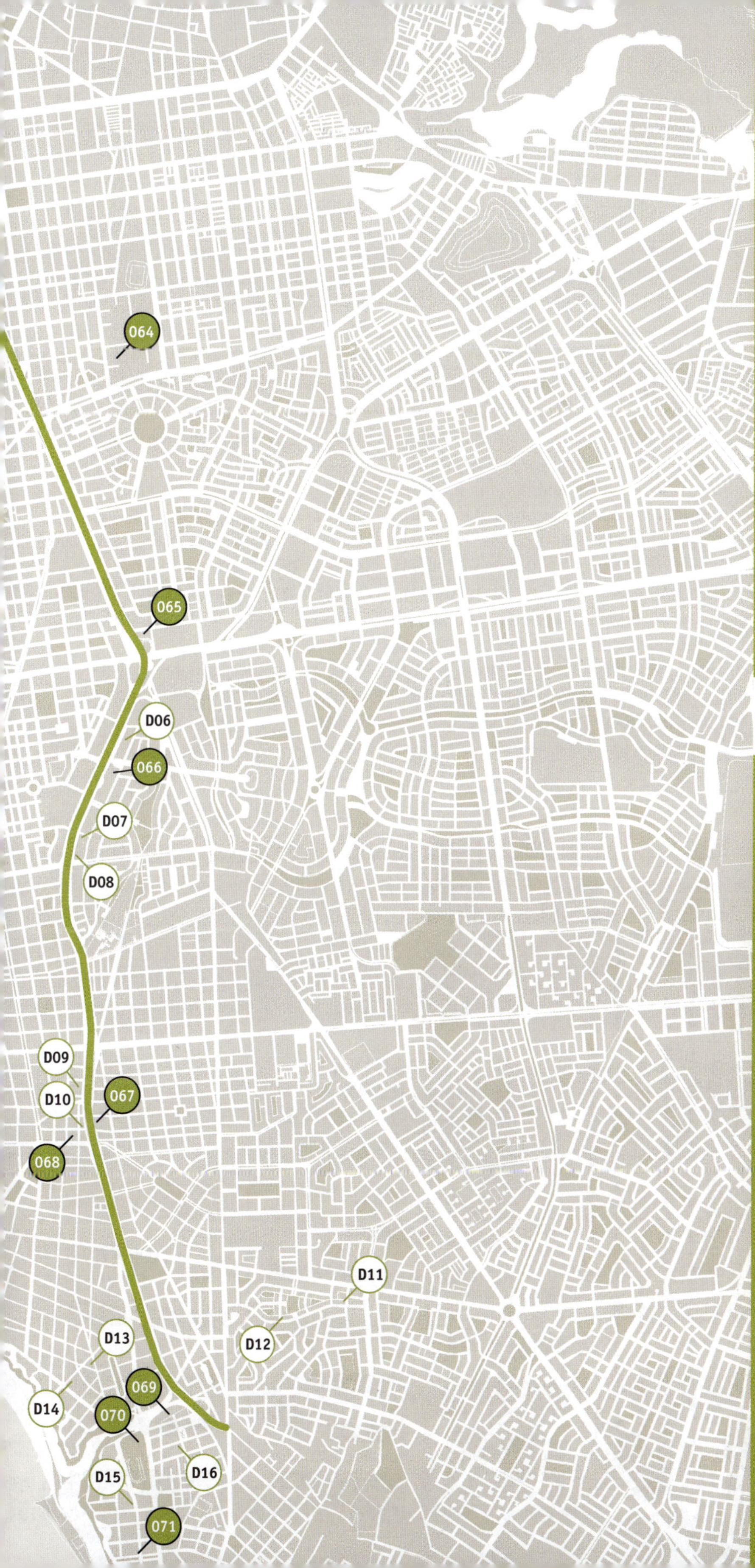

D

064

065

D06

066

D07

D08

D09

D10

067

068

D11

D13

D12

D14

069

070

D15

D16

071

Centro Cívico

Avenida Paseo de la República,
Cercado de Lima

*Adolfo Córdova, Jacques Crousse,
José García Bryce, Miguel Ángel Llona,
Guillermo Málaga, Oswaldo Núñez,
Simón Ortiz, Jorge Páez, Ricardo Pérez
León, Carlos Williams*
1970

060 D

In 1946, Fernando Belaúnde Terry, a member of parliament at the time, boosted the institutionalisation of urban planning by creating the Oficina Nacional de Planeamiento y Urbanismo (ONPU), which disseminated the principles of the Athens Charter and laid the foundations for the implementation of the Lima Pilot Plan. In this context, the construction of the Centro Cívico represented an attempt by the public administration to apply modernist theories. Located on a 3-hectare plot occupied at the time by the Lima penitentiary, the design – with contributions from Josep Lluís Sert and Paul Lester Wiener – contemplated commercial and government buildings on a highly ambitious scale, so ambitious that the design was rejected and the project was halted for two decades. In 1966, with Belaúnde now as president, the government revived the project and organised a competition, ultimately awarding the contract to a team of leading architects. Construction commenced after General Velasco's military coup and the project became one of the emblematic works of the new regime. The monumental complex includes a tower that remained the city's tallest edifice for 40 years, a convention centre and a series of seven-storey buildings organised around interior streets and squares connected by flights of steps, forming an interesting public space defined by its volumetry and the materiality of the concrete execution, painted over several decades later. Access is via a public square situated at the corner of the plot, at the end of Jirón de la Unión, one of the busiest streets in the city centre, which leads to the Plaza Mayor and the Puente de Piedra, the oldest bridge in Lima. In 1975, an insurrection by the police led to looting and severe damage to the buildings, including a fire at the main auditorium, followed by a period of decay that would last until 2007 when a private initiative remodelled the complex and turned part of it into a busy shopping centre. The history of the Centro Cívico is therefore entwined with the history of different models of urban management, from the modernist utopias promoted by the public sector to the commercial architecture of the private-sector.

Edificio de la Compañía de Seguros Rímac

061 D

Avenida Roosevelt 101,
Cercado de Lima
Ricardo de Jaxa Malachowski
1924

Situated at the end of the Paseo de los Héroes Navales, next to emblematic buildings of different styles and periods, this façade is defined by its elaborate composition and ornamentation. Built during the 11-year regime of President Leguía, a period of major real estate development, the academicist style reflects the European cultural influence and aspirations of Peruvian society at the time. The designer, Polish architect Ricardo de Jaxa Malachowski, was one of the first teachers of the architecture section at the Escuela de Ingenieros (now the Universidad Nacional de Ingeniería) and he was keen for the project to reflect the postulates of the École des Beaux-Arts in Paris, where he had previously trained: a tripartite composition with a rusticated stone base, a middle section of colossal pilasters and a slate mansard roof with spires to indicate the entrances and symmetrical axes. It was the first multi-family building in Lima, occupying an area of 5,200 square metres and containing 69 apartments in a complex floor plan organised around three courtyards. There are entrances on the three elevations and the building has one of the city's first mechanical lifts. It belonged to President Manuel Prado Ugarteche and housed the famous book publisher Populibros, an initiative promoted by the Peruvian writer Manuel Scorza in the 1960s to facilitate cheap access to national works of literature.

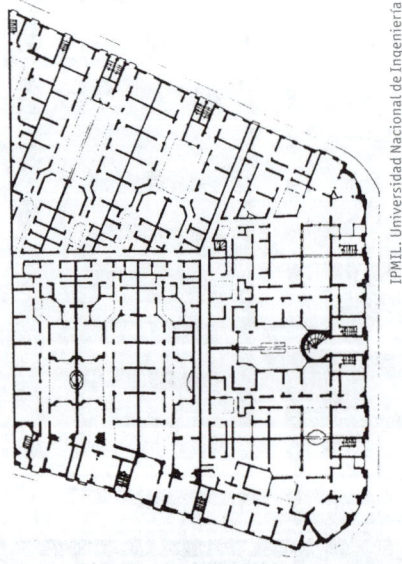

IPMIL. Universidad Nacional de Ingeniería

Hotel Sheraton

062 D

Av. Paseo de la República 170,
Cercado de Lima
Edward Durell Stone,
Ricardo J. Malachowski Benavides
1973

The Sheraton occupies part of the former site of the old Lima penitentiary, also known as the 'Panopticon' (1862–1961). Together with the Centro Cívico, it became a symbol of modernity in the 1970s, as well as the scene of political demonstrations due to its location at the entrance to the historic centre, opposite

Margaux Eyssette

a large public space and the Palacio de Justicia, designed by Bruno Paprowsky in the neoclassical style and opened in 1937. At its rear, on the Jirón Azángaro, there are various print shops that forge passports, university diplomas and any other type of document. The hotel project was entrusted to Ricardo J. Malachowski Benavides and Edward Durell Stone, the latter well known as the designer of the Radio City Music Hall at the Rockefeller Center and the Museum of Modern Art in New York. The result was a 20-storey volume preceded by a horizontal base in which the rigidity of the plan composition and the façade contrast with the exuberance of the decoration in the social halls, with mirrors, rugs and crystal-clear pools. Most outstanding of all is the atrium leading to the bedrooms, a spectacular vertical space typical of the American hotels that John Portman was designing in the United States at that time. The concrete parapets are decorated with pre-Columbian motifs reminiscent of the Mayan Revival architecture seen in the work of Frank Lloyd Wright. Although this is certainly not Durrel Stone's finest building, it nevertheless contains several hallmarks of his style, which some critics have called 'modernist populism.' Perhaps his greatest work – the US Embassy in New Delhi – was memorably caricatured in Tom Wolfe's classic book, *From Bauhaus to Our House*.

D

Palacio de la Exposición

063 D

Paseo Colón 125,
Cercado de Lima
Antonio Leonardi
1872

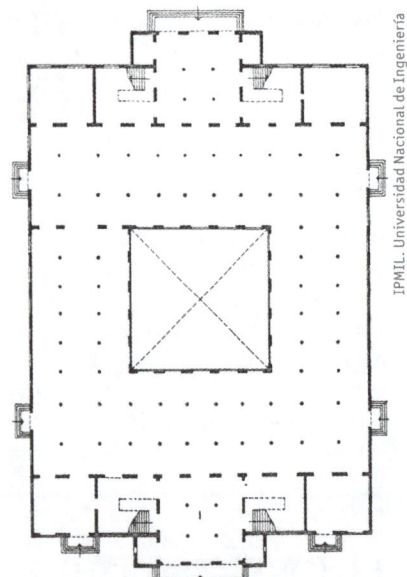

IPMIL. Universidad Nacional de Ingeniería

In 1868, the walls around Lima were demolished to make way for the city's expansion. The site of the old Guadalupe Gate became the city's first major public space, the Parque de la Exposición, created to accommodate the Lima International Exhibition in 1872. Several pavilions were built, the most important of which was the Palacio de la Exposición. Nowadays, the park occupies a smaller area than when it was originally developed. In 1898, it was divided into two separate parts after the Paseo Colón was opened up to traffic. In addition to the Palacio de la Exposición, this boulevard is lined with handsome mansions such as the Casa Augusto Wiese, the Casa Sal y Rosas and the Quinta Alania complex. The building is classical in its appearance, traditional in its construction and innovative in its structure and functionality. Symmetrical in both directions, it has a rectangular floor plan with two volumes projecting from the north and south façades to frame the entrances. It displays semi-circular openings, Ionic and Corinthian pilasters, decorated friezes and a balustrade on the roof. It is a two-storey construction with a brick ground floor and a top floor made of *quincha*, a vernacular building system based on reeds and clay. However, it was the first building in Peru with an iron structure. The metal columns form a regular grid that lends flexibility to a continuous and highly functional exhibition space with refined geometry, organised around a square courtyard. The palace has been the home of the Museo de Arte de Lima (MALI) since 1961. It has been remodelled on several occasions but its integrity remains intact. In 2016, an international competition was launched to build a new wing for contemporary art, won by Burgos & Garrido Arquitectos and Llama Urban Design. The latest intervention was the restoration of the façade, completed in 2022 by architect Carlos Torres.

Candy Torres

Renzo Rebagliati

Unidad Vecinal Matute

064 D

Avenidas México e Isabel
La Católica, Jirón Andahuaylas
and Jirón Abtao, La Victoria
Santiago Agurto, Enrique Ciriani
1954, 1964

D

In the 1940s, the government launched the Lima Housing Plan, determined to solve city's poor health conditions and shortage of housing through the construction of various neighbourhood units. These were working class districts with green spaces and recreational areas, good connections to workplaces and all the necessary services. The Unidad Vecinal III was the first one built and served as a model for subsequent units. Matute was the second neighbourhood unit built. Agurto's design combined linear four-storey blocks (some on pilotis and others at ground level) with groups of terraced single-family houses and different types of public spaces between them. It also included a civic centre and sports, religious, cultural and educational facilities. The project blended the rationalist language of the day with local

Jasip Curich. Courtesy of Revista CASAS

Passage constructed during the second phase

devices in a display of what Sharif Kahatt, in his book, *Utopías Construidas*, calls 'regional functionalism,' which can be seen in the use of pebbles and natural stone for bases, the colours on the façades and the articulation of the public areas in sequences that generate an interesting spatial diversity, evoking the traditional city. The south-east quadrant and the west end of the neighbourhood unit, including nearly 500 homes, respond to this first approach. After the completion of these sectors, the project was halted. A decade later, Enrique Ciriani was commissioned to reformulate the unit by increasing the density in order to include more homes. Consequently, this phase has no single-family constructions and is structured around five-storey linear blocks with single-storey apartments on the ground floor and split-level apartments on the upper floors, with accesses via sculptural staircases and external corridors. The distribution of the blocks generates alleyways and squares.

Edificio Interbank →

Calle Carlos Villarán 140,
La Victoria
Hans Hollein, Jaime Persivale
2000

065 D

The flagship headquarters of an important bank, this building is divided into two blocks due to its unique location between a busy cloverleaf interchange and the residential Santa Catalina neighbourhood. The first block, 20 storeys and 90 metres tall, adopts the form of an inclined sail over the road junction, dominating the city like a powerful totem. The curve of the façade, which complements the dynamic movement of the surrounding environment, is defined by its latticework, which is further underscored by the striking illumination at night that changes colour according to certain events. The second block, orthogonal and translucent, establishes a dialogue with the scale of the adjacent neighbourhoods and other

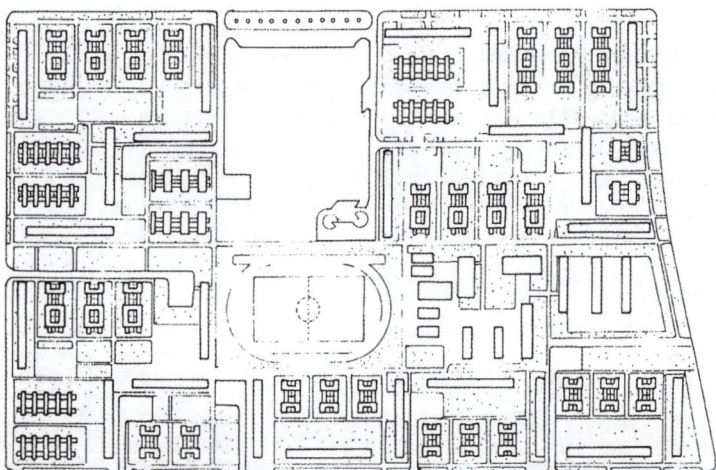

IPMIL. Universidad Nacional de Ingeniería

Josip Curich

Buildings of the first phase

D

nearby office buildings. The atrium rises to the full height of the building and contains two expressive staircases that contrast with the austere finishes. A spectacular cantilevered cube-shaped volume projects from the rear façade over the hustle and bustle of the road below. The building rests on a volcanic stone plinth that accommodates the basements. An independent volume that houses the auditorium, plus the heliport and a large sign, complete the construction. While the material aesthetics may fall short of the Viennese commercial premises that earned Hollein his Pritzker Prize, the changing image of this building maximises the kinetics of its context; in so doing, it becomes an urban landmark.

Edificio Petroperú

Avenida Canaval y Moreyra 150,
San Isidro
Walter Weberhofer,
Daniel Arana Ríos
1970

Brutalism, the architectural movement that emerged between the 1950s and 1970s and which is often associated with social utopias, was adopted as the official style of the military dictatorship of General Velasco Alvarado, reinforcing the image of power and economic independence that he sought to project. This group of buildings forms the headquarters of the state-owned oil company, located on a rectangular plot that occupies nearly 5 hectares parallel to the Vía Expresa, with a vehicle access from the Avenida del Parque and a pedestrian one from Canaval y Moreyra. Two architects with very different profiles joined forces for this project: Daniel Arana, who had used a more orthodox modernist language in the Edificio Las Gaviotas (1960) on the Playa Herradura; and Walter Weberhofer, an architect with great plastic talent and the designer of highly personal works with tortured forms. Hints of this language can be found in the plans and perspectives of this competition entry, awarded first prize and one of the finest examples of modernist architecture in Peru. The duo would go on to design several other interesting works, such as the Southern Peru Copper Corporation building in the Surco district. In this project for Petroperú, the primitive structure of the two horizontal volumes, which is accentuated by the bevelled-edge concrete, contrasts with the modernity of the main tower that was in its day one of the tallest in Lima. Its façade is defined by a hand-assembled curtain wall with empty joints between frames that has prevented the deterioration commonly found in similar envelopes from the same period. Moreover, in this case the architects took the extra precaution of applying a smoked filter to the glass and creating windows that open – a rare feature in buildings of this scale – to generate cross ventilation and counteract the exposure to heat and humidity in the summer months. The floor plan is distinguished in general by the order and clarity of the spatial distribution and, in particular, by the displacement of the vertical communication cores to the perimeter, in a structural solution designed by the engineers Gallegos, Casabonne and Arango, similar that employed by Norman Foster decades later in a tower he designed in Madrid for another oil company. The building is a work of total architecture, due to its balanced composition of volumes and the rhythm of the modulation on the façades, which has remained intact and in perfect condition to this day, thanks in part to the former head of maintenance, appointed when the building was inaugurated, who was careful to consult the architects over every alteration.

Candy Torres

Mercado de Surquillo 067 D

Av. Paseo de la República 53,
Surquillo
Alfredo Dammert
1940

Beyond the signs and billboards that saturate this context, it is still possible to glimpse the characteristic silhouette of what was the Miraflores market until the establishment of the Surquillo district in 1949 and which in 2013, after years of legal disputes, returned to its old status. This rationalist building occupies an P-shaped plot and consists of two spatially different constructions, each with their own programme. The market stalls are located in the oval space in the central area of the building. A vaulted structure, 14 metres high, 52 metres long and 36 metres wide, eliminates the need for columns. It consists of a succession of parabolic arches, four of them parallel to the central section, and six half-arches at each end arranged radially, all fragmented into straight segments to simplify the structure. Around this space, and contributing to its rigidity, the area where the shops are located is

resolved by means of a trabeated structure on load-bearing walls and a split-level flat roof. Natural light penetrates through the interval between the two roof levels and through the lower part of the dome. Today, an unfortunate remodel has distorted the view of the vaulted space, but this market remains one of the most interesting in Lima, allowing visitors to appreciate the rich variety of products in a diverse country whose cuisine has acquired the status of 'Cultural Heritage of the Americas.' An organic food fair is held every week in the pedestrian section of the adjacent Jirón Narciso de la Colina. The complex has served as the catalyst for a slow transformation in a district in need of regeneration.

Candy Torres

Hotel Holiday Inn

Avenida Ricardo Palma 355,
Miraflores
René Poggione, Susel Biondi
2019

068 D

Juan Solano

Located in the centre of the Miraflores district, this 17-storey building occupies a corner plot interrupted by a single-family home at the vertex. Although an obstacle for management purposes, this interruption nevertheless enhances the composition of the hotel, which is divided into two volumes to comply with municipal regulations and whose rear façade is set back with respect to the Casa Raúl Porras Barrenechea. The reinforced concrete structure, designed by René Lagos, displays a series of triangulations on the façade to counteract the shear force that buildings suffer in an earthquake. This solution frees the floor plan from the screen walls that often fragment the interior spaces of buildings of a certain height in Peru. Each diagonal brace spans two floors, distorting the scale of the building, which from the Vía Expresa appears lower than it actually is. The frames around the openings are painted black to emphasise the structure, which is concealed from the inside by counterbalanced windows. On the ground and first floors, the porticoes are slightly inclined towards the street, a Mannerist detail that creates a certain sensation of instability and in fact turns the hotel into a house of cards, able to sway and absorb the stress during an earthquake. This illusory fragility, accentuated by the location of a swimming pool on the roof, represents one of the finest structural effects in the city.

D

Renzo Rebagliati

Edificio UTEC

069 D

Jirón Medrano Silva 165,
Barranco
*Grafton Architects
(Yvonne Farrell, Shelley McNamara),
Alejandro Shell*
2015

Winner of an international competition launched in 2011, this building houses the Universidad de Ingeniería y Tecnología (UTEC) and is probably the most important Peruvian project of recent years, in terms of its impact. Although questioned in some quarters, awards such as the Silver Lion at the Venice Biennale in 2012 and the RIBA International Prize in 2016 are clear endorsements of its merits. It is located on an elongated plot whose north side faces a busy road junction and high-density constructions. The south side delimits a smaller-scale residential area in the Barranco district. This context, and its connection to the cliffs of the Costa Verde via one of the natural descents that link the city to the Pacific Ocean, shaped the entire project. With an uncommon scheme for this typology, the university building is conceived as a high-rise construction. A series of parallel reinforced concrete screens perpendicular to the longitudinal axis of the plot, whose geometry inclines the building over the highway on one side and sets it back on the other, articulate the structural base into which the different spaces of the programme are inserted. Towards Barranco, the teaching blocks and other enclosed spaces are arranged in steps, one on top of the other, generating terraces and establishing a dialogue with the scale of the adjacent residential fabric. The presence of abundant vegetation helps to soften the effect of the austere façade. The north side opens onto a complex network of roads and outdoor meeting spaces with multiple visual relationships designed to encourage social interaction. With its imposing presence, this massive elevation is the face the building offers to the metropolis and the collective imaginary.

Museo de Arte Contemporáneo

Avenida Almirante
Miguel Grau 1511, Barranco
Frederick Cooper,
Antonio Graña
2013

The origins of this museum date back to 1955, when the Instituto de Arte Contemporáneo was created with the aim of disseminating the latest artistic trends. Over the course of the following years, the Instituto amassed a large collection of works made by Peruvian artists and organised exhibitions in different venues around the city, prompting the idea for the construction of a permanent museum. In the 1990s, an auction was held to raise funds for the project, but works did not get under way until 2002. For its location, the municipal authorities allocated a large plot of land at the entrance to the district, occupied at the time by a park. After local residents campaigned to preserve the park, the building was ultimately relocated to the south of Barranco, to a small island in a pre-existing lake, taking advantage of the water and leaving a large part of the plot free. This green space absorbs the impact of the adjacent roads and simultaneously provides a recreational area. The project consists of a series of single-storey parallelepipeds arranged radially to generate different exterior spaces between them. The main volume contains the permanent collection while the rest of the programme is distributed across smaller volumes. Its simplicity reflects the tight budget, with an envelope of red fibre cement panels on the short side, like an industrial hangar. The structure is made of exposed steel and spans up to 20 metres with trusses that contain skylights – the most outstanding feature of the project – in a skilful reinterpretation of the old *teatinas* that characterise many of the roofs in this district. In recent years, the museum has hosted some interesting exhibitions, including 'Ecosistema del agua' (2019) by Ana Teresa Barboza and Rafael Freyre, an installation on the relationship between pre-Columbian cultures and water.

Hotel B

Jirón Sáenz Peña 204, Barranco
Claude Sahut, David Mutal
1930s, 2013

The Hotel B is housed in a Belle Époque summer mansion built in the 1930s, refurbished by David Mutal in 2013 in a way that respects the original geometry but challenges its materiality. It won the Hexágono de Plata at the 16th Peruvian Architecture Biennial in 2014 and was a finalist that same year at the 19th Pan-American Architecture Biennial. Access to the building is through an elliptical space situated at the vertex that serves as an antechamber to the reception area. The programme inserts social areas and 10 bedrooms into the existing two-storey structure, seamlessly integrating the installations and soundproofing. The marble staircase – a new element – is also integrated by means of its symmetry with respect to the reception desk and an ornate arch. Perpendicular to this axis is a courtyard connecting a new building, concealed behind a vegetal façade, with seven bedrooms spread across three floors, respecting the height of the cornice. The difference between levels is resolved by a three-flight staircase encapsulated in a cylindrical space that distributes and articulates the old and new, skilfully assembling and interweaving different materials and details. The latest extension, completed in 2019, has incorporated the spaces previously occupied by the Lucía de la Puente art gallery, preserving the art and design shop for a hotel that boasts nearly 300 artworks on its walls, ranging from pre-Columbian to contemporary. The project establishes the direction which the restoration of Lima's priceless historical heritage should ideally follow, solving a complex problem with a highly personal language in which the old and new come together with a resonance that recalls the craft of Carlo Scarpa. This is a memorable place to begin or end a tour of Barranco, with dinner in the courtyard or a cocktail at the bar under a painting by José Tola.

All photos: Gonzalo Cáceres

D

David Mutal Arquitectos

Other Works of Interest

D01 Dirección de Policía
Avenida España 323,
Cercado de Lima
Eduardo Orrego, Ricardo González
1980

D02 Palacio de Justicia
Avenida Paseo de la República,
Cercado de Lima
Bruno Paprowsky
1937

D03 Museo de Arte Italiano
Avenida Paseo de la República 250,
Cercado de Lima
Gaetano Moretti
1923

D04 Pabellón Morisco
Parque de la Exposición,
Cercado de Lima
M. Pachón
1872

D05 Polvos Azules
Avenida Paseo de la República 4,
La Victoria
Eduardo Orrego
2001

D06 Edificio Alide
Avenida Paseo de la República 3211,
San Isidro
*Frederick Cooper, Antonio Graña,
Eugenio Nicolini*
1981

D07 Edificio El Ejecutivo
Avenida Paseo de la República 3717,
San Isidro
*Carlos Arana, Antenor Orrego,
Juan Torres*
1976

D08 Sede de la Comunidad Andina
Avenida Paseo de la República 3895,
San Isidro
*Carlos Arana, Antenor Orrego,
Juan Torres*
1970

D09 Edificio Marsano
Parque Francisco de Miranda,
Miraflores
Américo Chini Sapori
1947

D10 Centro empresarial Narciso de la Colina
Calle Narciso de la Colina 421,
Miraflores
*Vértice Arquitectos (Sandro Moro,
Luis Miguel Becerra,
Hernani Canessa)*
2015

D11 Vivienda unifamiliar
Calle de Ciro Alegría 290, Miraflores
Javier Damiani
1972

D12 Vivienda unifamiliar
Calle Manuel Freyre 281, Miraflores

D13 Edificio multifamiliar
Avenida La Paz 1362, Miraflores
*Frederick Cooper, Antonio Graña,
Eugenio Nicolini*
1981

D14 Casa Zuzunaga
Avenida Núñez de Balboa 224,
Miraflores
Georg Rudolf
1962

D15 Edificio San Martín
Avenida San Martín 605, Barranco
Violeta Ferrand, Teodoro Boza
2014

D16 Edificio Torres Paz
Jirón Buenaventura Aguirre 292,
Barranco
*Vicca Verde (Horacio Goitre,
Gonzalo Zegarra, Mateo Peschiera)*
2019

**Right: Edificio San Martín
(Teodoro Boza, Violeta Ferrand)**

D

Arequipa and Larco

E

Bike lane on Avenida Arequipa

E

E01
E02
E03
E04
E05
072
073
074
E06
E07
E08
E09
E10
075
076
077
078
079
E11
081
082
E13
084

N

0   0.5   1km

E

Hospital Central del Empleado

072 E

Avenida Edgardo Rebagliati 490, Lince

Edward Durrell Stone, Alfred Lewis Aydelott, Ricardo J. Malachowski Benavides
1958

The creation of the worker's social security scheme in the 1930s and the construction of the associated hospital marked the beginning of the modernisation of healthcare infrastructure in Peru.

In 1948, the ruling military regime led by Manuel Odría introduced a similar scheme for salaried employees to provide health services for a sector of society with a higher income. The flagship infrastructure for this service was the Hospital Central del Empleado, or General Hospital for Employees, now known as the Edgardo Rebagliati Martins Hospital. Its construction commenced in 1951 on a plot of more than 16 hectares occupied at the time by the Huaca Santa Beatriz archaeological site. The project was entrusted to Edward

E

Durrell Stone and Alfred Aydelott, who had been selected by the United States Public Health Service and hired by the Peruvian government. With a gross floor area exceeding 90,000 square metres, part of the complex adopts a horizontal form consisting of low-rise buildings surrounded by large open spaces with gardens and car parks. It includes an area with surgeries and offices, an emergency zone, staff facilities, the medical director's house, a 300-seat auditorium and an austere chapel for 250 people. Rising from the centre of the plot is a long 14-storey prism with a wider middle section, including rooms on the façade and vertical communication cores, and two narrower lateral volumes occupied entirely by rooms. The whole programme is articulated by a long corridor that runs through the centre of the building from one end to the other. A healing machine with a capacity for 850 hospital beds, this is a canonical work of functionalism in its occupation of the plot, its floor plan organisation and its modular façade.

Centro comercial Arenales

073 E

Avenida Arenales 1737, Lince
Germán Costa, Luis Santiesteban
1982

After the city's first shopping gallery opened in 1956 on Jirón de la Unión, the typology gradually evolved until the appearance 20 years later of the first modern shopping malls. The Arenales was built in the district of Lince, occupying half a block with the main elevation on the avenue of the same name. The project also included two apartment buildings and an office block that were never executed. A four-storey construction with a basement, the centre and front of the building are given over to the commercial area. A central courtyard that allows natural light to reach the basement articulates the foot traffic. This is the main space in the building and, thanks to the sculptural treatment of the walkways, platforms and staircases, it is also the most outstanding. The top three floors at the sides of the building are occupied by the two car parks which, organised on half-storeys, enable a greater ceiling height for some of the premises. In the late 1980s, impacted by terrorism and the economic crisis, the shopping mall entered a decline. Most of its appeal today resides in its more recent unexpected transformation: since the end of the 1990s, it has become

a hotspot for a subculture of anime, manga and video game enthusiasts. Comics, costumes, collectible figures, Korean pop music and oriental restaurants can all be found here, as well as amusement arcades and numerous establishments filled with computers and teenagers. The volume that originally housed the two-screen cinema has been taken over by a Christian church known for its rather joyful mass gatherings.

Renzo Rebagliati

E

Edificio El Dorado
Avenida Arequipa 2450, Lince
Raúl Morey
1967

074 E

Architect Raúl Morey chose refined lines and meticulous modulation for the design of this high-rise office building at the intersection of the Avenida Arequipa and Avenida César Vallejo. With a rectangular floor plan, it occupies half a block and has three elevations facing the street. The 17-storey building rises from a base accessed by a flight of steps. The ground floor accommodates a double-height commercial area surrounded by a porticoed gallery that serves as a transitional space between the exterior and the commercial premises and lobby. The opulence that characterises this building can be seen from the entrance in the claddings, gold aluminium window frames and the design of the terrazzo paving, which underscores the modulation. On the next level, the open-air car park separates the commercial volume from the main body of the tower, developed as a free-standing volume. The curtain wall with gold aluminium profiles gives the building its distinctive appearance and name. The top floor is occupied by a Chinese restaurant with magnificent views of the city. The setback of this level and the thick cornice that covers it, creating a deep overhang, form the crest of a modern building that simultaneously reproduces the classical composition of base, shaft and chapter.

E

Renzo Rebagliati

E

Huaca Pucllana
Calle General Borgoño 8, Miraflores
Lima culture
200–700 CE

In contrast to post-conquest settlement patterns, pre-Hispanic land occupation was associated with the strategic location of urban centres in an integrated system of irrigation channels and large expanses of farmland. This is how the Lima culture developed an interconnected network of urban-ceremonial centres with a central base at Maranga, located in what is now part of the San Miguel district. Gradually emerging through the urban fabric of Miraflores, Huaca Pucllana was a ceremonial centre dedicated to the worship of a marine deity. It controlled the final section of the Huática, an irrigation channel that began in the River Rímac

Renzo Rebagliati

and discharged its surplus water at the present-day Bajada Balta. Built by the Lima culture, it was subsequently used by the Wari and Ychsma peoples as a burial ground. The site once extended across 16 hectares, but the city's expansion has reduced it to just 6 hectares today. Its main feature is the great pyramid consisting of seven stepped platforms linked by ramps. It is built with small adobe bricks 22 centimetres long and 7 centimetres wide, laid vertically in a way that simulates a bookcase, and then filled with pebble stones. This system is not only characteristic of the Lima culture but also an efficient anti-seismic technology. Since 1981, meticulous archaeological research and restoration works have made Huaca Pucllana an important tourist attraction. The fact that it is also home to one of the finest restaurants in the city, with views over the site, makes the place even more attractive.

Centro cultural Ccori Wasi

076 E

Avenida Arequipa 5280, Miraflores
Juvenal Baracco, Enrique Bonilla
2005

The present-day Avenida Arequipa was built in the 1920s to connect the historic centre to the summer resorts south of the city. The layout included a central promenade lined with trees, making it a popular location for the garden villas of the upper classes. Today, many of these old mansions have been refurbished to accommodate new programmes. Others have been replaced by high-rise multi-family buildings. In the late 1960s, the Universidad Ricardo Palma purchased one of these mansions, a neocolonial construction, using it for various educational and administrative purposes until finally transforming it into a cultural centre. The reuse of the house as part of the project preserves the memory of the avenue's residential past. The restoration has enhanced original features like the floors and mouldings, while partial demolitions have made way for a large exhibition hall with a metal structure on which the glazed volume of the library is suspended across the space. This hall also serves as the foyer for the auditorium, a separate volume built on the adjacent plot that assimilates the scale and the rhythm of the context and whose main façade incorporates a panel of stainless steel plates that reflect the light at night, creating a theatrical effect. Periodically, the building hosts wonderful exhibitions of projects and models by the university's architecture students. In fact, Juvenal Baracco's vertical workshop has produced some of the most important figures in contemporary Peruvian architecture.

E

Candy Torres

Edificio Bellevue ↓

Avenida José Pardo 715,
Miraflores
Miguel Forga, Celso Prado
1965

077 E

The Avenida José Pardo was the first boulevard developed in Miraflores, connecting the old railway station with the coastline. At the beginning of the twentieth century, the old ranches in this area gave way to elegant houses such as the Gutiérrez mansion, which is still standing today on the second block. In the 1960s, these were replaced by high-rise buildings, transforming the appearance of the avenue and significantly increasing the district's population. In 1953, the country's first American-style supermarket opened on the Avenida Larco and now the same company has established this one. The complex is composed of two differentiated parts with contradictory languages but both built with great precision. The first volume, a structure of parabolic vaults, accommodates the supermarket. The second, a 15-storey parallelepiped, has a curtain wall built with aluminium frames and blue panels, on top of a horizontal base that extends towards the supermarket. The tower clearly references the Lever House in New York. However, the concrete shell roof is a variant of Félix Candela's work in Mexico. The tower is in a reasonable condition and still stands out among the buildings on the avenue. The supermarket and part of the horizontal base are nowadays covered by the plasterboard panels of the current tenant, although the vaults are still there, emerging from the façade while they wait to be rescued.

Revista Arquitectura Peruana

Courtesy of Pool Porta Architect – AMPA

Edificio El Pacífico ↑

Avenida José Pardo 121, Miraflores
Fernando de Osma
1958

078 E

The public space formed by the Parque Kennedy and the Parque Central de Miraflores constitutes the district's centre of gravity, an epicentre of tourism and commerce. Located at the confluence of some of the most important avenues in the area, it is the site of notable works such as the Municipal Palace, a neoclassical building by Luis Miró Quesada, and the Virgen Milagrosa church by Ricardo de Jaxa Malachowski. This exemplary building occupies an irregular but privileged corner plot at the north vertex of the park. It has a mixed use, made up of a two-storey commercial base and a seven-storey residential block, separated by the void of the parking level.

The commercial base, which occupies the entire plot, is defined externally by glass façades and signage. Inside, a gallery lined with shops provides access to the apartments and what used to be one of the most modern cinemas in Lima. The apartment block is formally disconnected from the base and the geometry of the plot as an abstract volume of refined lines that rises above the city. It is composed of two rectangular prisms which, linked by the communications core, form a T-shaped floor plan. The main spaces open onto the glass façades with continuous windows. The secondary and service spaces are concealed behind opaque panels with windows protected by brise-soleils. The apartments originally had deep balconies with eaves to protect them from the sunlight, and although some of the owners have closed these spaces, the volume has preserved its appearance of lightness and transparency.

Edificio Diagonal ←

Calle Mártir José Olaya 201, Miraflores
Enrique Seoane
1959

079 E

Arcadia Mediática ↓

Calle Alcanfores 297, Miraflores
Michelle Llona, Rafael Zamora
2011

080 E

The construction of the Avenida Leguía in 1921, now the Avenida Arequipa, paved the way for the creation of a commercial hub around the Parque Central de Miraflores, driving both economic and demographic growth. The enactment in 1946 of the horizontal property law – promoted by architect and deputy Fernando Belaúnde Terry, who would later become president of the country – allowed buildings to be split into independent units and was an additional boost to this development that soon materialised in the Edificio Diagonal. This is a free-standing, mixed-use eight-storey building with commercial premises on the first two floors and apartments and offices on the remaining ones. The original design included ten floors, but during the construction, in different phases, it was finally reduced to eight. The floor plan is a symmetrical isosceles triangle. The longest side is the building's main elevation facing the busy Avenida Óscar Benavides, formerly known as the Avenida Diagonal, while the two short sides face onto a secondary road and a pedestrian passage. The convexity of the façades and the treatment of the corners modulate this geometry. At the rear, the obtuse vertex curves and the access is generated by a subtraction that leads to the lobby with the lifts. The corners facing the avenue incorporate double-height cylinders accommodating the stairs that rise to the second commercial floor. This gesture enhances the expressiveness of the cantilevered glazed spaces on the upper floors, the result of alterations to the original project, which contemplated balconies. The façade composition reflects the architect's quest for a regional interpretation of the modernist language, geometrically redefining traditional decorative motifs like the cornices to emphasise the structural axes. Similar strategies were used in the Edificio Limatambo, demolished in 2013 to make way for a 200-metre tower that has still not been executed.

Located on a corner in the Miraflores district, the Arcadia Mediática is the go-to bookshop for any architect who finds themselves in Lima and is looking for publications on Peruvian and Latin American architecture. The refurbishment project, carried out by Michelle Llona and Rafael Zamora in a space with irregular geometry and glass envelopes, is articulated around the design of modular shelving with wooden trays, ergonomically inclined and supported by a structure of white-painted steel tubes. The design was first created for an edition of the Casacor interior architecture fair in the Edificio Ronald in El Callao and subsequently adapted for this place. It has two functions: as a repository and showcase for books, and as a panel for protection from the sun, forming an abstract façade with skilful lighting. Another interesting element is the wooden furniture designed ad hoc to serve as a counter and consultation table. Other bookshops in Miraflores and San Isidro with a publishing tradition are the Librería Sur on Avenida Pardo y Aliaga, La Familia near Parque Kennedy, El Virrey in the Óvalo Bolognesi and Babel on Calle Arístides Aljovín.

Michelle Llona

Quinta en Tarata ↓
Calle Tarata 2, Miraflores
Augusto Guzmán
1938

 081 E

To explore Miraflores through its *quintas* is to journey back in time to the architecture that was practised in Lima in the early decades of the twentieth century, when modernist languages began to emerge amid eclecticisms and art deco ornaments. The *quintas* are clusters of houses grouped around a communal access courtyard or passage. They first appeared in the historic centre and then spread to the new districts. Miraflores is home to several exceptional ones, such as Leuro and Bustos on blocks 8 and 5 of the Avenida 28 de Julio. Conceived as quiet spaces away from the city, they became the fashionable typology in this coastal district where young architects of the day, such as Augusto Guzmán, tested their residential designs. The Calle Tarata is the location of this *quinta* affected by a Shining Path terrorist attack in 1992. Rationalist in its design, although clad with ornaments clearly inspired by art deco, it has characteristic elements of the Streamline Moderne style, such as round windows, metal frames, curved projections and tubular rails. Burnishing enhances the corners, defining the entrance and exit of the passage. Some *quintas* have been protected by the Ministry of Culture and the Miraflores municipal authorities, and have therefore preserved their façades and symmetry. In certain cases, the scale has been altered by the height of the buildings that have emerged nearby; in other cases, the state of conservation is not the best but the original atmosphere remains intact, hinting at the past existence of a city more attuned to a pedestrian scale.

Hotel Las Américas →
Avenida Alfredo Benavides 415, Miraflores
Walter Weberhofer,
Carlos López de Romaña
1978–1992

 082 E

Under the kitsch patina of an old-fashioned hotel aesthetic, it is still possible to appreciate the essential characteristics of a somewhat understated building by the renowned architect Walter Weberhofer, winner of the competition launched in 1978. Now known as the Hotel Estelar, at first sight it may not seem as impressive as his works in Santa María del Mar and the Edificio Petroperú, but it clearly demonstrates the architect's extraordinary command of his craft. The project originally consisted of a mixed-use building with a commercial base and a residential tower. The commercial area, which occupied the first five floors above ground and the first basement level, was structured like a helix. The spaces were arranged in ascending steps around a void that rose all the way up to the top of the commercial

base. The plan, an innovation at the time, contemplated three additional basement levels for parking, linked by a continuous ramp. This spatial programme was translated externally into a rich volumetric composition with an impeccable exposed concrete finish. A 14-storey tower for apartments was built on top of the base, aligned with the chamfered corner and with a meticulously executed continuous cladding of reflective glass. The construction works were halted in 1980, by which time the commercial gallery had been completed and partially sold and the tower structure and envelope were in place. For commercial reasons, the apartments were ultimately replaced by a high-rise hotel and the works recommenced in 1989 with a modified design by Carlos López de Romaña. A number of changes reduced the size of the commercial area to allow for a lobby, conference rooms and other hotel facilities. The skylight over the commercial atrium was covered to create a terrace on the sixth level and the tower gained an extra storey to accommodate a restaurant-bar with magnificent vistas of the city and ocean.

Edificio Alcanfores ↓→

Calle Juan Fanning 575, Miraflores
Alexia León, Lucho Marcial
2015

083 E

Until the 1980s, most buildings in Miraflores maintained a strong link with the street outside. Life spilled out of the houses – mainly single-family at the time – and onto the street through the front gardens and balconies. But with the increasing threat of terrorism, the occupants of these houses sought shelter behind high defensive walls. At the same time, new multi-family buildings gradually began to replace the traditional residential fabric. Both processes, still ongoing today, have redefined the relationship between interior and exterior. Located in a quiet residential area where the jacaranda trees cast a purple hue over the urban landscape, this building strives to retrieve the lost link between home and street. The project, which includes one and two-storey apartments of different sizes, stands on the corner of the Calle Alcanfores and

Edi Hirose. Courtesy of Leonmarcial Arquitectos

Calle Juan Fanning. It is developed in the irregular geometry resulting from the unification of three plots, responding with generosity to this complexity. Inwardly, the built mass absorbs the irregularities; outwardly, the limit is redrawn, set back from the boundary to generate an open area which is given to the street as a public square. This interruption of the perimeter fragments the built volume, which to a certain extent recognises the smaller, pre-existing scale. It also increases the façade area and controls the depth of the construction, therefore optimising the natural light and ventilation. Together with the public square, the wide cantilevered balconies underscore the building's quest to retrieve a dialogue between private and public life, simultaneously acting as a buffer to preserve the intimacy of the interior spaces. The sinuous forms, exposed concrete, subtle rails and exuberant vegetation give the building its characteristic appearance. Its exquisite execution has become a paradigm for the work of this office, whose standards are close to those of some of the best-known Swiss constructions.

Detail of the terraces

Centro comercial Larcomar

Malecón de la Reserva 610,
Miraflores
Eduardo Figari Gold
1998

084 E

The city of Lima is delimited physically by the Pacific to the west and the Andes to the east, with a geology shaped by the movement of tectonic plates and the ocean currents that batter the coast. These phenomena gave rise to the cliffs that run along more than 20 kilometres of coast line, rising to as high as 70 metres at certain points. This sheer drop, the natural border between the city and the sea, is the most characteristic element of Lima's coastal landscape. In the 1960s, the city launched an ambitious project at the foot of the cliffs known as the Circuito de Playas de la Costa Verde, which has gradually reclaimed land from the sea on which a coastal highway and a series of beaches have been developed. Larcomar is located on top of the cliffs at the end of the busy Avenida Larco. Conceived as a balcony over the ocean, this outdoor shopping centre not only takes advantage of the capital's mild climate but affords spectacular views as well. With no elevation facing the city, it is composed of several platforms embedded in the cliffs, forming the small squares and pedestrian streets that articulate the commercial and restaurant areas. Access is through the roof level from the pre-existing Parque Alfredo Salazar which, despite opposition from local residents, was completely transformed. The sculptural ventilation shafts of the parking area beneath the park stand out as urban landmarks and help to anchor the construction to the ground. The building, which strives to maintain a delicate balance between private investment and public interest, was intended to provide the metropolis with a new tourist attraction. It is now one of the most visited places in the city. However, its construction created a dangerous precedent in the interventions on the cliffs, and the proposed extension of the project is proving particularly controversial because it would entail the construction of a hotel and convention centre in a restricted area.

Renzo Rebagliati

Gonzalo Cáceres

E

Other Works of Interest

E01 Banco Minero del Perú
Avenida Garcilaso de la Vega 1464,
Cercado de Lima
J. Baracco, G. Benvenuto, A. Cavassa,
E. Nuñez, M. Chang Say, A. Hurtado,
C. Lizárraga, M. Wong
1966

E02 Edificio Guzmán Blanco
Avenida Guzmán Blanco 465,
Cercado de Lima
Manuel Villarán Freire
1952

E03 Casa Luza
Jirón Hernán Velarde 371,
Cercado de Lima
Enrique Seoane
1946

E04 Monumento a Fermín Tangüis
Circuito Mágico del Agua,
Jirón Madre de Dios,
Cercado de Lima
Héctor Velarde
1939

E05 EsSalud
Jirón Domingo Cueto 120, Lince

E06 Touring Automobile Club
Avenida General Trinidad Morán
698, Lince
Fernando Bryce,
Elsa Taramona de Arce, Julio Arce
1969

E07 Edificio Atenea
Calle Los Geranios 140, Lince
Marta Morelli, Sharif Kahatt
2017

E08 Casa Pun
Avenida Arequipa and
Calle Los Ángeles, Miraflores
Augusto Guzmán
1937

E09 Edificio de viviendas
Avenida Arequipa 4130, Miraflores
Augusto Choy Ma
1961

E10 Zaguán
Pasaje La Morena 122, Miraflores
Ghezzi Novak (Gustavo Ghezzi,
Arturo Ghezzi)
2015

E11 Banco de Crédito
Avenida José Larco 631, Miraflores
Jacques Crousse, Jorge Páez
1979

E12 Librería Babel
Calle Arístides Aljovín 421,
Miraflores
Ghezzi Novak (Gustavo Ghezzi,
Arturo Ghezzi), Blanco (Pamela
Remy), Lucho Marcial
2021

E13 Librería El Virrey
Avenida Bolognesi 510, Miraflores
1973

Right: Edificio Atenea (K+M Arquitectura)

E

West Lima: from San Miguel to Magdalena

F

F

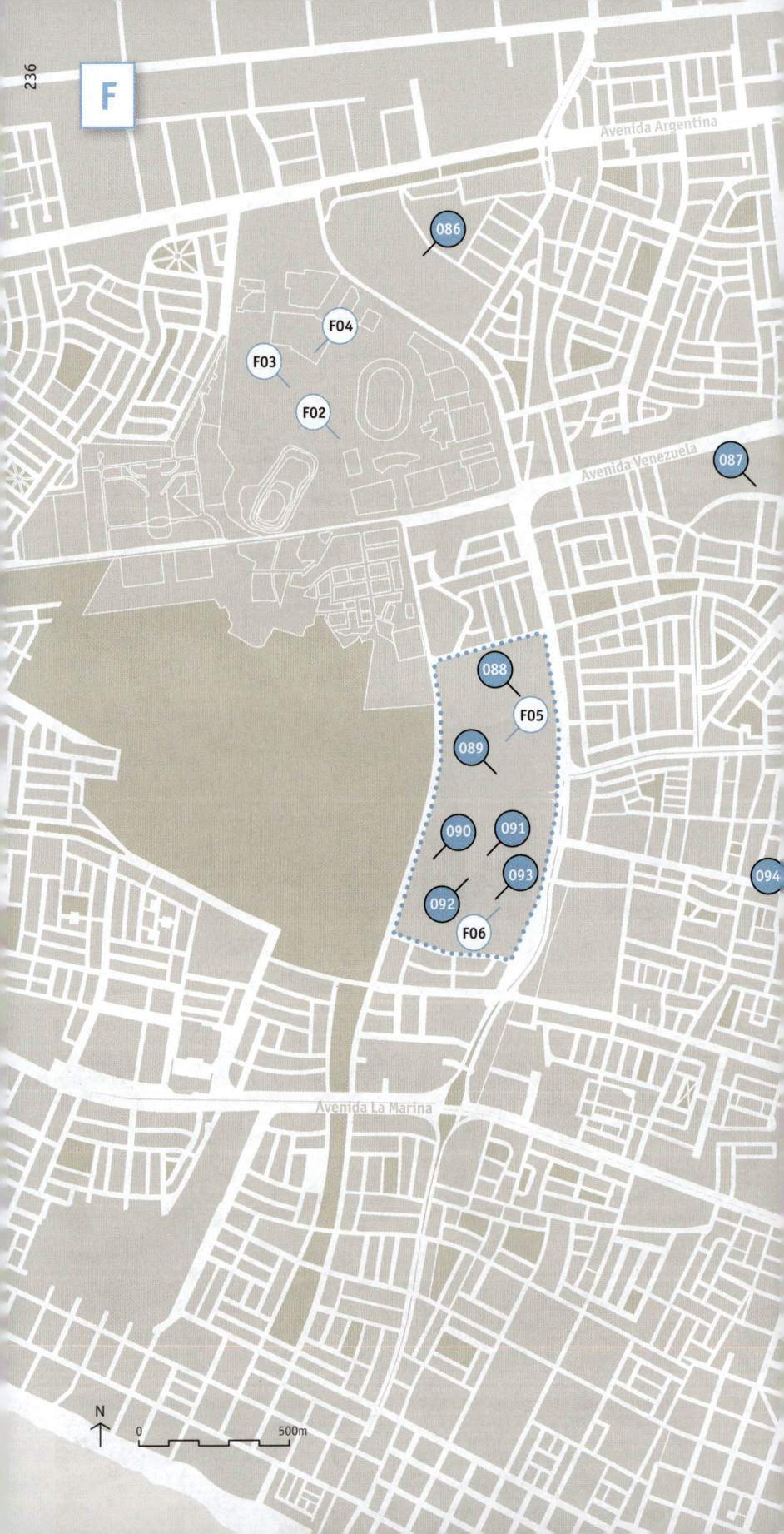

F

086

F04

F03

F02

Avenida Argentina

Avenida Venezuela

087

088

F05

089

090

091

093

092

F06

094

Avenida La Marina

N

0   500m

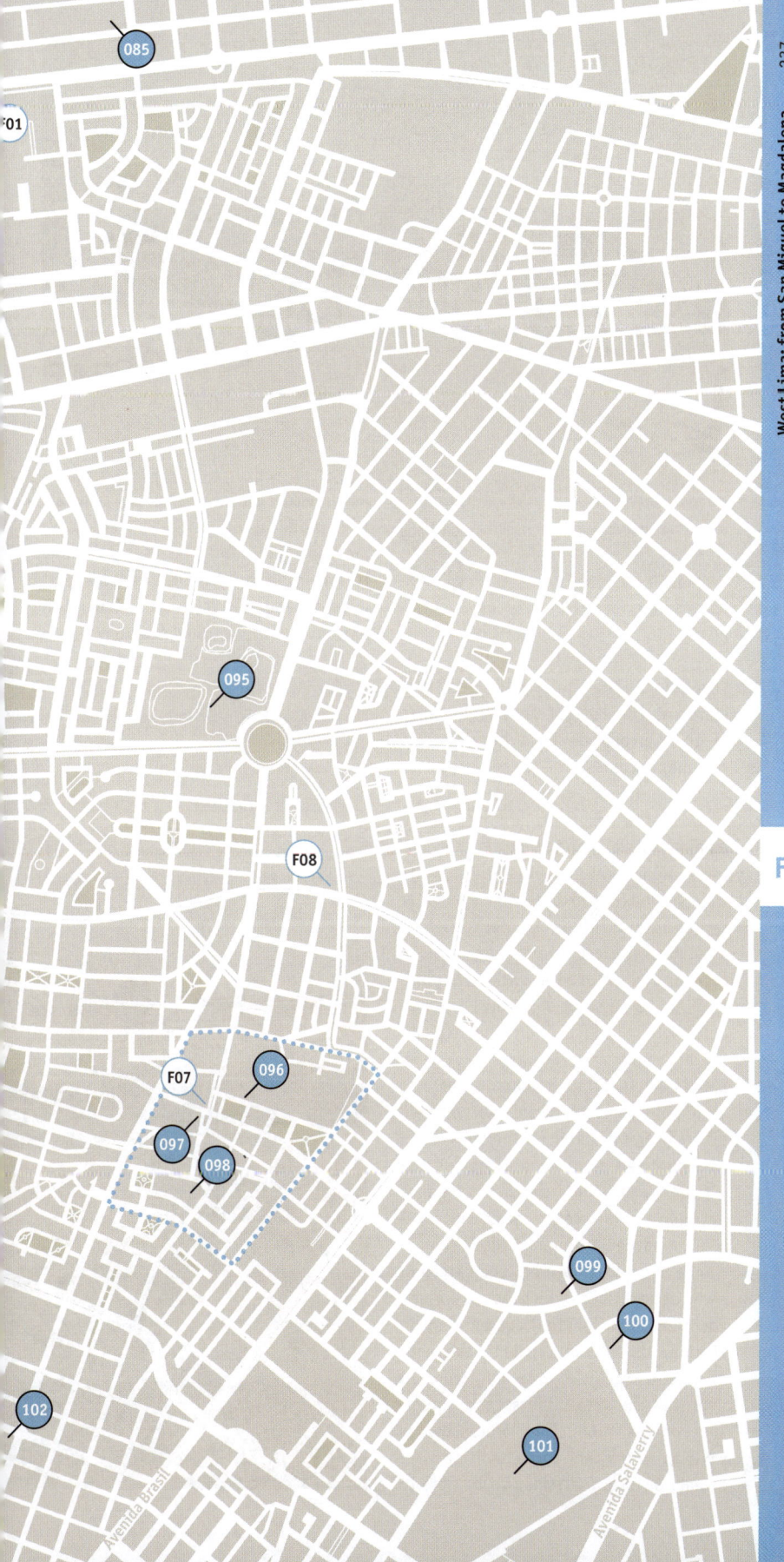

085

F01

095

F08

F

F07

096

097

098

099

100

101

102

Juan Solano

Nave industrial y oficinas AGP eGlass ↑

Calle Luis Carranza 1811, Cercado de Lima
V.oid (Felipe Ferrer)
2015

085 F

Located in the industrial area that starts at the Port of Callao and ends at the Cercado de Lima district, this building occupies an L-shaped plot with a double-height diaphanous interior where car windscreens are made. The administrative programme is concentrated in a longitudinal block with walkways around the top level, whose modular layout is interrupted at the corner by a cylindrical space at a tangent to both façades and wrapped in back-lit U-glass that is accessed obliquely through a funnel-shaped corridor. The exterior façade, built with discreet aluminium panels in neutral colours, contrasts with an ultra-modern interior defined by a continuity between the finishes in the robotised production areas and the offices, with a fine aesthetic balance between the different spaces. The integration of the lighting and ventilation in the ceiling and, above all, the choice of a white epoxy floor – which recalls Norman Foster's design for the McLaren plant in Woking, UK – is a distinct statement of intent. The use of architecture to improve the cleanliness and precision of the production processes, as well as providing the conditions for a team of local craftsmen to be able to manufacture an internationally competitive product, reflect the extraordinary ambition of this project. This is especially true considering the local context, just a few blocks away from Las Malvinas, an epicentre of the informal economy.

Unidad Vecinal III ↓ 086 F

Avenida Óscar Benavides,
Cercado de Lima
*Fernando Belaúnde Terry,
Juan Benites, Alfredo Dammert,
Luis Dorich, Eugenio Montagne,
Carlos Morales Macchiavello, Manuel Valega*
1949

When José Luis Bustamante was elected president in 1945, Fernando Belaúnde Terry became a member of parliament for the same party. The young architect found a favourable context for practising the theories he had been exploring in his magazine, *El Arquitecto Peruano*, which also served as a channel for disseminating the modernist projects of the time. To address deficiencies in health and living conditions in Peruvian society, Belaúnde launched the Housing Plan and created the National Housing Corporation to implement it. Rooted in the neighbourhood

unit, the plan was to create miniature cities for the working class close to workplaces and equipped with all the necessary services. The units limited and separated vehicular traffic, placing their emphasis instead on a landscaped environment through which residents could walk to their destinations, a measure also intended to encourage social interaction. Of the seven units planned, number three was the first one built. It is located near Avenida Colonial, opposite the industrial area and midway between the city centre and the Port of Callao, the aim being to minimise commuting time for workers. The total area occupied is 30 hectares, 88 per cent of which is open space. A fringe of trees visually protects the unit from the avenue. Vehicular traffic is confined to the ring road around the unit and service cul-de-sacs. The rest is pedestrianised and the size of the project was conditioned by the distance

Christopher Schreier

a person can reasonably walk to their destination. The services and infrastructure – shops, a school, a health centre, sports facilities, a church, a recreational centre and a police station – are located in the central area and surrounded by large green spaces. Around these amenities are the multi-family buildings, arranged in two-, three- and four-storey longitudinal blocks. Altogether, there are 1,112 homes of different types for 5,540 inhabitants. The execution of this project was a major milestone in the country. Although time has revealed the inadequacy of these initiatives to contain the informal sprawl of the city, the Unidad Vecinal III remains a landmark in national urban planning.

Conjunto habitacional Palomino

Avenida Venezuela, 28–30
Cercado de Lima
Santiago Agurto, Fernando Correa,
Luis Miró Quesada,
Fernando Sánchez Griñán
1967

In the 1960s, the government continued its efforts (begun in the 1930s) to provide Lima's lower classes with adequate housing and leisure areas. One of the most important developments at the time was the Palomino housing estate with its characteristic layout. The project is located near workplaces to minimise the commuting time for residents. The

services and infrastructures – schools, a market, sports facilities, a police station, a church and main square – are concentrated at the north end of the plot, on the Avenida Venezuela. This reduces the impact of the traffic on the residential buildings, which occupy the south end of the estate. The design is based on the compositional module of a housing unit. With slight variations, these are grouped into blocks of three units per floor in four-storey buildings. These are juxtaposed to generate curved buildings, distributed organically around the estate and leading to an interesting diversity of public spaces integrated into an urban landscape marked by the presence of the Huaca Palomino archaeological site. The

IPMIL. Universidad Nacional de Ingeniería

composition represents an interesting innovation in the conception of pedestrian flow, with users stumbling on streets and squares unexpectedly. The initial project also included six twelve-storey towers, but these were never built.

Leonardo Finotti

F

General view of the university campus

PUCP

The campus of the Pontificia Universidad Católica del Perú (PUCP) is located in an area occupied more than 1,500 years ago by Maranga, the pre-Columbian settlement where the Lima, Ychsma and Inca cultures once lived. Around the university, there are more than 60 archaeological sites with cultural heritage status, three of which are located on the campus itself, including Huaca 64, a gathering place for the Ychsma culture (circa 1200 CE), and Huaca 20 (500 CE), a Lima-culture burial ground.

The PUCP was the first private university in the country, founded in 1917 by Father Jorge Dintilhac. It initially occupied several buildings in the centre of Lima, but soon outgrew them. In 1944, José de la Riva Agüero donated the Pando estate in the San Miguel district to the institution, and in 1952 architects Santiago Agurto, Javier Cayo and Eduardo Neira won a competition to design the new campus, of which only the buildings for the faculties of Agronomy, Engineering and Chemistry were executed.

The master plan for the definitive development of the complex was drawn up in 1967 by the US firm Caudill Rowlett-Scott – designers of Larsen Hall at Harvard University – which devised a campus in the style of American universities, with buildings separated by green spaces and paths crossing the plot from north to south. The sports facilities are located at the ends of the campus and the car parks around the perimeter.

Over the years, architects of different generations have designed a series of interesting buildings. The firm Cooper Graña Nicolini Arquitectos carried out several of them with an austere materiality that is now part of the overall style of the university. For example, the

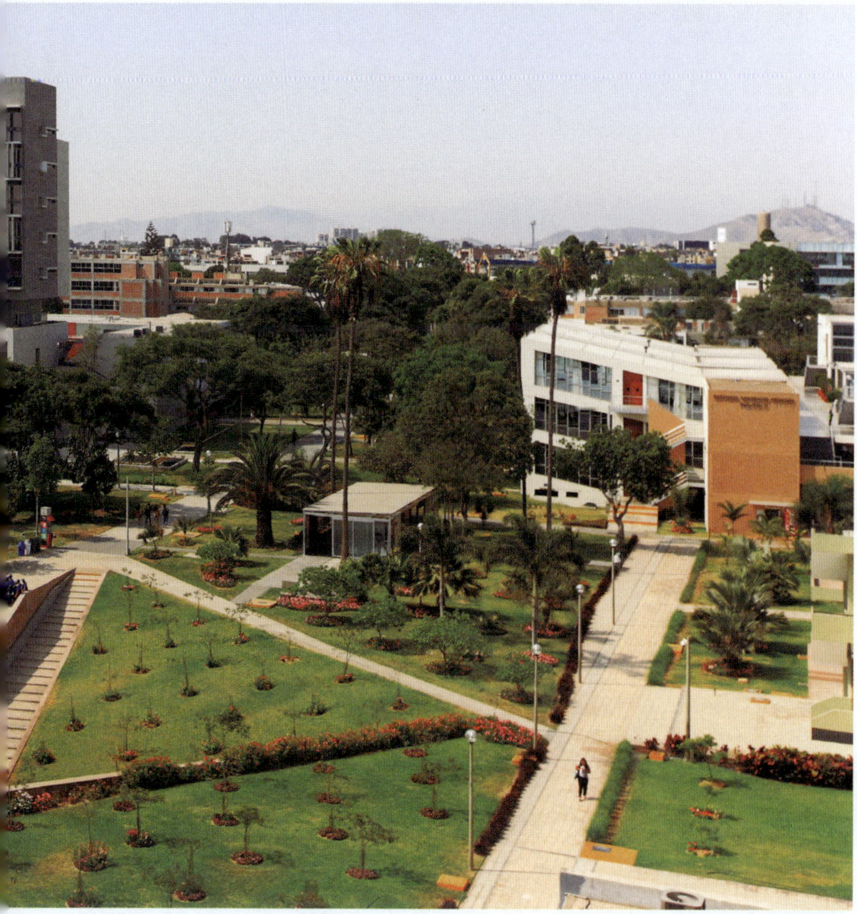

Facultad de Artes
Avenida Universitaria 1801, San Miguel
Reynaldo Ledgard, Óscar Borasino,
Guillermo Guevara, Sofía Rodríguez Larraín
2009

088 F

Map of the university campus

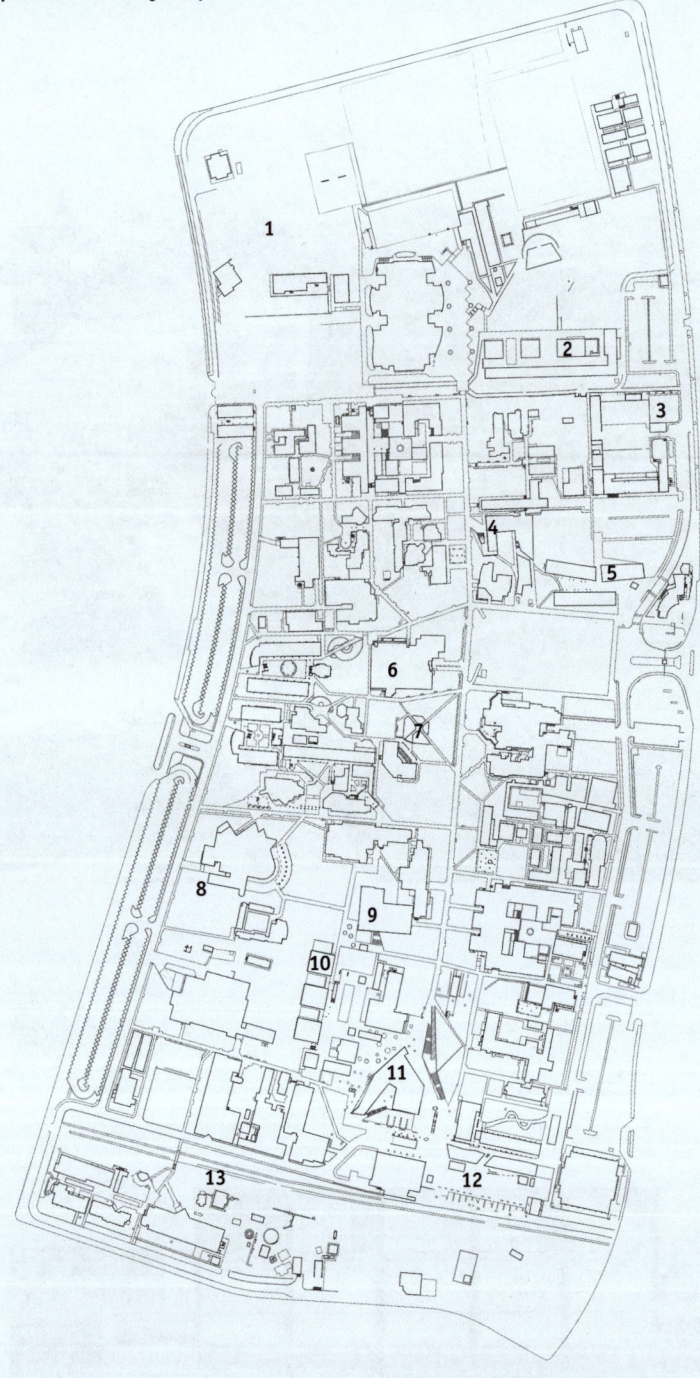

1. Huaca 20
2. Facultad de Artes 088 F
3. Huaca 64
4. Edificio Tinkuy
5. Complejo Felipe Mac Gregor
6. Biblioteca Central 089 F
7. Centro de Asesoría Pastoral Universitaria

8. Escuela de Gastronomía y Turismo 090 F
9. Complejo académico de Ciencias Sociales 091 F
10. Facultad de Arquitectura 092 F
11. Biblioteca de Ciencias 093 F
12. Aulario de Ingeniería y Ciencias
13. Camino Inca (*Qhapaq Ñan*)

Biblioteca Central
Avenida Universitaria 1801, San Miguel
Frederick Cooper, Antonio Graña, Eugenio Nicolini
1976

089 F

Escuela de Gastronomía y Turismo
Avenida Universitaria 1801, San Miguel
*51-1 Arquitectos (César Becerra, Fernando
Puente, Manuel de Rivero)*
2019

090 F

Complejo Académico de Ciencias Sociales
Avenida Universitaria 1801, San Miguel
Enrique Santillana, Tandem Arquitectura (Cynthia Seinfeld, Juan Carlos Burga, Jorge Draxl), Jonathan Warthon
2017

Juan Solano. Courtesy of Enrique Santillana

Biblioteca Central (089) is a concrete structure with exposed brick envelopes, three stepped levels and overhead lighting, while the Centro de Asesoría Pastoral Universitaria (1977) is made up of four concrete volumes with stained-glass windows by artist Adolfo Winternitz.

At a certain point, the university had to start growing vertically to increase capacity and preserve the green spaces. The Felipe Mac Gregor complex (Pedro Belaunde, Juan Reiser, Patricia Llosa and Rodolfo Cortegana, 2008) next to the main entrance is the tallest building on the campus and was the first one conceived according to that principle.

In recent decades, the university has promoted works of a certain size designed by teachers of the School of Architecture (092), which itself was designed by Reynaldo Ledgard, Pedro Belaúnde and Frederick Cooper and occupies three concrete volumes linked by walkways. The classrooms, resolved with grids of concrete beams and seamlessly integrated lighting, have become the emblematic image of the workshops.

Ledgard is also the architect, with Óscar Borasino, Guillermo Guevara and Sofía Rodríguez Larraín, of the Faculty of Arts (088), an L-shaped building organised around galleries with three beautiful glass-fronted wings. Patricia Llosa and Rodolfo Cortegana designed the Tinkuy student services building (2011), a small concrete structure that houses a series of meeting places, as well the teaching block (2014) with its expressive support

Detail of the Faculty of Humanities

structure for the external staircases, located next to the Faculty of Engineering. The Biblioteca de Ciencias (093) is one of the most powerful buildings on the campus, accessed through a basement level that is connected to the central path on the campus by means of fractured geometry folds. The structure, built in a skilfully executed earth-coloured concrete, contrasts with the fragility of the glazed envelopes with windows that open for natural ventilation.

The Complejo Académico de Ciencias Sociales (091) has a sunken courtyard that illuminates two basement levels and a volume above ground with a double glass façade and concrete slats. Lastly, the Escuela de Gastronomía y Turismo (090) is accessed through a spectacular palm grove and has a steel grid structure that exposes all the mechanical installations for didactic purposes.

The Inca road system (Qhapaq Ñan), a communication, trade and defence network covering 30,000 kilometres, runs across the southern border of the campus. Some 467 metres long and protected at certain points by 4-metre high walls built with adobe, *quincha* and rammed earth, this section connected the Parque de las Leyendas and Huaca Mateo Salado archaeological sites.

Inserted into a deeply stratified social fabric, the PUCP is an oasis of civilisation that is consistently rated the best university in the country in international rankings. It has built a top-class faculty of staff and a diverse community of students who shine with their knowledge in nearly every company and institution across Peru. The university plays a pivotal role in social mobility, the current lack of which is hindering the country's competitiveness and progress.

Facultad de Arquitectura

Avenida Universitaria 1801, San Miguel
Reynaldo Ledgard, Frederick Cooper, Pedro Belaúnde
2005

092 F

F

PUCP

Biblioteca de Ciencias
Avenida Universitaria 1801, San Miguel
Patricia Llosa, Rodolfo Cortegana
2014

093 F

All photos: Juan Solano. Courtesy of Llosa Cortegana

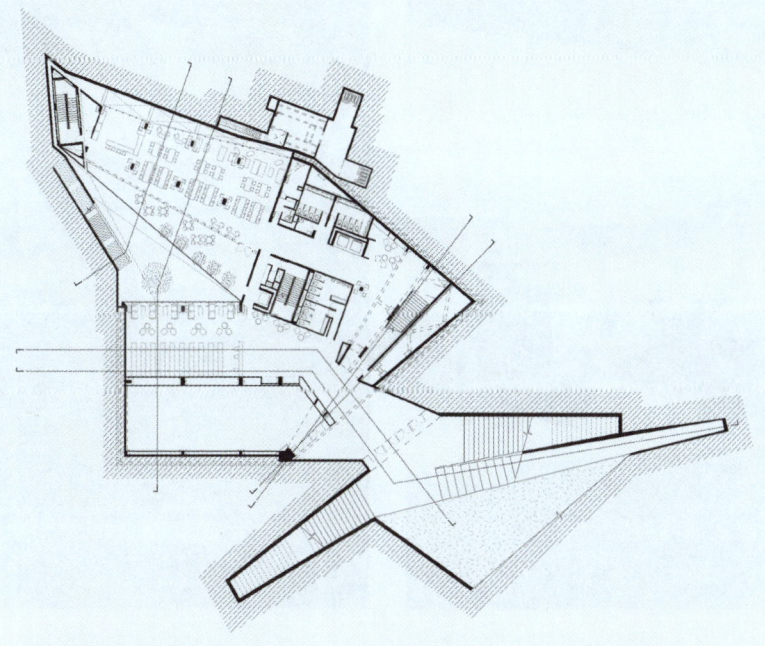

Basement floor plan

Margaux Eyssette

Margaux Eyssette

Museo Arqueológico Rafael Larco Herrera

094 F

Avenida Simón Bolivar 1515, Pueblo Libre
Rafael Larco Hoyle
18th century
Remodelled from 1950 onwards

The history of this collection began at a small house at the Hacienda Chiclín in Trujillo, northern Peru, where pre-Columbian artefacts were kept, most of them of Mochica origin. In 1926, Rafael Larco Hoyle turned the house into a museum to avoid the dispersion of objects removed from archaeological sites, and in 1950 he transferred the collection to the Hacienda Cueva in Lima, which had been built centuries earlier on top of archaeological ruins. The restoration exercised good judgement in terms of the choice of the ceramic flooring and ornaments, incorporating grilles, doors and wooden beams from the demolished

Museo Larco Herrera

house of the Marquises of Herrera in Trujillo's main square and reconstructing a viceregal atmosphere. Today, this 'decorated shed' houses what is probably the finest private collection of pre-Columbian art in Peru: 45,000 artefacts encompassing more than 5,000 years of history that have been part of exhibitions at the world's greatest archaeological museums and are displayed at this museum and at the Cusco branch. In addition to a deposit open to visitors, the museum hosts a magnificent collection of gold and an amusing display of erotic ceramics. A ramp leads down to one of the most charming gardens in Lima, with desert vegetation, bougainvilleas climbing up the perimeter walls and a charming fern pergola that shelters an excellent café-restaurant. Altogether, a highly recommended visit.

Huaca Mateo Salado 095 F

Avenida Maríano Cornejo,
Cercado de Lima
Ychsma and Inca cultures
12th–16th century

Following the suppression of idolatry by the Catholic Church in the mid-sixteenth century, during the viceregal period the *huacas* fell into a gradual state of neglect. It was in this context that French Protestant Matheus Saladé set up a provisional residence amid the ruins that today bear his name. Accused of heresy by the Tribunal of the Holy Office, in 1573 the hermit became the first person to be executed by the Spanish Inquisition in Lima's main square. However, the origin of this ceremonial administrative centre dates back to the peak of the Yschsma culture in the Rímac Valley, at a site that was subsequently occupied by the Incas in the fifteenth century. It consisted of a 30-hectare precinct with five pyramidal buildings distributed asymmetrically around a large open space. The main pyramid stands on a platform connected to the central area by a ramp. This typology was used to create public spaces on different levels and with different hierarchies, interconnected through an articulated system of corridors and stairways. Following the urban expansion of Lima in the twentieth century, the preservation of the archaeological complex was threatened by the emergence of informal quarries and illegal invasions of land. The much-needed rescue works began in 2007 and the results are visible today: Mateo Salado has become a contemporary paradigm for the management of archaeological heritage in a way that is meaningful to the local community, thanks to the organisation of cultural and educational activities.

F

Candy Torres

In the midst of the high-rise development that the central districts of Lima have experienced in recent years, the historic centre of Pueblo Libre has preserved its scale and the aura of a bygone era. Located on pre-Hispanic farmland furrowed by irrigation channels, it was originally founded as an indigenous town in the sixteenth century. Haciendas were emerging at this time to structure the agricultural exploitation of the area during the colonial period, and the church of Santa María Magdalena (097) was also built, lending the village its traditional name of Magdalena Vieja. The land for the church was donated by the Franciscans, in charge of teaching Christian doctrine to the Native Americans who settled there. The appearance we see today dates from the eighteenth century, earlier versions having been destroyed by earthquakes.

It has a simple configuration with a nave and a choir loft over the entrance. With a barrel vault roof, reconstructed on several occasions, the most outstanding elements of the Baroque interior are the main altarpiece and the pulpit in dazzling gilded wood. The neocolonial portal dates from the 1930s.

From its foundation, Magdalena Vieja was a quiet rural village surrounded by vegetable gardens and olive groves. With its bucolic atmosphere and dry, sunny climate, it became a popular recreational space for many residents of Lima, including Andrés Hurtado de Mendoza, third Viceroy of Peru, who in the mid-sixteenth century established his country residence there. His successors did the same, and in 1818 the penultimate viceroy even made the village his permanent abode, at what was known as the Palacio de la Magdalena

Quinta de los Libertadores
Plaza Bolivar, Pueblo Libre
Architect unknown
1818

096 F

Gonzalo Cáceres

Iglesia Santa María Magdalena

Avenida San Martín 1172, Pueblo Libre
Architect unknown
18th century

Candy Torres

IPMIL. Universidad Nacional de Ingeniería

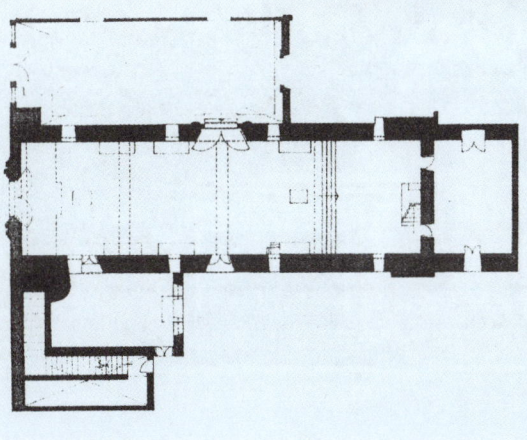

F

(096). Although the façade is similar to that of a ranch house, the palace has elements of the 'viceregal *quinta*,' a residential typology for country recreation, usually located on the outskirts of the city and best exemplified by the Quinta de Presa in the Rímac district. The building has two porticoed galleries on axis with the entrance. The one on the front façade, with grilles and raised from the ground, has slender wooden columns and a double flight of steps at the entrance. The rear gallery, which opens onto the vegetable garden, currently constitutes one side of a large porticoed courtyard. The building has witnessed important moments in the history of Peru. During the independence struggles, it was briefly home to José de San Martín and then Simón Bolívar, after which the palace was renamed Quinta de los Libertadores and the place became known as Pueblo Libre. In the War of the Pacific, President García Calderón set up his residence and government there during the Chilean invasion. Today, the building houses the National Archaeology, Anthropology and History Museum, which also incorporates the adjacent building with a neo-Peruvian portal by Héctor Velarde.

But this is not the only interesting civic building in Pueblo Libre. In addition to the characteristic ranch houses with railed porches that can still be seen in the area, another fine example is the Casa Orbea Hacienda (098), restored in

1940 by Emilio Harth Terré and still in good condition. A two-storey building with galleries on the top floor, where the living quarters were once located, it has a beautiful chapel and other handsome interior spaces. The entrance portal, flanked on one side by a tower and on the other by an exuberant bougainvillea, serves as a finishing touch to the end of Avenida San Martín.

Bearing witness to this farming tradition is the Queirolo tavern, whose piscos and wines have formed part of Lima's collective memory since the nineteenth century. With its old-fashioned interior and *teatina* skylights, the bar is an obligatory stop on the local gastronomic circuit. It was recently restored by Enrique Bonilla Di Tolla, reinstating the rich merits of this historic complex.

Casa Hacienda Orbea

Calle Juan Roberto Acevedo 105, Pueblo Libre
Architect unknown
18th century

098 F

Candy Torres

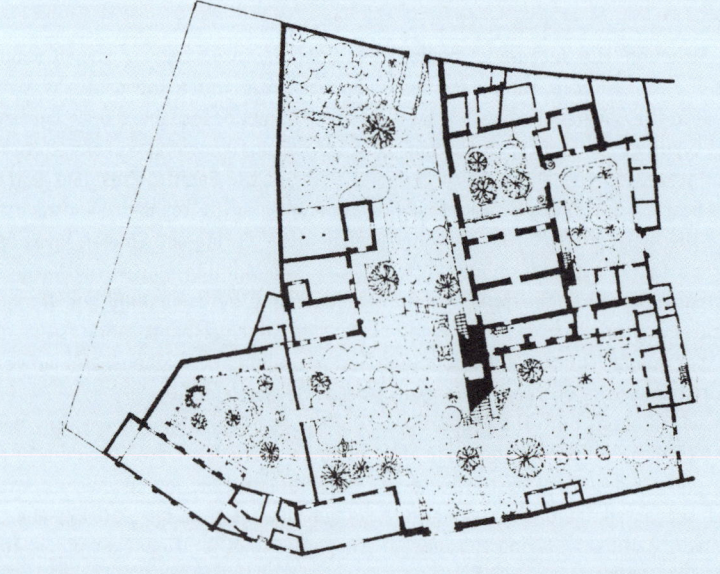

IPMIL. Universidad Nacional de Ingeniería

Iglesia San Antonio de Padua 099 F

Avenida San Felipe 571,
Jesús María
Roberto Wakeham
1968

In the 1960s, Jesús María was a residential district of affluent homes with gardens and a small-scale urban fabric. However, in recent decades large multi-family towers have proliferated, like the ones that now surround this austere yet impeccably designed church with its abundance of fine details and nuances. The plasticity of the construction evidences the influence of Le Corbusier, in whose office the author worked as a young man. The building comprises several sculptural volumes, including the striking bell tower. Load-bearing walls, slab stones and huge beams, executed in reinforced concrete and exposed brick, form intersecting planes that generate different atmospheres and modulate the penetration of natural light. The interior space is continuous and fluid. The altar, covered by a pyramidal dome, invades the nave, dividing it into two bays and permitting different orientations and forms of celebration. The aisle at the side, with a lower ceiling height, contributes to this spatial flexibility and diversity. The result is a total work of art in which the architect Wakeham, the glazier Adolfo Winternitz and the sculptor Anna Maccagno integrated their artistic disciplines to great effect. The polychrome stained-glass windows lend protagonism to the natural light. The 'Magnificat' is depicted on the west elevation and in the evenings splashes colour across an otherwise almost achromatic interior. On the east side, the 'Through Him, With Him and In Him' stained-glass window bathes the altar in the morning light. In terms of the sculptures, the most outstanding are the relief carvings on the vast concrete beam that compensates the difference in ceiling height between the nave and aisle, and the Via Crucis integrated into a band of concrete that runs along the east and south walls. It is interrupted by the wooden confession booths, recessed in the brick panel, and the large bronze statue of Saint Francis of Assisi that stands in a niche with overhead lighting.

Candy Torres

Casa Huiracocha

Jirón Huiracocha 2265,
Jesús María
Luis Miró Quesada
1947

100 **F**

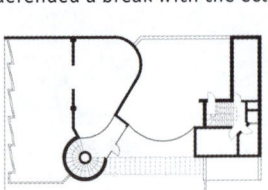

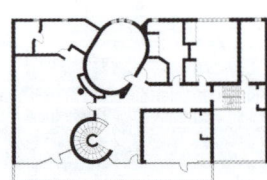

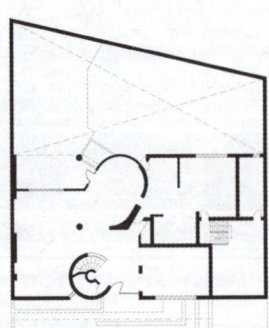

Luis Miró Quesada wrote the seminal essay on the Modernist Movement in Peru, *El espacio en el tiempo* ('space in time'), and was the driving force behind Agrupación Espacio, whose famous manifesto defended a break with the eclectic architecture that was practised at the time. He designed this house – the first genuinely modern home in the country – for himself. A horizontal volume between party walls, most of the programme is organised around two storeys. The ground floor comprises the lounge, living room, dining room and kitchen, designed as a continuous, fluid space that opens onto the garden. The bedrooms and a reading area are located on the top floor. The service areas occupy a lateral lower-height, three-storey volume with a staircase linking it to the rest of the house. A rooftop terrace, part of it covered, completes the programme. On the façade, the ground floor is blind to ensure privacy, while the top floor has a continuous balcony to afford views of the vicinity and protect the interior from excessive sunlight. In his studies of the house, Sharif Kahatt points out the influence of Le Corbusier in the continuous window and the volumetry of the rooftop terrace, notes the reference to Frank Lloyd Wright in the treatment of the materials on the ground-floor façade and the use of different heights as spatial dividers, and even sees a nod to Mies van der Rohe in the curved wall of the dining room and the folds of the staircase cylinder on the roof; all of these features sitting neatly with the local woodwork tradition, the use of pebble stones, the furniture and the colonial and pre-Columbian objects, evidencing the author's well-known quest for a specifically Peruvian modernity.

Gonzalo Cáceres

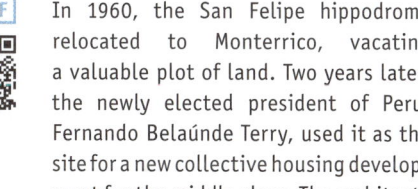

Residencial San Felipe

Avenida Gregorio Escobedo,
Jesús María

*Enrique Ciriani, Mario Benuy,
Jacques Crousse, Oswaldo Núñez,
Luis Vásquez, Víctor Nikita Smirnoff,
Víctor Ramírez, Jorge Páez*
1969

101 F

In 1960, the San Felipe hippodrome relocated to Monterrico, vacating a valuable plot of land. Two years later, the newly elected president of Peru, Fernando Belaúnde Terry, used it as the site for a new collective housing development for the middle class. The architects of the Junta Nacional de Vivienda (JNV),

F

Building and central square of phase I

Carlos Palomino

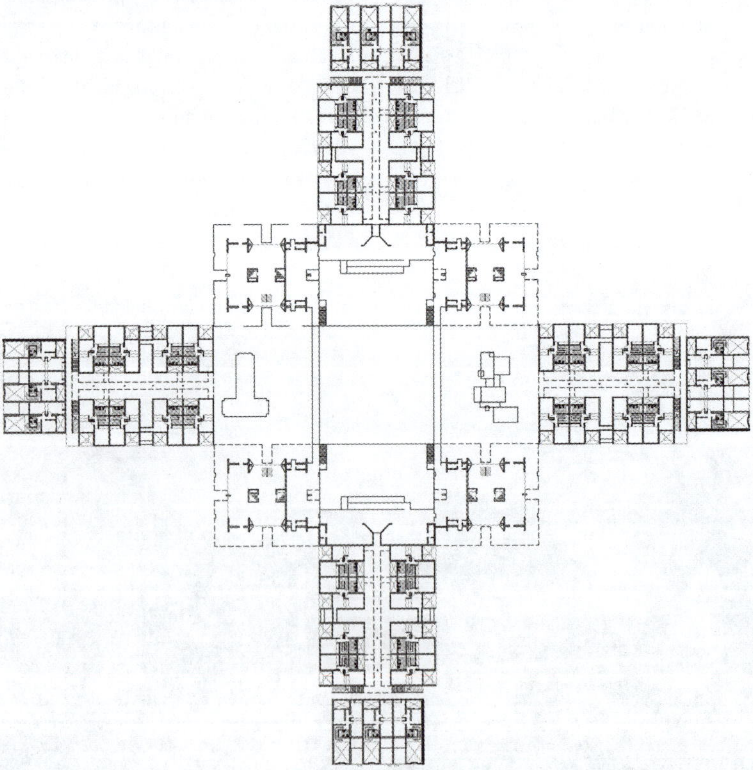

Phase I, first floor

or National Housing Board, developed three versions of the project, which would occupy 26 hectares. The first one, by Enrique Ciriani and Mario Bernuy, consisted of the repetition of a group of Greek-cross plans, although in the end only one was built at the south-west end of the plot. The centre of the cross forms a central square, with four 14-storey towers at the vertices. The arms of the cross are formed by four-storey buildings with split-level apartments next to three two-storey single-family homes. Walkways surround the square and link the homes. Perfectly symmetrical, rotund and abstract, the development acquires a monumental quality. While this first phase was under construction, the JNV decided that it was necessary to achieve a greater density with a lower budget and in a shorter time than realistically demanded by the project. Jacques Crousse and Oswaldo Núñez developed a second version in which Ciriani and Bernuy's module was repeated at the north-east end of the plot. Running between the two blocks was a raised pedestrian street linking these volumes as well as several multi-family buildings. Due to budgetary and timing issues, this design was also rejected and Luis Vásquez and Víctor Nikita Smirnoff developed the version that was finally executed. To the complex already built by Ciriani and Bernuy were added the multi-family buildings proposed in the second version, in greater numbers and distributed all over the site: five-storey buildings with a central courtyard that relate to each other, 10 storey linear blocks on pilotis and 15-storey towers with a commercial ground floor. In the central area, there is service pole with attractive architecture. This phase is not as powerful as the first one built, but on the whole the project is positive. Its construction gave the city a pedestrian-friendly urban oasis protected from the traffic with interesting modern buildings and plenty of public spaces and green areas. It also enabled the government to proclaim that modern times had arrived.

F

Gonzalo Cáceres

Building of phase II

Iglesia del Sagrado Corazón de María 102 F

Calle 28 de Julio 523,
Magdalena del Mar
Padre Simón Llobet (Promoter),
Julio Ernesto Lattini
1957

This striking religious building, also known as the 'dome church,' is a landmark in the urban fabric of the Magdalena district due to its height of nearly 70 metres and its colours: aquamarine and pastel pink. Its design and construction were promoted over the course of a decade by Father Simón Llobet, who opened it to the public in 1957 before it was completed. The original project included a 10-metre-high statue of the Virgin Mary on top of the dome but it proved too heavy for the structure and was replaced in 2006 by a fibre glass statue made by Arequipa artist Fredy Luque Sonco. The original sculpture was transferred to the end of the

Avenida de Brasil. Many people consider the church to be the tallest in the city, and it is rumoured that its neo-Renaissance design was inspired by the famous Santa Maria del Fiore in Florence because of the great ribbed dome and the plan composition: a central regular octagon buttressed by smaller-scale geometries. However, the proportions in this building are less refined, the transition between façade walls and the dome is awkward, and the bell towers seem incongruous.

The composition of orders at the entrance is somewhat confused, although the drum of the main dome is skilfully integrated. The reference to Florence gives an idea of the disproportionate ambition of this kitsch church. Even so, its bright colours reflect the modern air of a flourishing district with a young population, an increasing number of services and a vibrant business community that is worth visiting to gain a feel for the Peruvian new society.

Other Works of Interest

F01 Unidad Vecinal Mirones
Avenida Óscar Benavides,
Cercado de Lima
Santiago Agurto, Carlos Cárdenas,
Luis Vásquez
1955

F02 Campus de la Universidad Nacional
Mayor de San Marcos
Avenida Venezuela, Cercado de Lima
Alfredo Dammert, Carlos Morales
Macchiavello, Manuel Valega Sayán,
Jorge Garrido Lecca, Henry Biber
1949

F03 Rectorado de la Universidad
Nacional Mayor de San Marcos
Universidad Nacional Mayor de
San Marcos, Cercado de Lima
Reynaldo Ledgard
2003

F04 Biblioteca Central de la Universidad
Nacional Mayor de San Marcos
Universidad Nacional Mayor de
San Marcos, Cercado de Lima
1999

F05 Edificio de servicios estudiantiles
Tinkuy (PUCP)
Avenida Universitaria 1801,
San Miguel
Patricia Llosa, Rodolfo Cortegana
2011

F06 Aulario de Ciencias e Ingeniería
(PUCP)
Avenida Universitaria 1801,
San Miguel
Patricia Llosa, Rodolfo Cortegana
2014

F07 Taberna Queirolo
Avenida San Martín 1090,
Pueblo Libre
1880

F08 Clínica Stella Maris
Avenida Paseo de los Andes 923,
Pueblo Libre
Paul Linder
1950

Right: Rectorado de la Universidad Nacional Mayor de San Marcos (Reynaldo Ledgard)

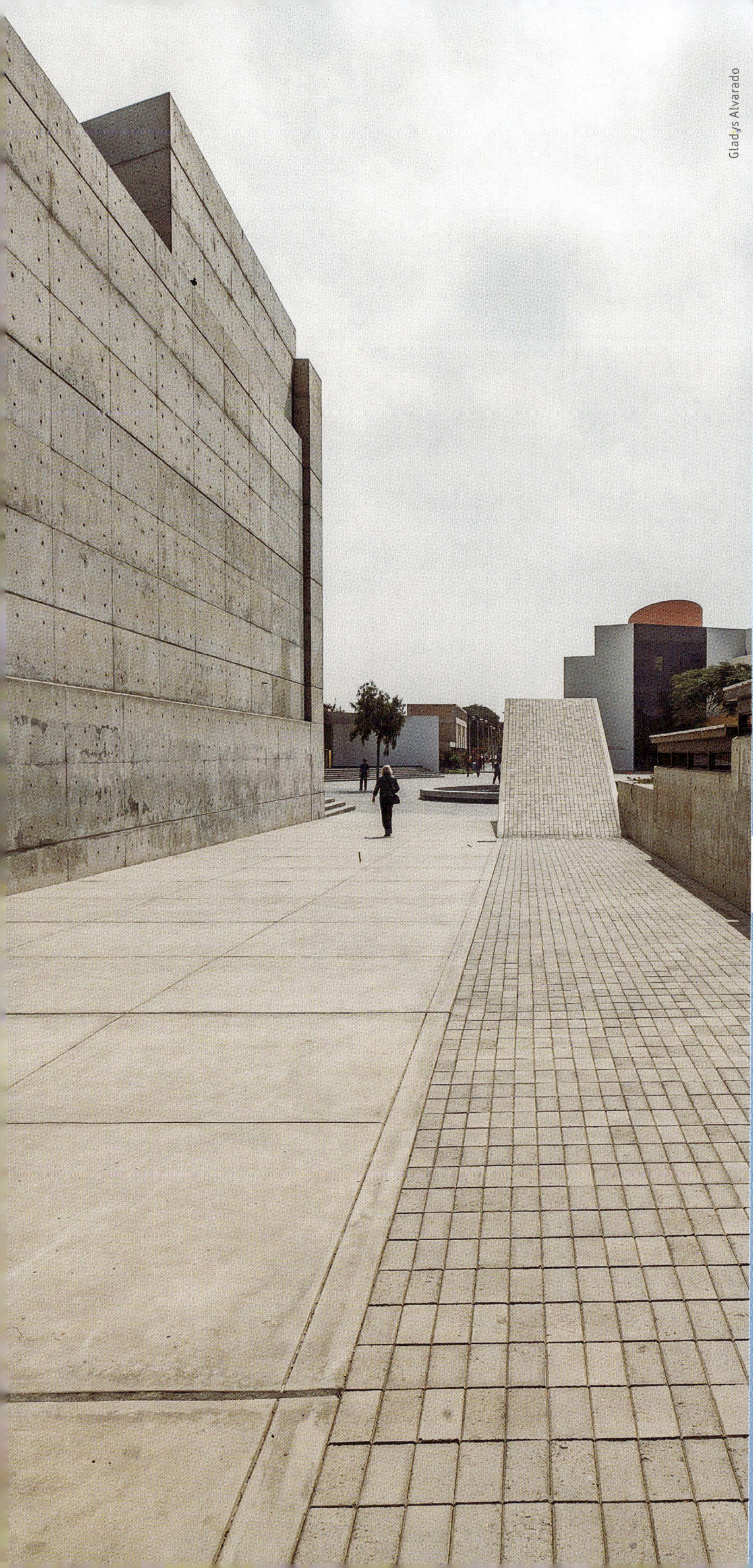

Gladys Alvarado

San Isidro

G

Parque Roosevelt

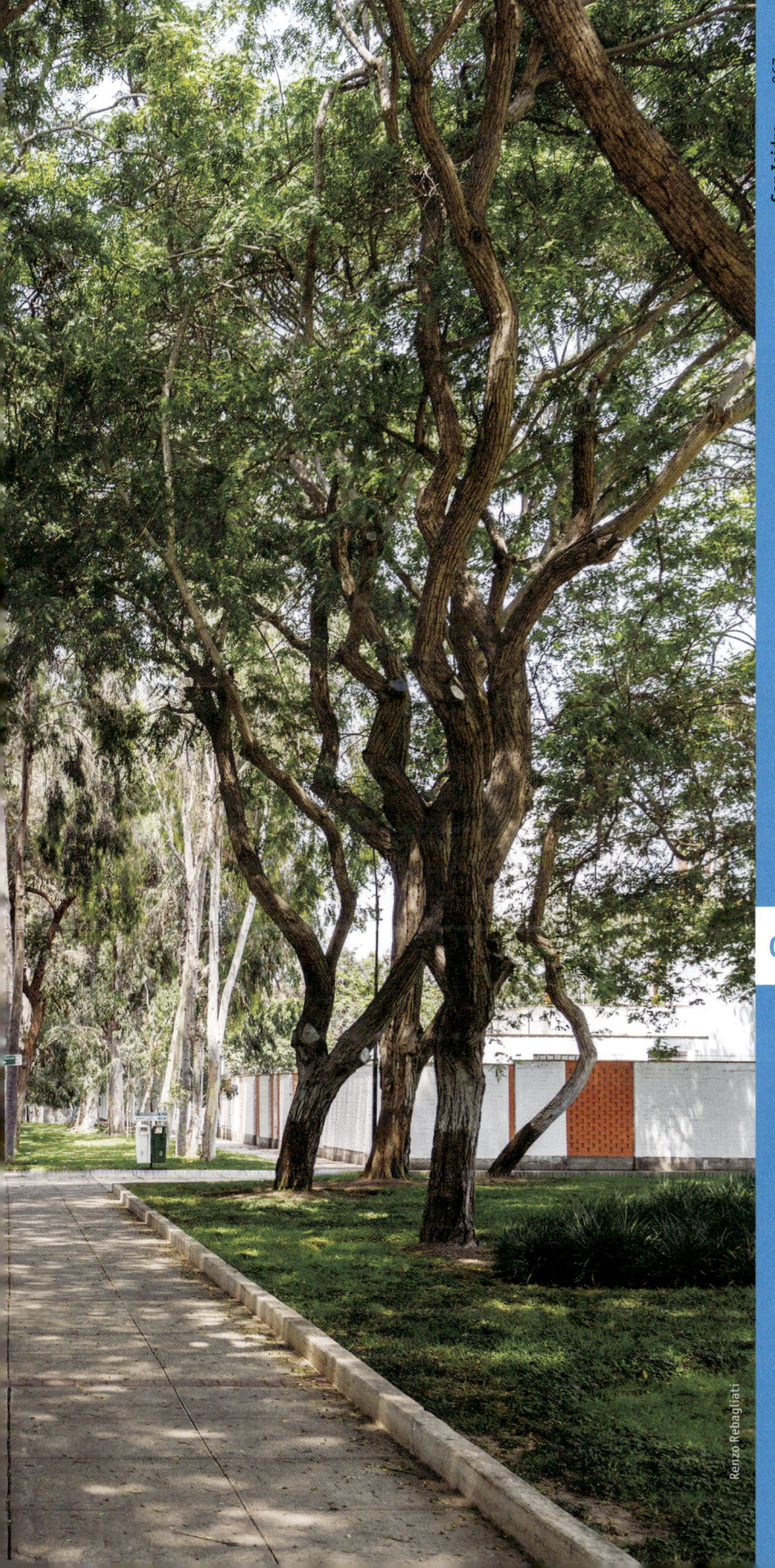

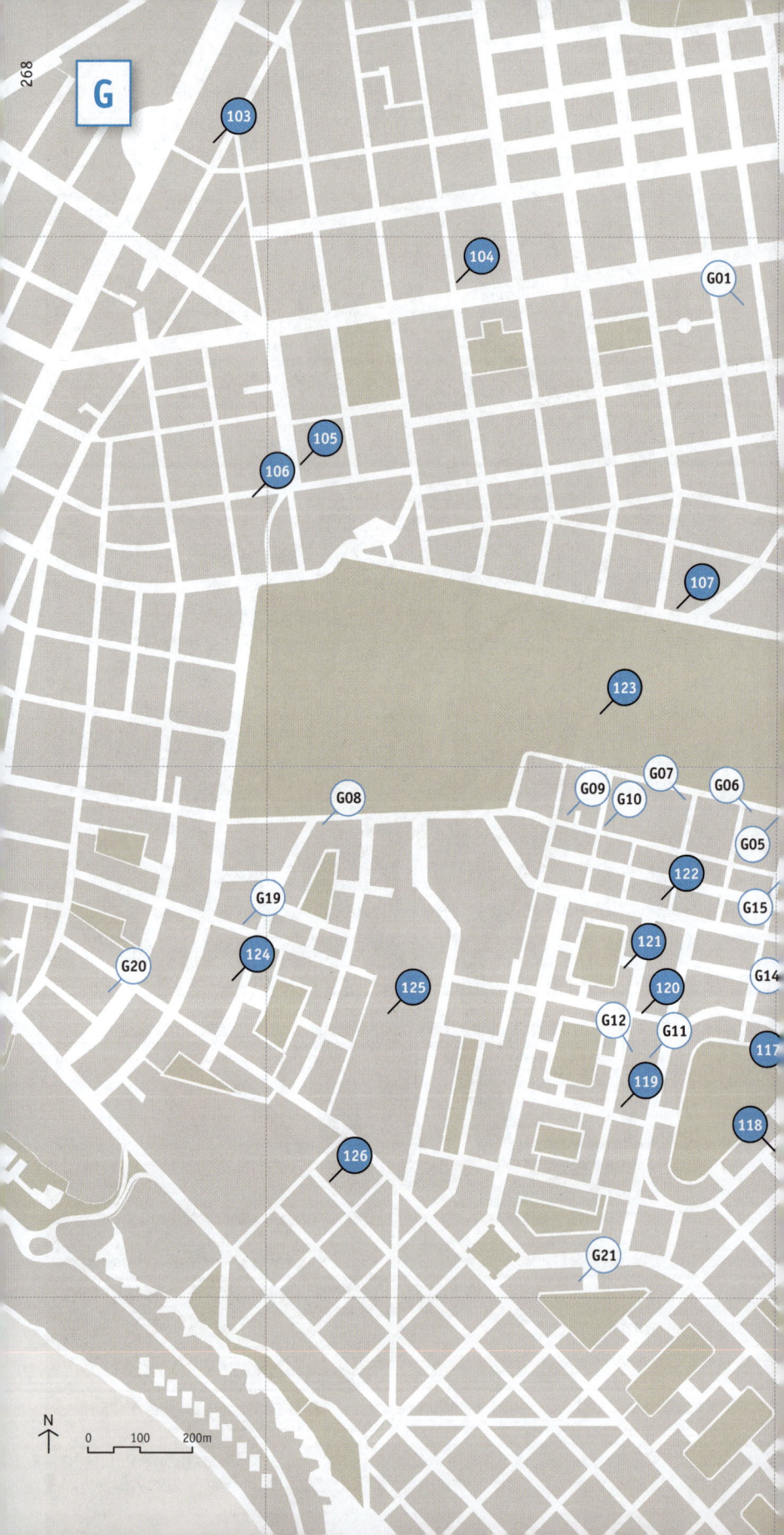

G

103

104

G01

105

106

107

123

G08

G09

G07

G10

G06

G05

G15

122

G19

121

G14

G20

124

120

117

125

G12

G11

119

118

126

G21

N

0   100   200m

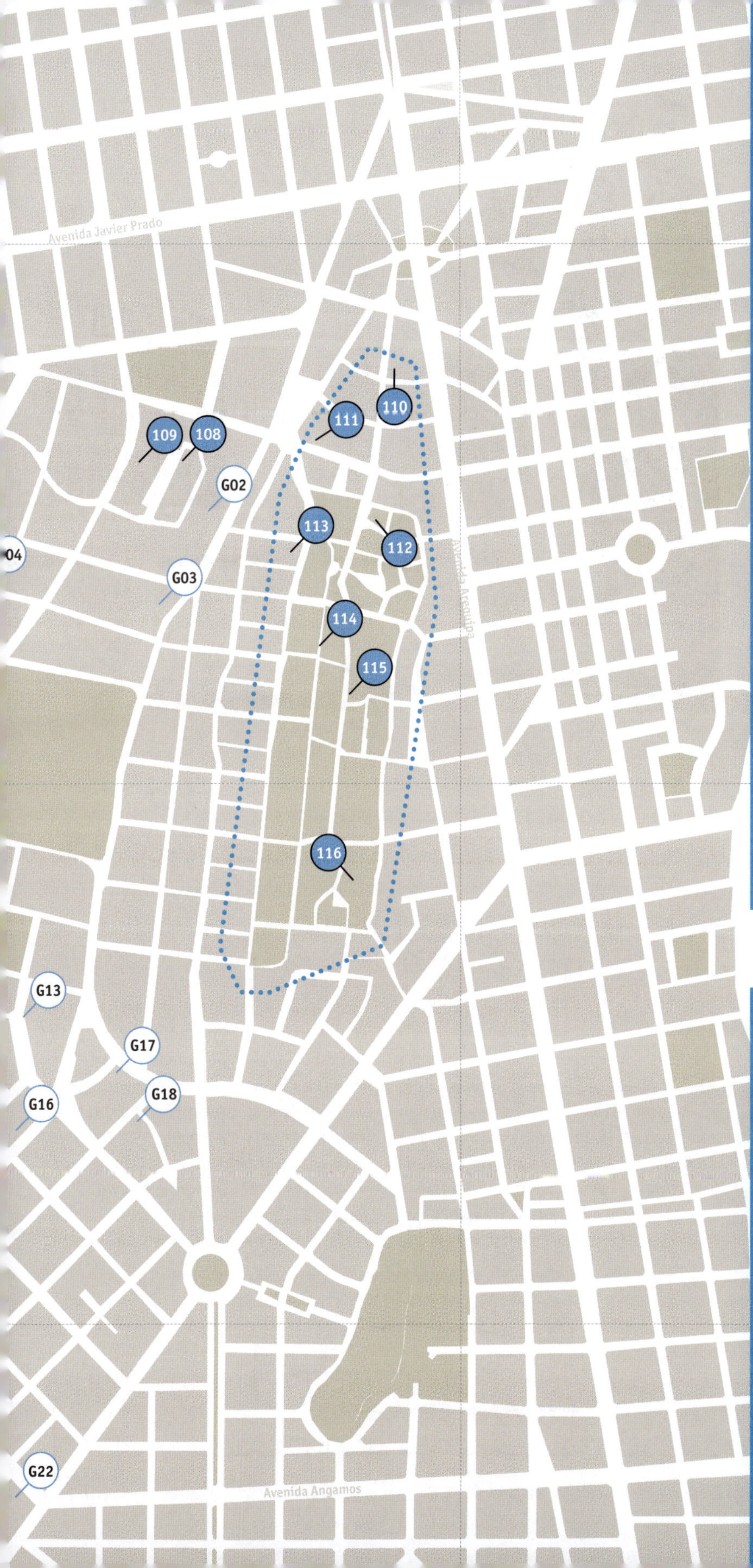

109 108
G02
O4
G03

111 110
113
112
114
115

116

G13
G17
G16 G18

G22

Avenida Javier Prado

G

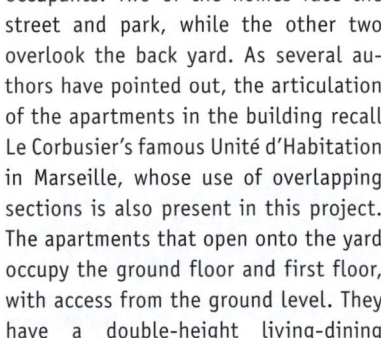

Edificio Roma

Calle Roma 390, San Isidro
Theodor Cron
1950

103 G

The Swiss architect's first work in Lima already reveals an interest in reconciling his modern affiliation with the Peruvian architectural tradition. This small but exquisite three-storey building between party walls, which achieves enormous spatial quality in a limited area, includes four split-level apartments for single occupants. Two of the homes face the street and park, while the other two overlook the back yard. As several authors have pointed out, the articulation of the apartments in the building recall Le Corbusier's famous Unité d'Habitation in Marseille, whose use of overlapping sections is also present in this project. The apartments that open onto the yard occupy the ground floor and first floor, with access from the ground level. They have a double-height living-dining room and a bedroom or studio on the

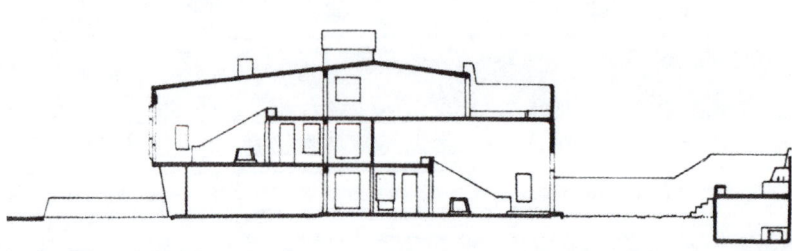

IPMIL. Universidad Nacional de Ingeniería

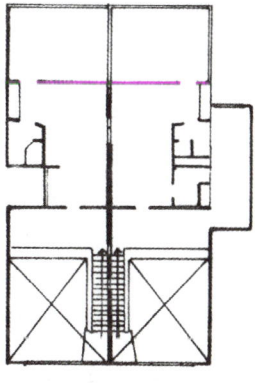

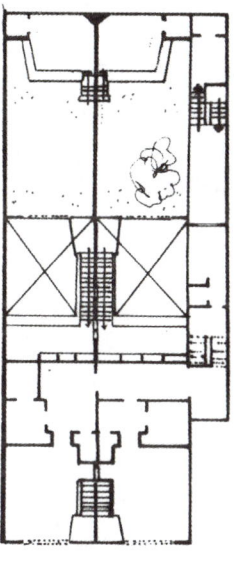

mezzanine. Each apartment enjoys half of the landscaped yard and an independent studio with a terrace at the far end. The first floor provides access to the homes overlooking the street, which occupy the top two floors. These apartments are also articulated around a double-height public area, but in addition to the space on the mezzanine they also have a separate bedroom and balcony on the top floor. The refined volume that accommodates the living rooms dominates the composition of the main façade, in which the large picture windows with latticework hark back to viceregal architecture. This volume rests on five trapezoidal brick piers that accommodate garages in the interstices between them and mark the building's rationalist structure. A narrow section on the north side contains the entrance, set back, as well as the vertical communication cores and services.

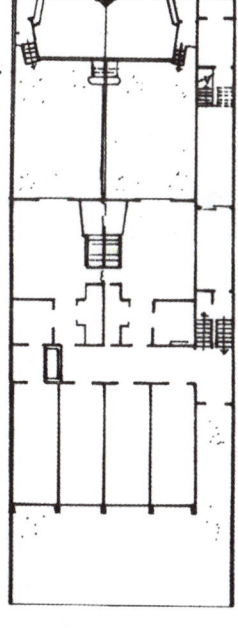

Renzo Rebagliati

Sede OIT

Calle Las Flores 275,
San Isidro
Ruth Alvarado, Óscar Borasino
2004

104 G

At the beginning of the 1930s, three incipient real estate developments located along Avenida Javier Prado were separated from Miraflores and formed a new district called San Isidro. After the Vía Expresa was completed in 1967, this exclusive residential area became one of the most important financial and commercial centres in the capital, prompting rapid growth. As a result, high-rise office buildings and low-density housing now coexist on the same street. In response to this changing urban context, the building for the World Trade Organisation's regional headquarters in Lima consists of a six-storey L-shaped building that turns inwards to a landscaped courtyard and presents a closed face to the outside. The stepped floors – a clear reference to the pre-Hispanic platforms – generate terraces with access from the offices and the communal and administrative areas, enabling them to extend their activities outside. They also provide adequate lighting for the interior spaces. The main façade is austere and rational, with three continuous windows protected from the sun by horizontal eaves and connected by a vertical window aligned with the main entrance, all against a uniform granite background. In 2004, the building won the Hexágono de Oro – the highest distinction conferred by the Colegio de Arquitectos del Perú – at the 11th edition of the Architecture Biennial.

Renzo Rebagliati

Casa Cooper

Calle Los Castaños 461,
San Isidro
Frederick Cooper
1975

 **105** **G**

This two-storey house in San Isidro was built using the same techniques that had been used in austere constructions on the outskirts of Lima: a reinforced concrete structure with exposed concrete blocks for the envelope. It contains modern spaces, eclectic details and a tropical garden in a work that defies all classification, replete with nods to ancient and modern architecture, both local and international. The house is set back from the street, creating a small entrance area where the garden wall meets the house wall, forming a small chamfer – the characteristic element of its urban presence – which contains a wide window with oblique frames, a coloured iron door, a lintel shaped like a Saint Andrew's cross and a porthole window. The references in this *povera* construction – the private residence of the architect, founder of the School of Architecture at the Pontificia Universidad Católica del Perú and editor of the magazine *Arkinka* – transport it to another place. While the façade has nods to Louis Khan and James Stirling, the materiality of the interiors recalls works by Aldo van Eyck and their spatial, longitudinal and double height attributes, particularly in relation to the garden, evoke the Eames House in California. To cite Rafael Moneo, this is a pre-digital house, as evidenced by the interior accumulation of photos and paintings on the walls that form a palimpsest or visible trace of another culture and its legacy.

Renzo Rebagliati

Edificio multifamiliar

106 G

Calle José Granda 315,
San Isidro
Theodor Cron
1962

Theodor Cron was born in Basel in 1925 and graduated as an architect from ETH Zürich in 1946, where he was a student of Max Bill. He arrived in Lima in 1948, building this exquisite multi-family construction with nine double-height apartments in 1962. Located on a corner plot between Calle José Granda and the Pasaje Country, the building has a curved access to the car park and a colourful garden inspired by Burle Marx's finest works in Brazil. The building materials are simple: an exposed reinforced concrete and brick structure painted over in white on the façade, terrazzo floor tiles in the communal areas, a variety of local woods for the doors, hardly any window frames, and a large awning on the roof finished with esteras or rush matting as a filter. Together, these elements form a light, attractive work. The interior is defined by meticulous attention to detail, from the wooden finish of the staircase leading to the mezzanine in each apartment to the kitchen units, bathroom tiles and even the washbasins and taps. The position and scale of the building with respect to the urban context, the geometry of the apartments and the materiality of the finishes generate a work of superior quality – possibly one of the finest apartment buildings in Lima – in an exercise that balances European rationalism with Latin American exuberance.

Renzo Rebagliati

Renzo Rebagliati

G

Edificio Golf Millenium

107 G

Avenida Aurelio Miró Quesada 3,
San Isidro
Ruth Alvarado, Óscar Borasino,
Guillermo Málaga
2009

The imposing void created in the urban fabric of San Isidro by the Lima Golf Club is surrounded by a series of juxtaposed towers that present an almost continuous flat, hermetic façade over this large green space. The Golf Millenium multi-family building occupies a generous plot in a privileged central position on the golf course, with the main front on the Avenida Aurelio Miró Quesada and two elevations on the side streets. In order to minimise its impact, the complex is divided into four towers, achieving a certain degree of permeability while progressively reducing its height at both

sides. To maximise the views, the towers are arranged around the three sides of the plot and rotated outwards, forming a fan. The interior part of the plot is given over to the underground garages and the gardens, with a swimming pool and a play area. Each tower is composed of two volumes turned outwards, with two apartments per floor, and a core that functions as an intermediate hinge, articulating both the main and the service communications. The front façades, glazed and with aluminium carpentry, have a tripartite structure. The first three floors form a plinth and have colonettes to emphasise the verticality. Above them, the transparent envelope is interrupted by the floor slabs which, from approximately halfway up each tower to the top, are underscored by eaves. On the side façades, vertical blades preserve the privacy of the interior spaces.

G

Renzo Rebagliati

Edificio Real 2

Vía Principal 155,
Centro Empresarial Real,
San Isidro

Jean Nouvel, Miguel Rodrigo Pérez-Araníbar
2017

108 G

In the second half of the twentieth century, different institutions began to build new premises in the developments south of the city, to the detriment of the historic centre. At the same time, and most notably since the 1980s, corporations started relocating their headquarters to San Isidro. It was in this context that the Centro Empresarial Real – a complex of office buildings designed by architects such as Alfredo Montagne, Cooper Graña Nicolini and others – was inaugurated in 1995. On the last free plot on the site, the French Pritzker Prize winner and local architect, Miguel Rodrigo, built a 14-storey construction that establishes a relationship with the surrounding heterogeneous environment through the attractive chromaticism of its envelope, the centrepiece of the project. Very simple in construction, it consists of large ultra-transparent panes of glass on minimalist steel profiles. Sliding multi-coloured panels provide solar protection to the interior spaces. This system offers a constantly changing image because of the collective action of the users, creating a sense of community in a context in which each company strives to reaffirm its own personality. The chromatic treatment continues on the ceiling of the double-height lobby. On the ground floor, the façade is set back to incorporate a vegetal filter, while the rooftop garden affords panoramic views of the city.

Gonzalo Cáceres. Courtesy of *Revista CASAS*

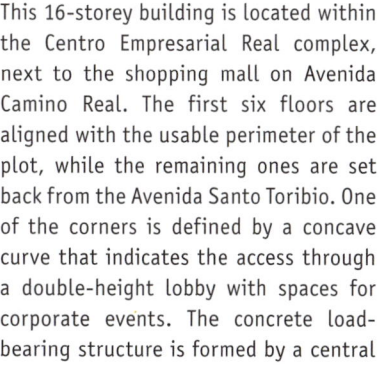

Edi Hirose

G

Edificio Real 8

109 G

Vía Central,
Centro Empresarial Real,
San Isidro
*Hünerwadel Arquitectos
(Nicolas Hünerwadel, Víctor Pazos)*
2014

This 16-storey building is located within the Centro Empresarial Real complex, next to the shopping mall on Avenida Camino Real. The first six floors are aligned with the usable perimeter of the plot, while the remaining ones are set back from the Avenida Santo Toribio. One of the corners is defined by a concave curve that indicates the access through a double-height lobby with spaces for corporate events. The concrete load-bearing structure is formed by a central core with six lifts and a grid of columns independent from the façade that support a system of flat beams. The façade is composed of horizontal bands and parapets rendered with natural stone, cut into concave slabs, which define the corners in a singular way. The modulation of the windows changes on each floor, with trapezoidal frames finished in wood occupying the space between the glass and the sun shades and creating a deep envelope that differs considerably from the curtain wall solutions typically found in office buildings. The interior finishes are of superior quality, with soft-coloured carpets and natural stone for the floors, wooden panels for the walls and skilfully designed lighting. The result is undoubtedly the finest corporate building that has emerged in Lima in recent years.

El Olivar

The Spanish introduced the Mediterranean olive tree to Peru in the mid-sixteenth century and two centuries later El Olivar had nearly two thousand specimens. When the area was developed, the woods became the largest public green space in the district, although nowadays it has been reduced to a rectangle of approximately 250 metres wide and 850 metres long. Two parallel streets define the perimeter, while a central avenue, the Avenida Los Incas, traces a winding path from north to south. The residential area of El Olivar extends its limits beyond the woodland, southwards along Avenida Agustín de la Torre up to its intersection with Avenida Pardo y Aliaga, eastwards along the continuation of Avenida Arenales and northwards along Avenida El Bosque, always maintaining its density and quality of vegetation. On the latter avenue, Barclay & Crousse designed El Bosque Boutiques (110), a small concrete building with volumes arranged radially, slightly set back from the corner to generate a pleasant public space.

Bearing witness to its colonial past as an agricultural holding is the Casa Moreyra (111), an eighteenth-century hacienda that once cultivated these olive trees and still displays elements of viceregal architecture, such as the side chapel, the double entrance steps and the octagonal tower. The floor plan is composed of concatenated spaces, without any corridors, organised in an L-shape around a gallery of Doric columns and semi-circular arches, which form a semi-open courtyard with a fairly rustic decorative programme of mouldings, tiles and balustrades.

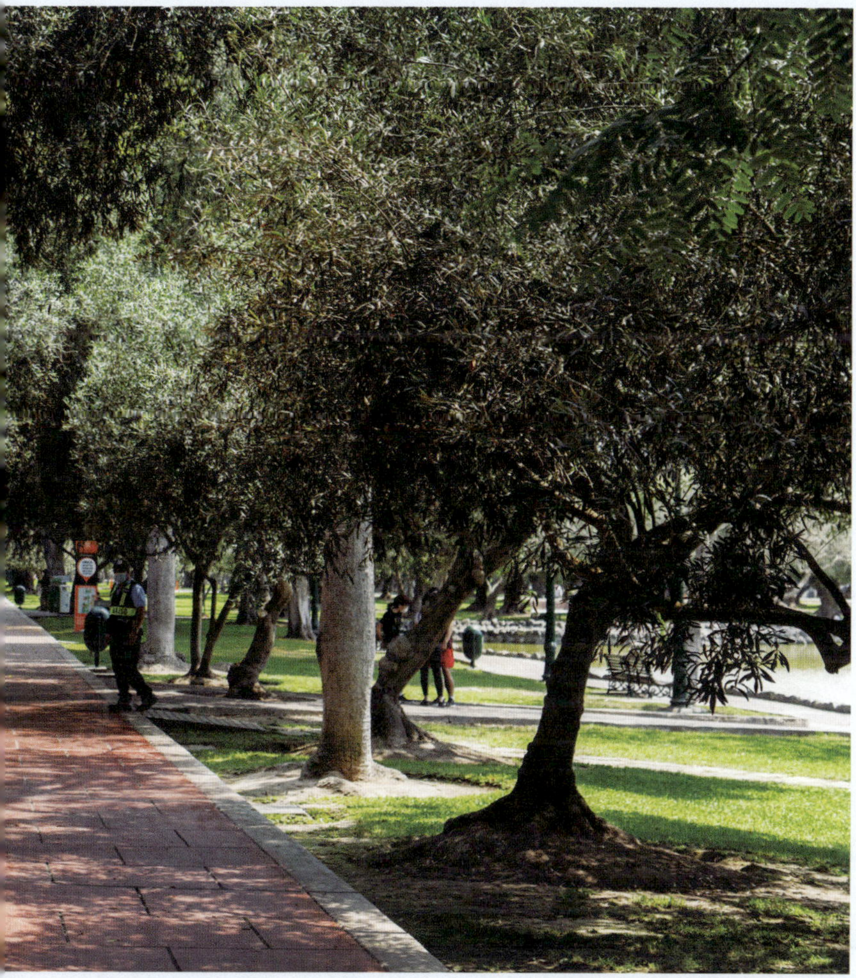

Renzo Rebagliati

Main pedestrian path in El Olivar

El Bosque Boutiques

110 G

Avenida El Bosque 277, San Isidro
Sandra Barclay, Jean Pierre Crousse
2014

Christopher Schreier

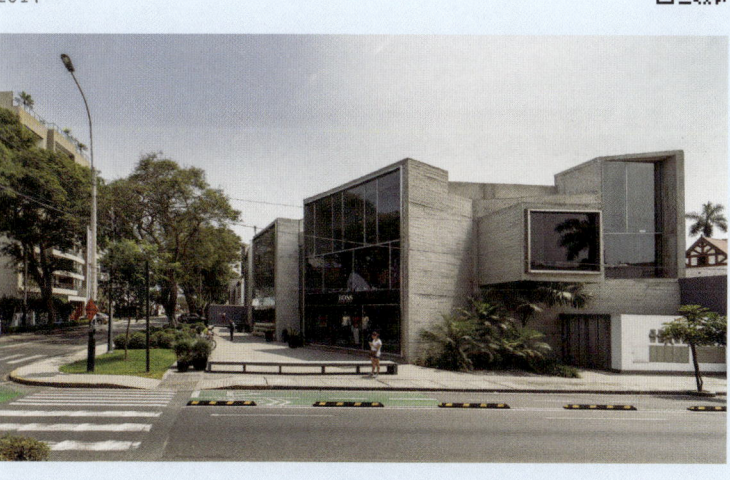

Casa Moreyra

111 G

Avenida Paz Soldán 290, San Isidro
Architect unknown, 51-1 Arquitectos
(César Becerra, Fernando Puente, Manuel de Rivero)
18th century, 2014

Iván Salinero and Antonio Sorrentino. Courtesy of 51-1 Arquitectos

The building was refurbished in 2015 by the studio 51-1 Arquitectos to house the restaurant Astrid y Gastón, flagship of the La Macha business group owned by famous chef Gastón Acurio. The restrained, luminous intervention removed elements that had been added to the structure, opting instead to highlight the original carpentry. Of particular note are the wooden floors, the door ornaments and the ceiling structures, with skilfully integrated mechanical ventilation. The project restored the perimeter walls around the front garden to

Edificio El Olivar

112 G

Calle Francisco Tamayo 180, San Isidro
Manuel Villarán
1966

Edificio La Ponciana

Calle La República 110, San Isidro
Sandra Barclay,
Jean Pierre Crousse
2015

113 G

Juan Solano

Urbanización El Olivar

Avenida Los Incas, San Isidro
Manuel Piqueras Cotolí
1920

114 G

Gonzalo Cáceres

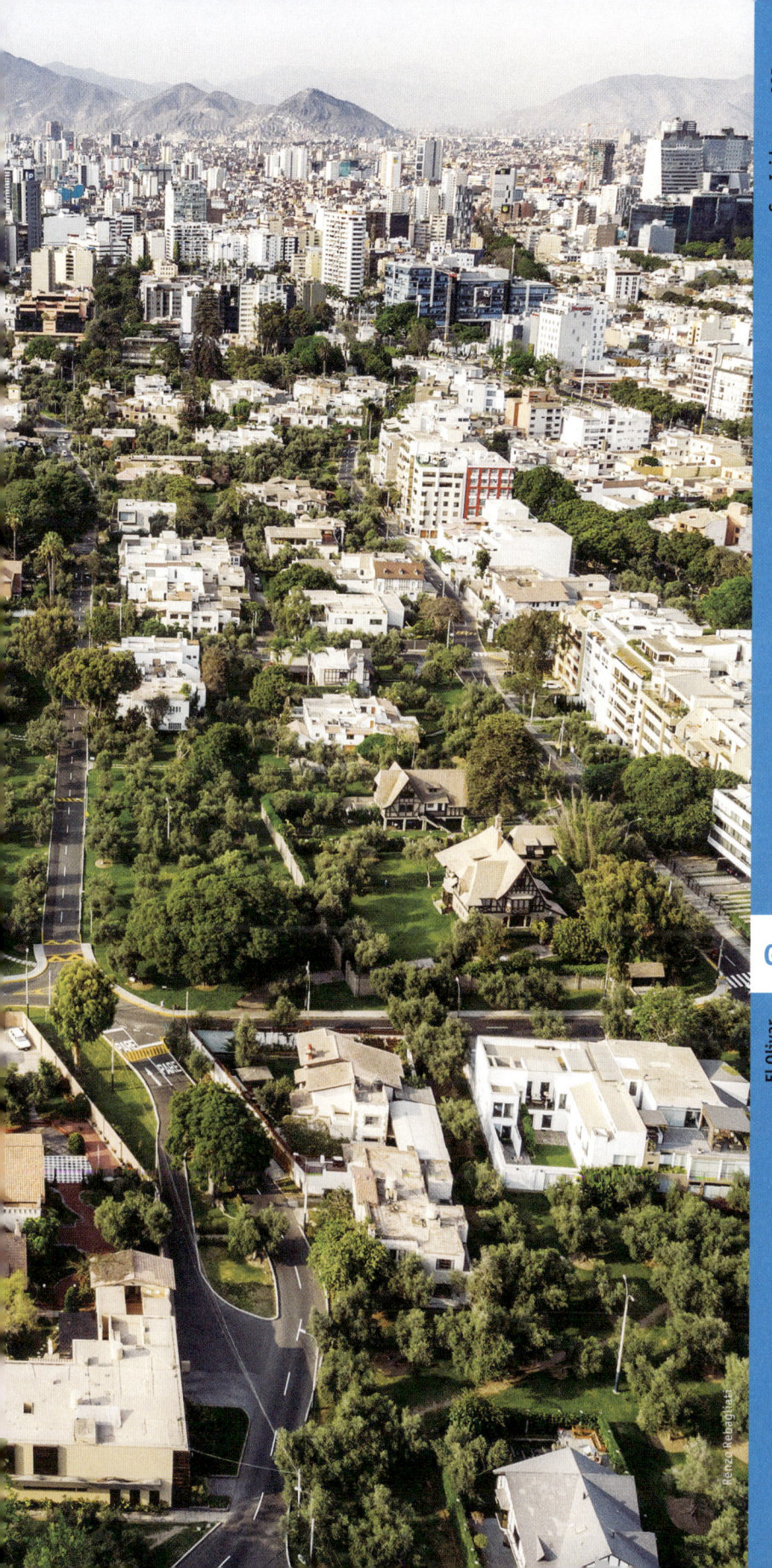

G

Renzo Rebagliati

Casa El Olivar

Calle Hermilio Hernández 250, San Isidro
Ruth Alvarado
2010

Stella Watmough

their original height, adding a new vegetable garden and a greenhouse to service a culinary research centre.

The nature of the area changed in 1920 with its urban development (114). The Spanish sculptor Piqueras Cotolí designed an irregular layout with a picturesque appearance. The project overlapped with the grid geometry of the olive grove, with trees spaced at distances of between 6 and 8 metres in both directions to facilitate their exploitation. The constructions – mostly detached single-family homes – are inserted into this layout mainly without fences around the private gardens, blurring the ownership structure and generating an exceptionally attractive housing development in a public park. A red cement path, skilfully separated from vehicular traffic, runs through the woods parallel to Avenida Los Incas, part of it lined by Tudor-style houses designed by architects such as Emilio Harth-Terré and José Álvarez Calderón. The municipal mandate to preserve this eclectic English style inspired the ironic project of the Casa Tudor (116)

by 51-1 Arquitectos. Ruth Alvarado's Casa El Olivar (115), on the other hand, did not need to meet that requirement, incorporating the verdant context into the design by means of a façade with leaf-shaped perforations.

The growth of Lima's population in the mid-twentieth century led to densification and the appearance of multi-family buildings, many of them in a modernist style. Although El Olivar was caught up in this process, it managed to preserve its scale and character. In this context, Manuel Villarán designed the building known as the Edificio El Olivar (112), with a rigorously modern floor plan and a façade composed of panels of glass interrupted by windows with wooden frames. That construction marked the beginning of a process that has continued around the edges of the park, as reflected by two projects designed by Masuno Estudio and Barclay & Crousse. The first is a small three-storey work skilfully executed in exposed concrete, with interesting finishes and rails. The second, called La Ponciana (113), has six

Casa Tudor

Avenida Los Incas 575, San Isidro
*51-1 Arquitectos (César Becerra,
Fernando Puente, Manuel de Rivero)*
2015

116 G

Gonzalo Cáceres. Courtesy of *Revista CASAS*

G

El Olivar

floors and is split into two volumes with the entrance located between them. The glass façade is protected from the sun by wooden latticework, pointing the way forward for new buildings in the area.

El Olivar is undoubtedly one of the finest spaces in Lima and well worth visiting on foot or by bike. Its merits are not so much the buildings but an almost perfect balance between nature and density that combines high-rises, small-scale multi-family constructions and single-family homes with spectacular vegetation. Commerce, housing and offices mix in a way that is neither American nor European, accompanied by all the necessary amenities. This is one of the few places in the city where public space is the protagonist, with hardly any fences or private streets. El Olivar challenges nearly every cliché about luxury zones in Latin America.

Renzo Rebagliati

Courtesy of Emilio Soyer Nash archive

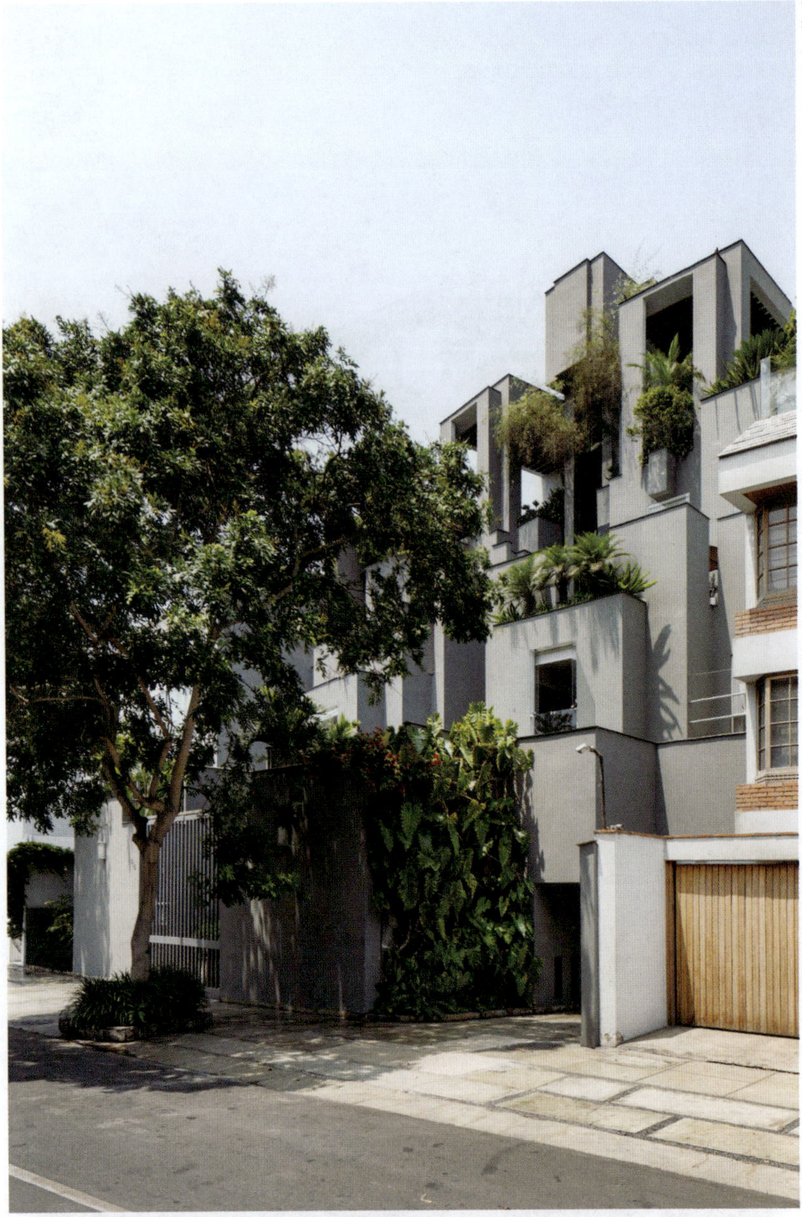

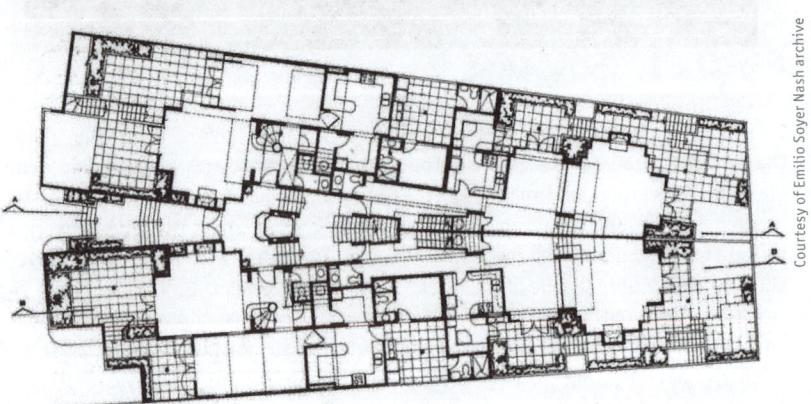

Edificio Ajax-Hispania

117 G

Calle Alfredo Salazar 607,
San Isidro
Emilio Soyer
1983

In the context of the postmodern architecture built in Latin America in the 1980s, this project presents a volumetry with references to pre-Columbian coastal constructions and a floor plan that has nods to the Italian Renaissance, in an eclectic work with an otherwise attractive materiality discreetly located in one of the greenest parts of San Isidro. Built on a narrow plot on a block of semi-detached constructions around an amoeba-shaped park, the structure is resolved with an axis of symmetry based on the access. The entrance leads to a panoramic lift that is flanked by stepped volumes incorporating balconies and window boxes. Each volume operates as a separate unit with a scale typically found in stacked Mediterranean houses. The homes are accessed from the Italian-style central staircase, with three flights of steps and a vanishing perspective, which widens and branches off to the interior garden. The wet rooms and installations are articulated along this central spine, leaving the perimeter free to open outwards in an organic manner, with double heights and evocative outdoor spaces that ignore the geometry of the party walls. This is a Mannerist building, very different from the prevailing Peruvian architecture at the time yet still contemporary, with roots in the Aldo Rossi school and reminiscences of some of Ricardo Bofill's 1970s works, such as Xanadú and Kafka's Castle.

Renzo Rebagliati

G

Edi Hirose. Courtesy of Leonmarcial Arquitectos

Edificio Balcón

Calle Víctor Maúrtua 245,
San Isidro
Alexia León, Lucho Marcial
2015

118 G

Since the second half of the twentieth century, the residential fabric in San Isidro has been undergoing a process of densification whereby single-family homes are gradually being replaced by multi-family housing. This impeccable building is one of the most recent examples. The pedestrian access is conceived as an interior passage that crosses the building from front to back, connecting the street to a back yard that also serves as a buffer zone between this property and the neighbouring one. The volume is set back from the street in a series of stepped planes, which generate a second free space along one side of the plot. This strategy of emancipation from the boundary allows the building to stand apart from the homogeneous street façade, made up of conventional constructions between party walls. Instead, multiple diverse relationships are established between the interior spaces and the environment. Furthermore, the multiplication of the façade area, combined with the back yard, maximises the natural light and

Edi Hirose. Courtesy of Leonmarcial Arquitectos

ventilation. The project includes four spacious residential units, two with a floor area of 300 square metres and two with an area of nearly 600 square metres. The first of the larger units, which is split-level and occupies the semi-basement and ground-floor levels, is perceived as the typical family house thanks to its connections with both yards. The two smaller units occupy the levels immediately above, one on each floor, and the split-level attic is given over to the other large unit. The exposed concrete and green rails form an austere palette of materials, with trees camouflaging the building and minimising its presence.

Edi Hirose. Courtesy of Leonmarcial Arquitectos

G

Vivienda unifamiliar

Calle Carlos Graña 277,
San Isidro
Studio MK27 (Marcio Kogan)
2016

119 G

The Calle Carlos Graña is lined with a series of modernist houses dating back to the 1950s and 1960s alongside more contemporary buildings designed by some of Lima's finest architects. Developed in conjunction with Samanta Cafardo, Elisa Friedman and Jorge Baerti, this house is the first Peruvian work by the well-known Brazilian architect, whose style is characterised by the use of exposed concrete, wooden frameworks and finishes and furnishings in the best modern Brazilian tradition. On a plot that is 16 metres wide and 30 metres deep, the building divides the programme of uses by creating different layers of privacy on three stepped horizontal volumes, set back from the party walls. The entrance, raised half a storey above street level, is finished with compact panelling made of strips of Brazilian wood. The next floor has a façade of grey micro-perforated corrugated iron sheets and the top floor, cantilevered over the rest area, is concrete with digital-aesthetic latticework. These façade mechanisms are actually typical elements of viceregal architecture in Peru, present in the wooden balconies of the mansions in the historic centre. They respond to the extreme exposure to sun and humidity of this desert area by means of interfaces that filter the light, allowing the breeze to pass through and generate spaces with optimal climate comfort from which to see without being seen.

Casa Vertical

Calle Alfredo Salazar 892,
San Isidro
Alexia León
2005

120 G

Located on a square plot between three party walls, the Casa Vertical does not have a lift. Instead, it is structured around a varied collection of impeccably executed staircases that combine pairs of materials such as steel with terrazzo floor tiles and tropical wood with marble, finished with banisters made out of rectangular-section galvanised steel or *metal deployé* painted in green. The house consists of four levels and a basement, which includes double-height ceilings, terraces, balconies and skylights. The abstract geometry of the floor-plan composition and the ultra-refined materiality – expressed, for example, in the enormous pieces of white marble – take this small work to another level, referencing Italian fascist architecture and Giuseppe Terragni's Villa Bianca (1937) in particular, where every functional element, including the skylights, doors and furnishings, also fulfils an aesthetic purpose. The entrance, located in a context of meticulous urban landscaping, skilfully resolves the transition to the street by replacing the recurring wall with railings and generating a chromatic

Edi Hirose. Courtesy of Leonmarcial Arquitectos

Edi Hirose. Courtesy of Leonmarcial Arquitectos

G

Edi Hirose. Courtesy of Leonmarcial Arquitectos

continuity between the paving inside the plot and the footpath outside. The façade, concealed behind a cedar tree, is composed of concrete walls rendered in white, sliding aluminium carpentry and vertical blinds. The result is a remarkably light and cheerful work, far removed from the brutalism that prevails in contemporary Peruvian architecture. The Casa Vertical was one of the first works in Alexia León's career, but it already contains design elements that she has subsequently deployed in buildings on Calle Juan Fanning and Calle Victor Maúrtua.

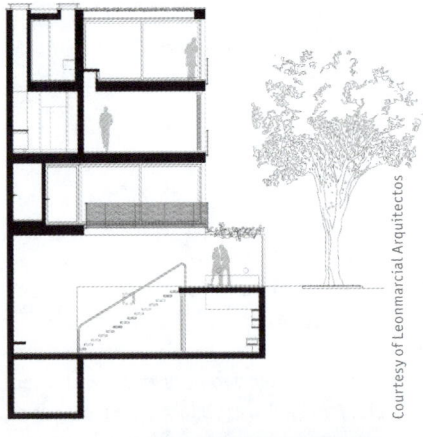

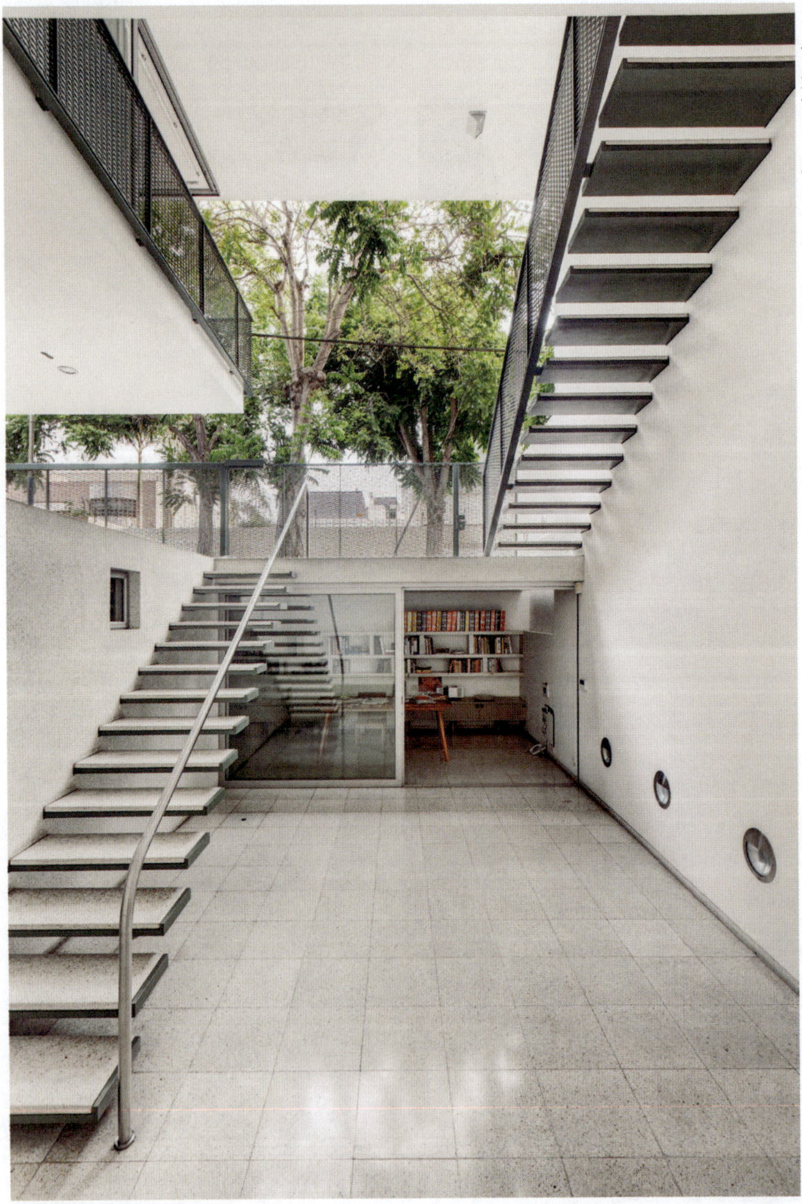

Underground spaces

Edificio Carlos Graña

Calle Carlos Graña 160,
San Isidro
Óscar Borasino
2001

121 G

G

Between the Avenida Santa Cruz and Avenida Álvarez Calderón, the urban lay-out has left a series of voids in the form of large courtyards in the middle of the block that function as public parks. These parks, which, because of their position, can be explored sequentially, offer quiet havens away from the city hustle and bustle and form one of Lima's finest residential areas. This building is located in one of these parks, on a privileged plot with three fronts: one faces the street, another gives onto the park and the third overlooks the pedestrian access pas-sage. A concrete plinth accommodates the car park. Above this level, the street and passage façades have an opaque ceramic skin, meticulously designed with a 10-centimetre square module, where the service spaces and smaller bedrooms are located. Numerous holes punctuate the street façade, while on the passage side the perforations are reduced to little more than fissures. By contrast, on the park side the walls disappear and the building opens onto the vegetation. A refined metal structure supports the transparent façade, where different types of balconies echo the diversity of the apartments. The building appropriates the park, but the park also appropriates the building. To a certain extent, the in-terior is incorporated into the landscape, so gazing out at it allows the beholder to somehow participate in the hedonistic experience of actually living in it.

Edificio Álvarez-Calderón

122 G

Avenida Álvarez-Calderón 530,
San Isidro
José García Bryce
1963

José García Bryce designed this housing project in the San Isidro district in 1963, using slabs of reinforced concrete and a whitewashed brick envelope with singular wooden carpentry. It is a rationalist building in which, according to the project description, 'the visual appearance is the expression of the construction.' Built at a time when single-family housing was the norm in the district, the volume is set back from the streets and adjacent plots, generating a continuous façade in its treatment that is interrupted at the rendered entrance area by the water tank on the roof, which has been converted into an ornamental element to indicate the placement of the stairwell. The urban design around the plot and landscaping are finely executed with two access ramps connecting the car park in the semi-basement to the public footpath. An 'extraordinary building due to its construction truth and simplicity' is how Miguel Cruchaga described it in the magazine, *El Arquitecto Peruano*. It would surely be a masterpiece if it were not for certain details of the floor plan distribution, such as the location of the maid's bedroom next to an unnecessary courtyard in a building with six façades, where narrow winding staircases double and segregate the foot traffic.

Renzo Rebagliati

Renzo Rebagliati

G

Avenida General Portillo

G

Lima Golf Club

Avenidas Pezet, Portillo,
Miró Quesada and Camino Real,
San Isidro
1924

One of Lima's largest green spaces belongs to a private golf club, which has nevertheless generated a spectacular urban setting around its edges with high-rise buildings from which to gaze down on this historical anomaly that does not even have a continuous tree-lined perimeter path to service the large numbers of cyclists and joggers who use it every morning. The view of a savannah landscape with mustard green lawns and ancient desert trees has enormous appeal from a real estate point of view and has led to the construction of some remarkable buildings, designed by Óscar Borasino, Ruth Alvarado, Arquitectónica, Hans Hollein, Reynaldo Ledgard and Guillermo Málaga. Others of a more picturesque nature, like Robert Stern's designs on Avenida General Pezet – three buildings at numbers 195, 375 and 561 – reproduce the materiality and forms of the Chicago School in the late nineteenth century. The last one completed, at number 195, echoes the twin towers of the El Dorado building in the upper west side of Manhattan. Unfortunately, there are no public viewpoints from which to gaze at this Latin American 'Central Park,' whose history began in 1923 when a group of associates belonging to the British colony purchased a large plot of land from the Moreyra Paz Soldán family to build a golf club and develop the surroundings at a time when Lima was expanding outwards, away from the historic centre. The greens opened in 1924 and were followed two years later by the Country Club, a neocolonial building designed by Augusto Benavides, José Álvarez Calderón and T. J. O'Brien. During the course of successive acquisitions, the club became an independent entity and a road for vehicular traffic now separates it from the golf course. It was refurbished in the 1990s and now houses one of the best-known hotels in Lima, with an English-style pub and terrace where excellent cocktails are served in a Visconti film-like atmosphere.

Pezet 561 residential tower (Stern, Jones, Whalen, 2018)

Peter Aaron / OTTO. Courtesy of Robert A. M. Stern Architects

The Country Club Lima Hotel

Courtesy of Los Portales

G

Renzo Rebagliati

G

[Full-width photograph of a modernist house with a large tree in front, spanning the upper portion of the page]

Casa Ausejo

Avenida Alberto Chabrier 250,
San Isidro
Carlos Ausejo
1965

124 G

Located in a quiet residential street opposite one of the parks that forms the urban fabric of San Isidro, this is arguably the house that best addresses the security requirements that have conditioned architectural design in Lima over the last few decades. A key element of the project is the property's exterior wall, dignified in a similar way to the one at the Smithson's Upper Lawn Pavilion finished a few years earlier which, like this house, was built for the use and enjoyment of its designers. Placed on top of that white brick wall is one of the two volumes that make up the house, accommodating the bedrooms: a refined, emphatic prism with a glazed façade affording views of the neighbouring park and wider city. The meticulous execution conceals the union between the interior partitions and the aluminium carpentry, with a delicacy that evokes the works of the American grand masters of the period. The raised, cantilever quality of this volume generates a porch on the street façade, marking the beginning of a spatial sequence that leads to the house and continues at the large opening in the wall that constitutes the threshold of the interior courtyard. From here, five steps lead finally to the door in wooden panelling that forms the façade of the second volume. This part of the house is situated at an intermediate height, opening onto the back garden through a porch that allows social activities to spill outside. A flight of steps connects the two volumes.

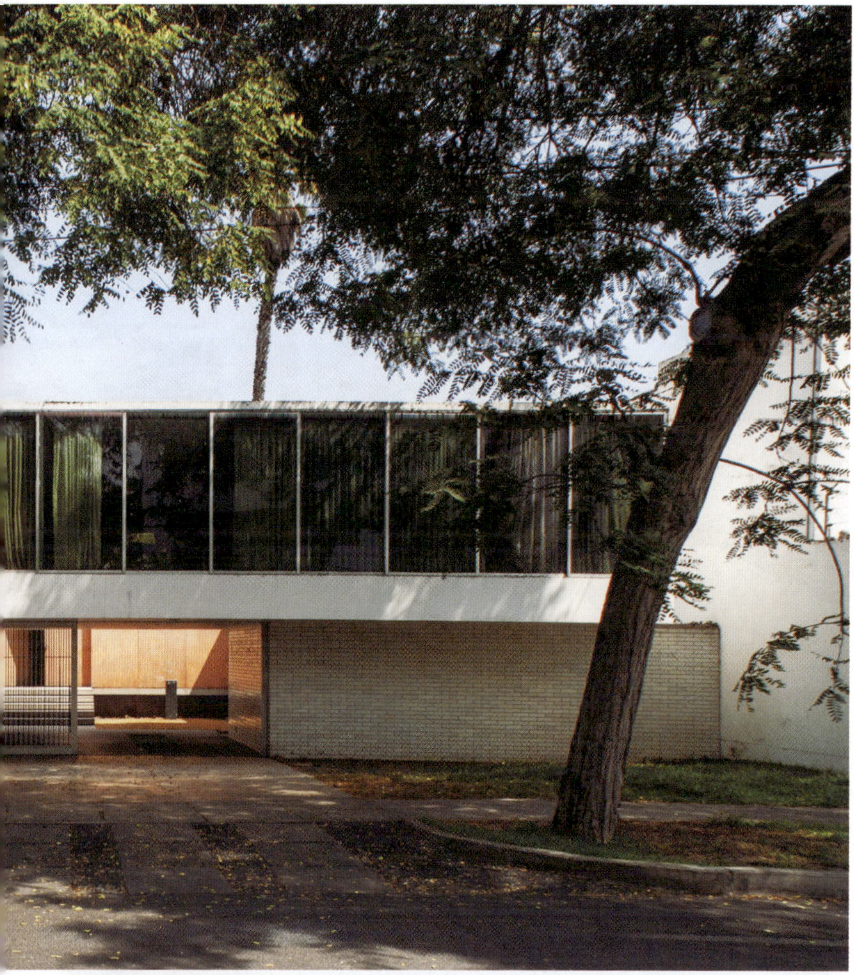

Gonzalo Cáceres

Gonzalo Cáceres

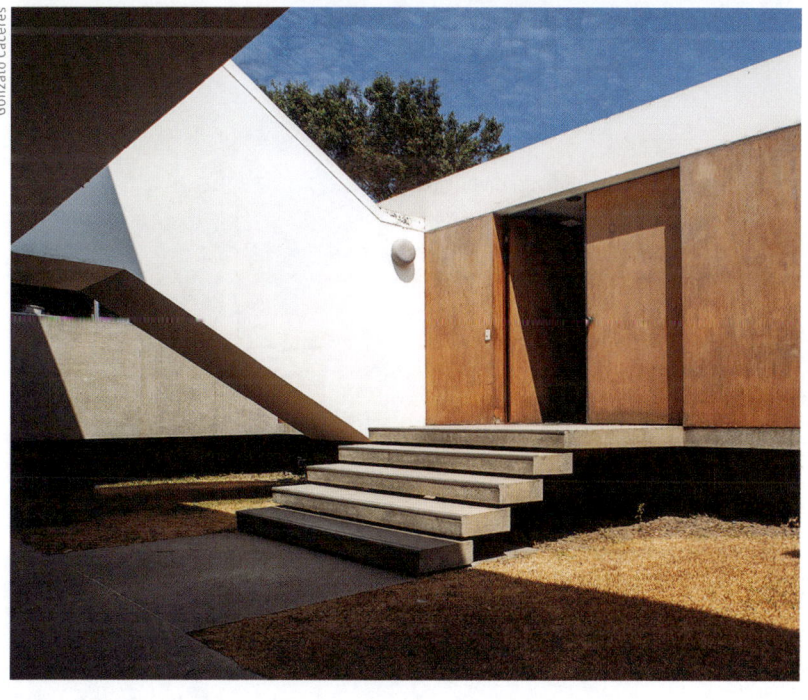

Residencial Santa Cruz

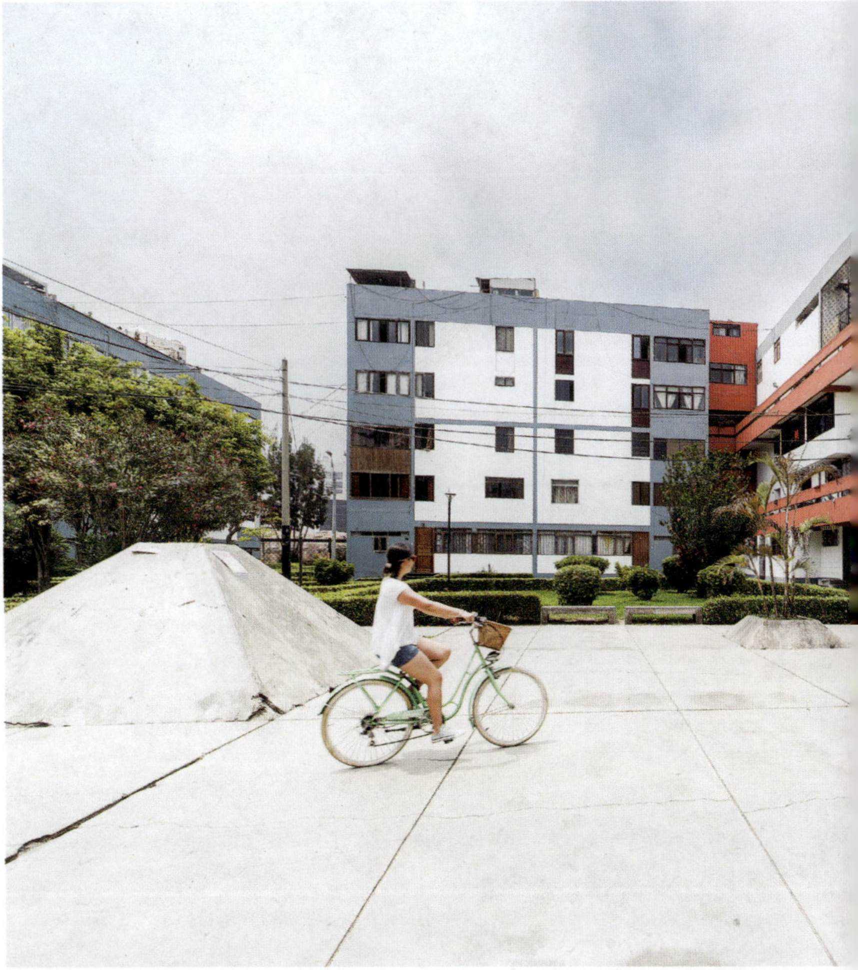

Avenida Belén, San Isidro
Jacques Crousse, Luis Vásquez
1966

While the development of his emblematic San Felipe residential complex was under way, the architect and president, Fernando Belaúnde Terry, promoted other collective housing projects for the middle class through the National Housing Board. The Residencial Santa Cruz is located in one of the most affluent residential areas of the city, a stone's throw from the San Isidro golf club. It occupies a 7 hectare plot originally belonging to the Ministry of Defence, which gave it up in exchange for the construction of a row of 44 single-family homes for the military along its west side. The complex features both cross-plan and linear blocks, as well as a small building housing the

remaining apartments are split-level with access from external corridors on the first and third floors. The sculptural stairs in the linear blocks lend a unique identity to the project. The arrangement and combination of the two typologies generates and articulates different green spaces and public squares with unusual truncated cone-shaped planters. The linear blocks perpendicular to the longitudinal axis of the plot fragment it, reducing the scale of the open spaces but nevertheless leaving the ground floor free to maintain continuity with the footpaths and facilitate a sequential route through the different squares and gardens. As a whole, the complex achieves an intimate scale, with less impact than Residencial San Felipe but more warmth.

neighbourhood association and shops. All the residential buildings have five floors and in each case the ground floor accommodates single-storey apartments accessed directly from the street. The

G

Christopher Schreier

Diego Franco Coto. Courtesy of Nómena Arquitectos

Diego Franco Coto. Courtesy of Nómena Arquitectos

Edificio Morphology

126 G

Avenida Mariscal La Mar 1332, Miraflores
*Nómena Arquitectos
(Moris Fleischman, Diego Franco,
Héctor Loli, Jorge Sánchez), Talia Valdez
2016*

The Santa Cruz neighbourhood, one of the least affluent parts of the otherwise prosperous Miraflores district, has been undergoing constant transformation in recent years. The car repair shops, modest houses and traditional stores are giving way to high-end restaurants, design shops and modern office and apartment buildings. As a 'concept store,' this building of impeccable architecture represents a brand-new typology in the city. The long plot between party walls is occupied in its entirety. The commercial, office and restaurant programmes are located on the street side, with premises stacked on all five floors, with the top floor functioning as an outdoor space. The rear of the plot is given over to a large landscaped void where Lima's only butterfly pavilion has been installed. A perimeter ramp winds its way up this void, allowing users to enjoy the space. The ground-floor façade is transparent, establishing a commercial link with the street, while the remainder has a double skin of concrete latticework and glass. This feature echoes the modern Latin American tradition and typical Lima balconies, also serving to filter the view over parts of the neighbourhood that have not yet been transformed.

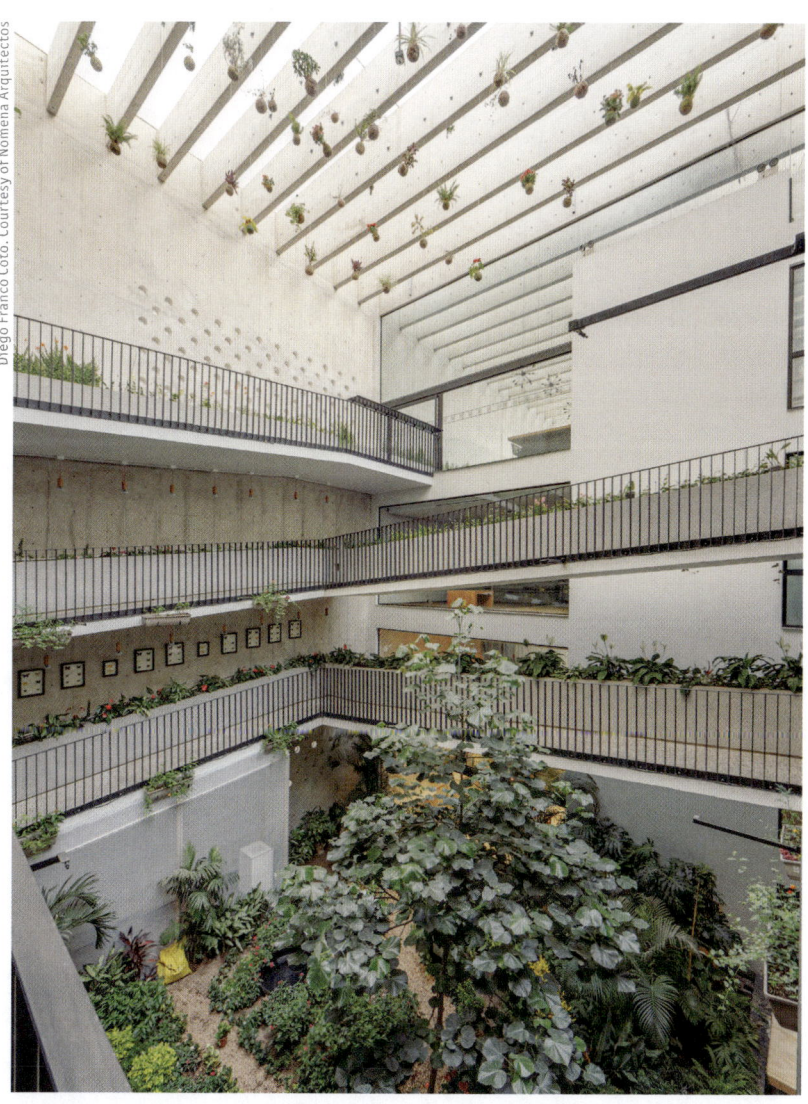

Diego Franco Coto. Courtesy of Nómena Arquitectos

G

Other Works of Interest

G01 Casa Canziani
Calle Los Alamos 338,
San Isidro
Mario Gilardi
1951

G02 Centro comercial Camino Real
Avenida Camino Real 390,
San Isidro
Daniel Arana Ríos
1980

G03 Parque urbano
Avenida Camino Real 598, San Isidro
Augusto Román, José Bauer,
Juan Caycho
2022

G04 Casa Mulder
Calle Lizardo Alzamora Oeste 170,
San Isidro
Arquitectónica (Bernando
Fort Brescia, Laurinda Spear)
1985

G05 Edificio multifamiliar
Avenida General Juan Antonio Pezet
345, San Isidro

G06 Torres residenciales
Avenida General Juan Antonio Pezet
195, 375 and 561, San Isidro
Robert A. M. Stern, Michael D. Jones,
Paul L. Whalen
2018

G07 Edificio Pezet 515
Avenida General Juan Antonio Pezet
515, San Isidro
Hans Hollein, Alejandro Shell
2011

G08 Edificio Santa Amelia
Avenida Juan Antonio Pezet 1181,
San Isidro
Guillermo Málaga
1967

G09 Edificio de viviendas
Calle Manzanilla 195, San Isidro

G10 Vivienda unifamiliar
Calle General Muñiz 197, San Isidro

G11 Casa Matos
Calle Mariscal Blas Cerdeña 282,
San Isidro
Adolfo Córdova, Carlos Williams
1961

Right: Casa Canziani (Mario Gilardi)

G

Other Works of Interest

G12 Viviendas unifamiliares
Calle Carlos Graña 243 and 269,
San Isidro

G13 Lila
Calle Miguel Dasso 125, San Isidro
*Ghezzi Novak (Gustavo Ghezzi, Arturo
Ghezzi), Blanco (Pamela Remy)*
2021

G14 Vivienda unifamiliar
Avenida Álvarez Calderón 275,
San Isidro

G15 Casa Toro
Calle Francisco Eguiguren 207,
San Isidro
José García Bryce
1952

G16 Restaurante Cosme
Calle Tudela and Varela 162,
San Isidro
*51-1 Arquitectos (César Becerra,
Manuel de Rivero, Fernando Puente)*
2014

G17 Librería SUR
Avenida Pardo y Aliaga 683, San Isidro
2012

G18 Casa Gross
Calle Almirante Lord Cochrane 171,
Miraflores
Héctor Velarde
1954

G19 Edificio Chabriez
Calle Paúl de Beaudiez 310,
San Isidro
*Nómena Arquitectos
(Moris Fleischman, Jorge Sánchez,
Diego Franco and Héctor Loli)*
2019

G20 Vivienda unifamiliar
Avenida Octavio Espinosa 310,
San Isidro
Walter Weberhofer

G21 Edificio de viviendas NU
Parque Naciones Unidas, Miraflores
Sandra Barclay, Jean Pierre Crousse
2017

G22 Edificio de viviendas
Avenida Angamos Oeste 1115,
Miraflores

G

Lila (Ghezzi Novak, Blanco)

H

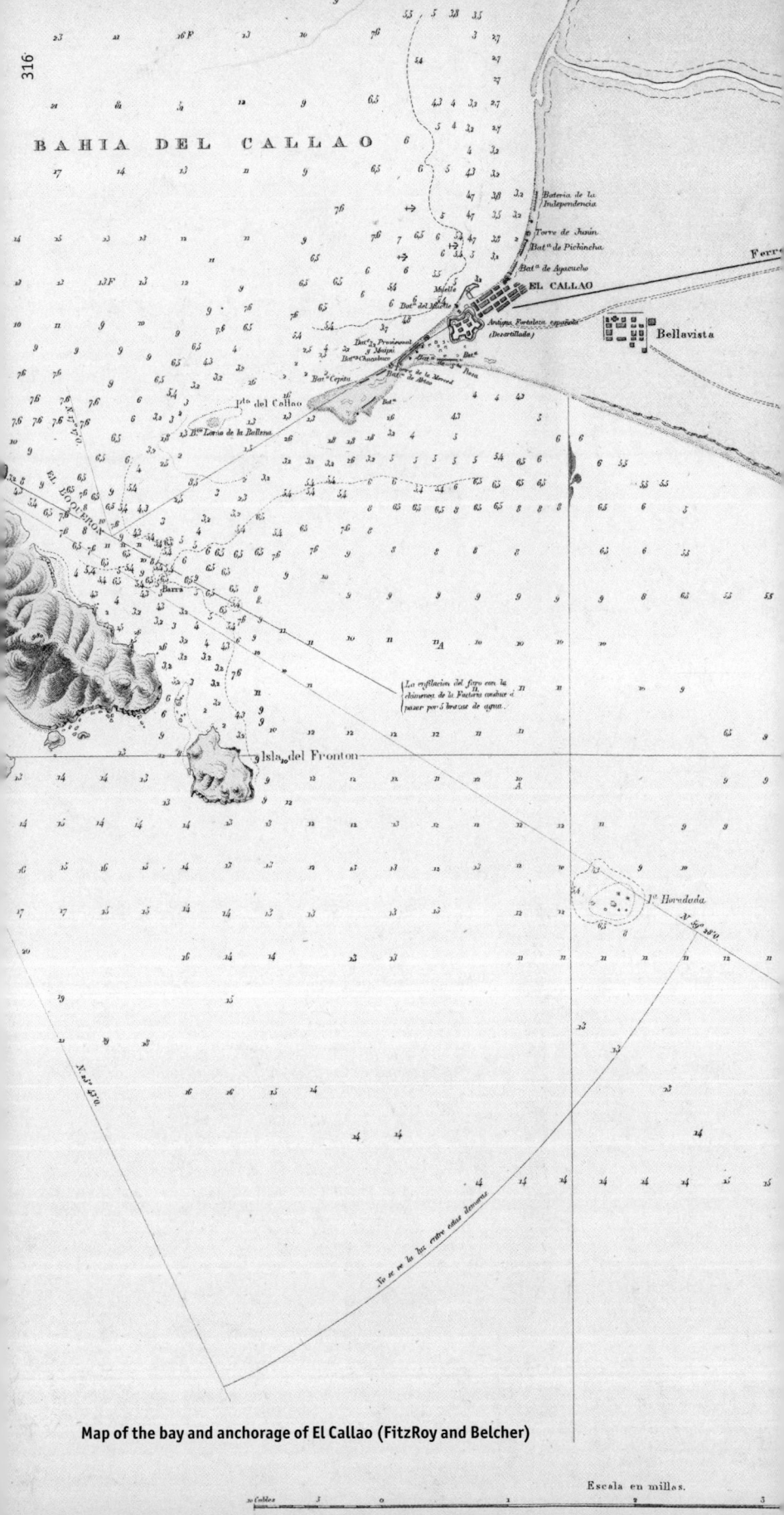

Map of the bay and anchorage of El Callao (FitzRoy and Belcher)

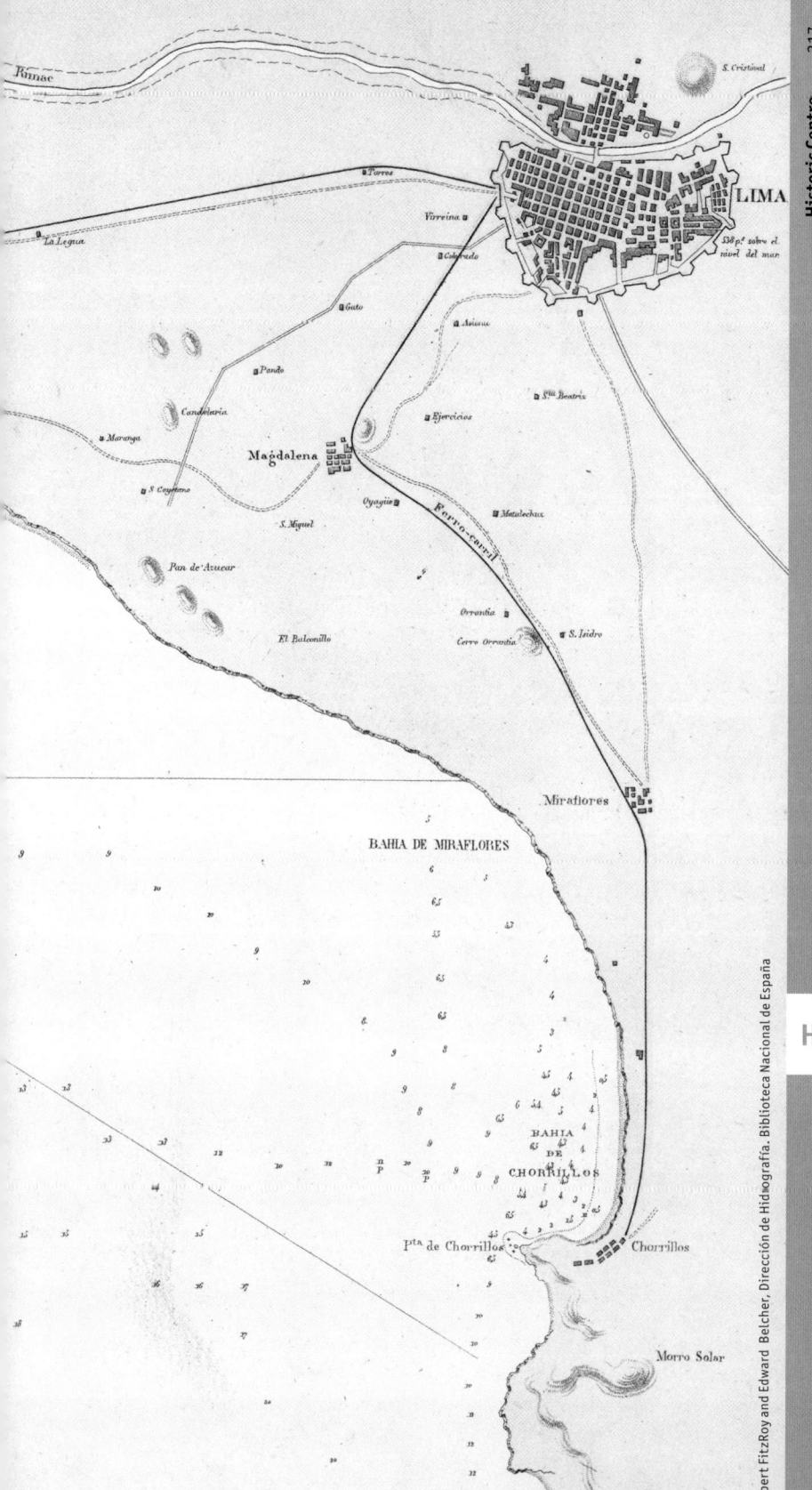

H

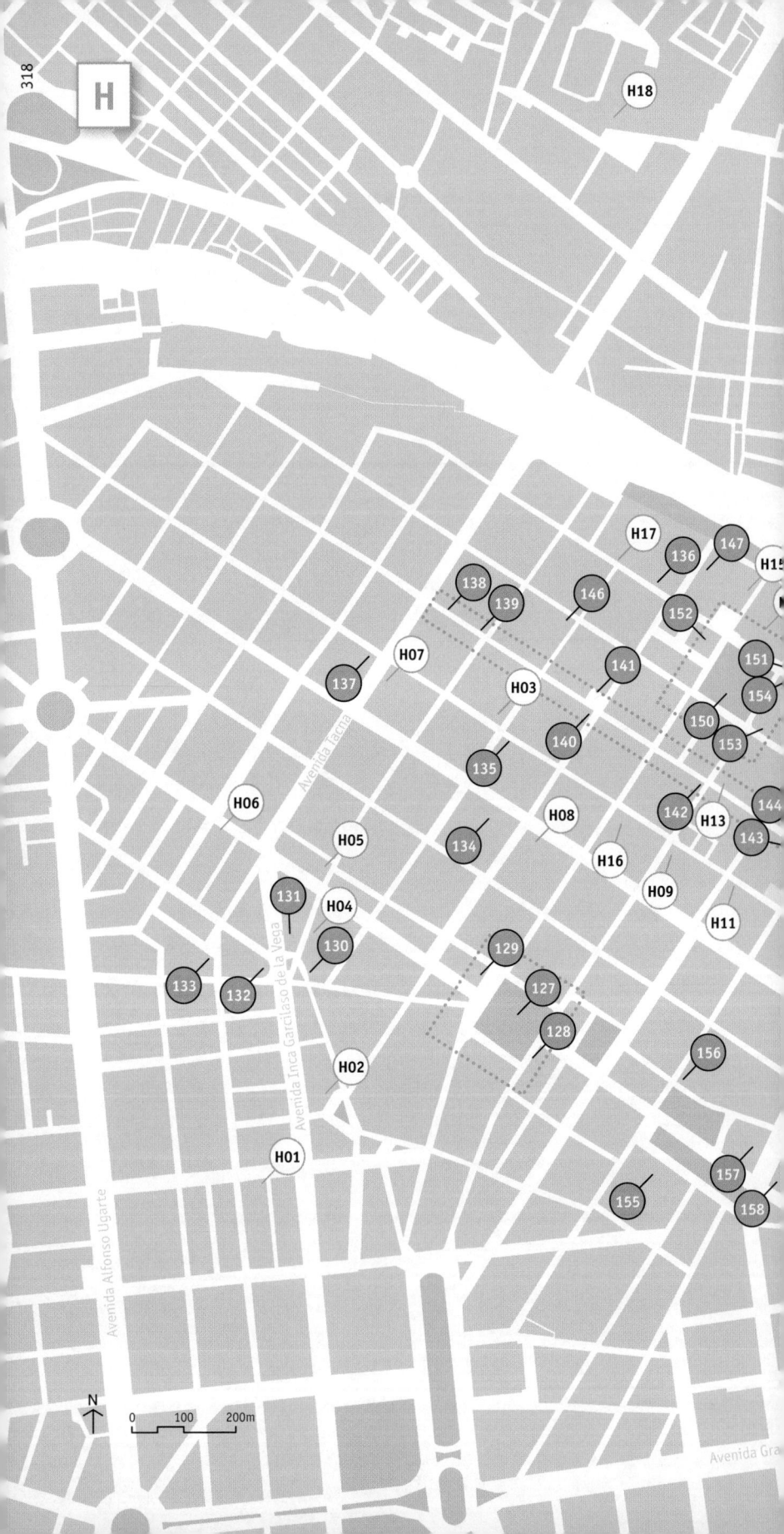

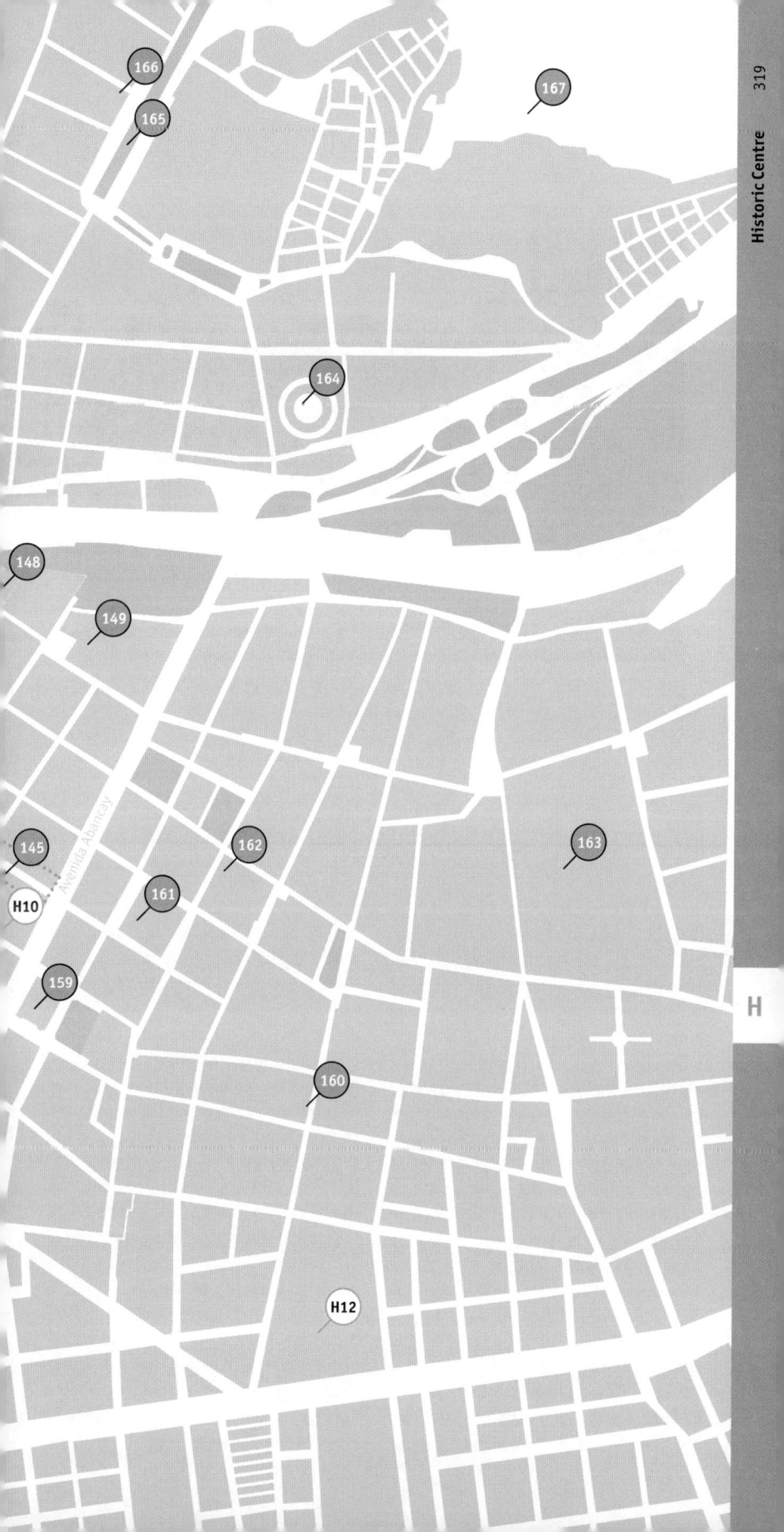

166

165

167

164

148

149

145

H10

Avenida Abancay

162

161

163

159

H

160

H12

Plaza de San Martín
Cercado de Lima
Manuel Piqueras Cotolí
1921

127 H

Plaza de San Martín

The demolition of the fortified walls around Lima in 1868 marked the beginning of a process of urban expansion that was halted by the War of the Pacific. The subsequent reconstruction helped to open up the centre towards a new fringe through modern squares and avenues inspired by European boulevards and Haussmann's renovation of Paris. One of the new arteries was Avenida Nicolás de Piérola, popularly known as La Colmena ('The Beehive'), which begins at the Plaza del 2 de Mayo, designed by Ricardo de Jaxa Malachowski, and includes in its trajectory some of the most important public spaces on the perimeter of the historic checkerboard plan, such as the Parque Universitario and Plaza de San Martín (127).

In the sixteenth century, the square had been occupied by the San Juan de Dios hospital complex with its ornate Baroque church. Part of this ensemble was demolished in 1851 to make way for the Lima-Callao railway station. Finally, in 1919, the entire block was torn down and to make way for the square.

The projects submitted by architects Ricardo de Jaxa Malachowski and Bruno Paprocki were rejected and the contract was finally awarded to Spanish sculptor Manuel Piqueras Cotolí. The Greek-cross plan designed for the square defined four quadrants with flowerbeds and fountains at the vertices and included steps along three of the arms to absorb the difference in height. A monument to General José de San Martín by Mariano Benlliure was placed in the centre of the square.

Although the buildings around the square were built in different phases over the course of three decades, they preserved the design features of the original project. The consistency of the height, the use of concrete with quartz as the single façade material and the designs in diverse but coherent architectural styles (academicist, eclectic and neocolonial) lend uniformity to the urban space. The first buildings on the north-west side were inaugurated in 1914 before the contract for the project had been awarded: the Teatro Colón by Claude Sahut and the Edificio Giacoletti by the Masperi brothers.

Gonzalo Cáceres

The inauguration of the square on 27 July 1921 was a major public event, coinciding with celebrations to mark the centenary of the country's independence. To provide an appropriate backdrop, an ephemeral structure, popularly known as the 'Cardboard Palace,' was erected on the still incomplete north-west side for the National Industry Exhibition. After it was dismantled, the Hotel Bolívar (129) was built in commemoration of the centenary of the Battle of Ayacucho. It originally had three floors plus a semi-basement level that served as the plinth, but in 1938 it gained an additional two floors with the same aesthetic as the initial design. An eclectic building, its main façade is symmetrical and divided into three sections with a cornice between the top two floors that is interrupted in the central panel. The elevation on Avenida Nicolás de Piérola is set back from the ground floor to generate a terrace over the plinth that accommodates a restaurant. The lobby is circular and has a stained glass dome through which natural light penetrates.

In 1929, this side of the square was completed with the construction of the Club Nacional by Ricardo de Jaxa Malachowski and Enrique Bianchi, providing a meeting point for city's ruling classes. It is a symmetrical building in the academicist style, with a double-height loggia on the façade formed by semi-circular arches on geminate columns.

Rafael Marquina's design for the Zela and Pumacahua colonnades maintains the initial aesthetic of Piqueras Cotolí's porticoed galleries. The project provided a single, symmetrical façade with Baroque features to hide the diverse irregular constructions on the north-east and south-west sides.

The south-east side of the square was the last to be executed, with works commencing in the 1930s. It is defined by the height of the Boza and Sudamericana (128) buildings (both designed by José Álvarez Calderón and Emilio Harth Terré). The latter is a neocolonial construction with a three-storey portal and a narrower upper section that culminates in a turret. The Cine Metro (Guillermo

Edificio Sudamericana
Jirón Carabaya 933, Cercado de Lima
José Álvarez Calderón, Emilio Harth-Terré
1938

128 H

Candy Torres

Payet), the Edificio Fénix (130) and the Edificio Cerro de Pasco complete this side of the square.

The Plaza de San Martín has been a cultural and political hub since the day it was inaugurated. Its proximity to the San Marcos and Federico Villarreal universities cultivated an intellectual and bohemian atmosphere centred on the local cafés and bookshops, immortalised by writers like Mario Vargas Llosa and Oswaldo Reynoso. Despite the progressive closure of these establishments, the immediate vicinity around the square preserved a counter-cultural momentum concentrated on Jirón Quilca, a pre-Hispanic street whose diagonal layout resisted the imposition of the Spanish grid plan. All major political demonstrations start and end at this square and every day people gather on the marble crescent-shaped seats to hold debates.

Hotel Bolívar
Jirón de la Unión 958, Cercado de Lima
Rafael Marquina
1924, 1938

129 H

Edificio La Fénix
Jirón Rufino Torrico 981,
Cercado de Lima
Enrique Seoane
1948

130 H

The architecture syllabus at the Escuela Nacional de Ingenieros was designed in 1912 by Ricardo de Jaxa Malachowski, who had trained at the École des Beaux-Arts in Paris. That classical approach gradually changed, especially after the 1946 reform when teachers like Paul Linder (trained at the Bauhaus) and Luis Miró Quesada joined the recently created Department of Architecture and defended the new rationalist ideas of the Modern Movement. Enrique Seoane maintained a neutral position in the debate between the two trends, although his projects transitioned from a predominantly neocolonial style to modernism. The building for La Fénix, an insurance company, was one of the architect's first works to evidence this change. A remarkable feature of this project is its skilful relationship with the environment, achieved through its curved and concave volumetry with respect to the old Plaza de la Salud, which is further complemented by the convex profile of the Edificio Ferrand (1947) located opposite. The ground floor accommodates a lobby with access from the rear elevation. This provides the main façade with a larger commercial area whose floor plan, counter-curved with respect to the remainder of the volume, creates a striking presence in the square. The façade is symmetrical and has a central seven-storey panel with continuous windows and a band of geometric motifs along the top, a device frequently used by this architect. Two lower lateral panels project slightly from the main panel and once had terraces and wooden pergolas on the top floor that are now enclosed with glass. The typical floor resolves the residential and office uses in a similar way, around a circular staircase illuminated by glass bricks and a long central corridor. The design of this building earned Seoane the prestigious Chavín Prize in 1950.

H

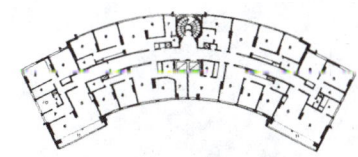

Typical floor plan

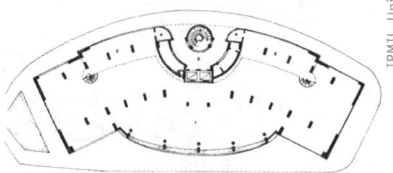

Ground floor

IPMIL. Universidad Nacional de Ingeniería

Edificio Wilson
Avenida Inca Garcilaso de la
Vega and Jirón Rufino Torrico,
Cercado de Lima
Enrique Seoane
1946

131 H

Seoane's quest for a modern architecture with a distinct Peruvian character first materialised in this project. Its construction coincided with that of the Tacna-Nazarenas building, with which it shares many compositional elements, although this building is more refined. Its location at the corner of two streets that form a sharp angle enhances its presence and allowed the configuration of a U-shaped floor plan with three façades. The volume is organised around three parts with different languages, separated by cornices. The double-height ground floor forms the plinth and accommodates the lobby and commercial areas. With a neocolonial aesthetic, it has a marble cladding and elaborate mouldings that incorporate pinnacles flush with the façade plane. The middle part, with four apartments per floor, is more austere and its flat surface, rendered and painted, is defined by the continuous windows typically found in modern architecture. The fifth floor, with the same façade distribution as the previous ones, is incorporated into the building's crest and characterised by a pre-Columbian-inspired cladding of geometric reliefs similar to the ones that Seoane subsequently used in his building for the Ministry of Education. The sixth floor, with two apartments and the same language, is set back to generate a perimeter terrace. The building culminates in a volume to house the installations, once again with identical treatment. Several details enrich the design, such as the semi-circular staircase with a delicate metal banister and natural lighting provided by its glass brick envelope, and the meticulous demarcation of the corners of the volume with a concave profile.

Edificio Ferrand
Avenida Inca Garcilaso de la
Vega 874, Cercado de Lima
Fernando Belaúnde Terry,
Alejandro Alva
1947

132 H

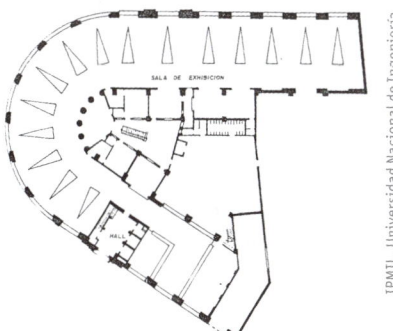

IPMIL. Universidad Nacional de Ingeniería

H

Despite his rationalist academic training, Fernando Belaúnde Terry's early works in Peru alternated between the neocolonial style and a pre-modern aesthetic. After he returned to Lima in 1936, single-family homes for the elite represented the bulk of his output. Following the success of his residential project for Neighbourhood Unit No. 3, from 1945 the architect's works evidence a definitive shift towards modernity. For the commission to design the Ferrand building, Belaúnde borrowed formal concepts from earlier projects to resolve a more complex programme on a larger scale. However, both the client and the municipal authorities were reluctant to accept such a modern proposal and commissioned architect Alva Manfredi to modify the façade and add neocolonial decorative details, which included a stone entrance portal and different types of mouldings. The building consists of a curvilinear volume on a corner plot that establishes a dialogue with Plaza de la Salud opposite. With eight storeys and a basement, the ground floor was conceived as a car showroom for the firm Ferrand Hermanos, with large shop windows and a mezzanine level. The first to the fifth floors all have the same plan with offices arranged radially, while the top two floors have stepped setbacks to generate large terraces.

Cine Tauro

Jirón Washington 8,
Cercado de Lima
Walter Weberhofer
1958

During the first half of the twentieth century, the increasing importance of cinema as a form of entertainment was translated into the construction of large movie theatres that became landmarks of the historic centre. By the 1960s, the central checkerboard district contained no less than 39 such premises, reflecting the boom in this typology and its expansion to new areas of the city. Some examples, such as the Roma (Theodor Cron, 1956) and Tacna (Alejandro Alva, 1949) cinemas, have survived to this day. This project by Walter Weberhofer stands out as one of the best pieces of modern architecture in Lima. The original design featured a 10-storey building with commercial areas, apartments and offices, but only the first four storeys and a cinema with a capacity for 1,280 people were executed. The site of the project on a corner plot adds great plasticity to the volume, accentuated by the dynamic appearance of elements such as the typography and a mosaic mural crest. The entrance hall has a circular staircase connecting it to the stalls and mezzanine level through a foyer that receives natural light from an oblique curtain wall and echoes the interiors of the Berliner Philharmonie by Hans Scharoun. The floor plan is dotted with a collection of staircases where structure and partitions do not quite fit together, unusual for a work that was 30 years ahead of the deconstructivist movement and whose material decadence has only served to heighten its expressiveness, recalling the drawings of Lebbeus Woods. In the 1980s, the historic centre entered a process of urban decay that impacted the cinema's commercial activity and led to its current state of neglect. Despite this, the building has not suffered any major alterations and has preserved the rich quality of its architecture while it awaits a new use.

Héctor Abarca

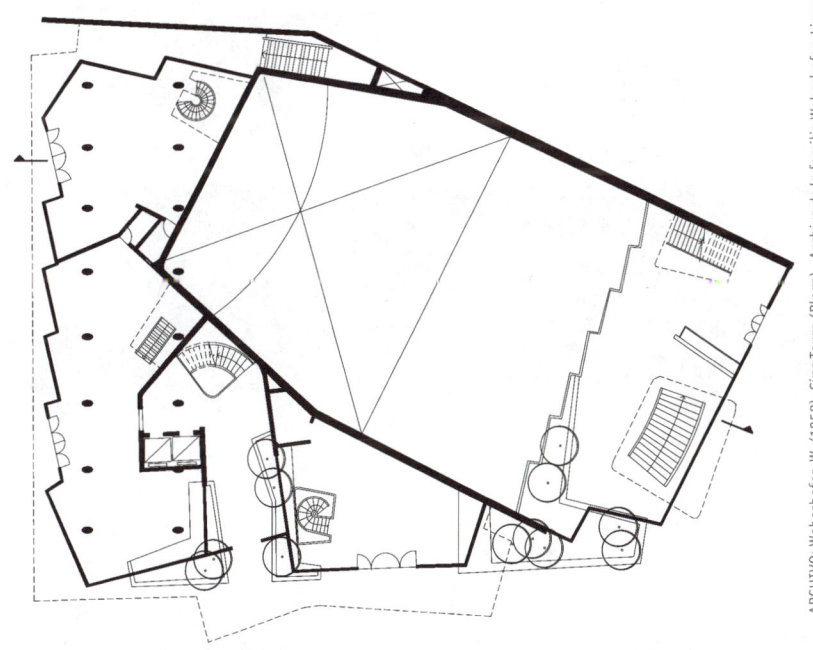

ARCHIVO: Weberhofer, W. (1958). Cine Tauro (Plans) . Archivo de la familia Weberhofer, Lima

H

Galerías Gallos-Mogollón

134 H

Avenida Emancipación 271,
Cercado de Lima
Raúl Morey
1958

With an architecture inspired by the Parisian covered passages of the nineteenth century, Lima's first shopping galleries reflected the ambitious aspirations of the city's aristocrats during the 1920s. Works like the Pasaje del Carmen (1924) and the Edificio Ronald (1929) were constructed around a central corridor with a glass roof, with entrances from two perpendicular streets and a varied programme of uses, from shops and restaurants to apartments and offices. In the mid-1950s, modern architecture reinterpreted this typology with new technological and building concepts. The Galerías Gallos-Mogollón stands out from other works of the time thanks to

a spatial sequence that transcends the academicist monotony and offers spaces with singular characteristics. Whether entering the building from the busy Avenida Emancipación or from the much quieter Jirón Moquegua, one is inevitably drawn to the circular plaza in the centre: a double-height space crowned by a concrete roof alleviated by holes of different sizes that evokes an abstract starry sky and in which the light and sound produce unexpected effects. The project was designed on plots with different developers, differentiating the sectors by colour, composition and finishes while retaining an overall consistency. The volumes on the upper floors, with up to 11 storeys, accommodate apartments and offices. Although many of the shops are closed today, the building remains in good condition. The place was immortalised in Melina León's internationally acclaimed film, *Canción sin nombre*, in 2019.

H

Edificio Atlas
Jirón Huancavelica 279,
Cercado de Lima
Walter Weberhofer,
José Álvarez Calderón
1955

135 H

Following the approval of the 1949 Pilot Plan, the infrastructure in the historic centre underwent a series of urban and architectural modifications associated with the arrival of modernity. The widening of the Avenida Abancay (1947) and Avenida Tacna (1959) led to the total or partial demolition of numerous historic buildings in the central checkerboard district, such as the church of Santa Rosa and the convents and monasteries of Santa Teresa, La Concepción, San Francisco and Nazarenas, making way for the construction of new buildings with up to nine storeys. In this context, a competition to design the headquarters of the Atlas insurance company in 1953 marked the beginning of the prolific production of Walter Weberhofer, who teamed up with José Álvarez Calderón to propose an 11-storey commercial building with two basement levels. Located next to the Segura Theatre and opposite the Plazuela del Teatro , the project deliberately shuns a formal relationship with its immediate historical environment. The volume occupies a corner plot and is composed of a two-storey commercial base and two tall office blocks connected by a central core. The tallest block is separated from the plinth by an open diaphanous floor on the third level. The north elevation has an aluminium curtain wall façade culminating in a rooftop garden with a free-form crest which, like the grid of sunshades on the west façade, is inspired by modern Brazilian architecture. The building won a gold medal from the municipal authorities in 1955 but is nowadays considerably deteriorated. In 2020, it was purchased by a real estate developer specialised in the refurbishment and rental of properties with historical or artistic value.

Convento de Santo Domingo 136 H

Jirón Camaná 1,
Cercado de Lima
Manuel de Amat, Juan de la Roca,
Juan García, Diego Maroto
16th–19th century

The ensemble of the basilica and monastery of Nuestra Señora del Rosario, more popularly known as the convent of Santo Domingo, is composed of five cloisters with rooms arranged around them. The arcade on the top floor of the main cloister, built around a garden with a fountain, represents one of the finest examples of woodwork in the world. It is formed by semi-circular arches with a balustrade and intermediate panels perforated by two ovals with ornaments carved from the same wood. The result is an extraordinary piece of craftsmanship, well worth a visit on its own. The ground-floor arcade is clad with *azulejos* from Seville. The most important spaces, such as the church, the chapter house and the porter's lodge with its splendid Mudejar coffered ceiling, are located around this cloister. The Baroque chapter house is where the Universidad Nacional Mayor de San Marcos was founded in the mid-sixteenth century. With checkerboard floor tiles and wooden furniture, it is adorned with classical scrolled ornaments on a mismatched scale that lend the space an over-elaborate appearance. The church has two entrances from Plazuela de Santo Domingo, one on either side of the octagonal Rococo tower, a slender 46-metre-high structure that stands out from the rest of the complex. The rectangular floor plan comprises a nave and two aisles, with a wooden rib vault over the former and a dome at the crossing. Located beside the church is the more austere Vera Cruz chapel built by Diego Morales and Diego de Guillén, with a proto-Baroque doorway. Together with the church, it forms a little public square outside. The entire complex is built with adobe walls, wooden columns and ceilings, and brick arches. It has been reconstructed on several occasions due to earthquake damage and today holds one of the finest old libraries in Lima. The convent is also the resting place of Saint Rose of Lima and Saint Martín de Porres, important symbols for the city.

H

Capilla de la Reconciliación

137 H

Jirón Huancavelica 515,
Cercado de Lima
Óscar Borasino,
José Antonio Vallarino
1990

The Lord of Miracles, also known as 'Christ of Miracles,' was an image painted on an adobe wall that escaped the 1655 earthquake unscathed. In 1715, it was adopted as the patron saint of Lima and a series of chapels and other facilities gradually grew up around it to protect the image, eventually forming the Nazarenas convent where the Carmelite nuns continue to guard it to this day. The Rococo shrine was inaugurated in 1771 and is nowadays open to the public. The procession held every October in honour of the image has become a form of collective catharsis that transcends faith. It is a popular celebration in which the purple colour of the nuns' habits infuses the participants'

clothes, the posters for the event and even the food and drinks served, forming an astonishing iconography and a spectacle that is well worth witnessing. The growth of Lima's population in the 1980s overtaxed the capacity of the complex, prompting the need to extend and enhance the facilities. A new chapel, almost parallel to the church but facing the opposite direction, was added. The chapel and church are connected at three strategic points, two at ground level and one at the height of the choir loft, leaving an open space between the two buildings. The roof is a barrel vault homothetic to the main one. Its scale softens the chapel's external presence and is the key to the success of the intervention. The transition between spaces was resolved by a series of large-format doors built with wooden stretcher frames whose square modular design was extended to the windows, including the stained-glass ones, as well as the grilles and railings.

Gonzalo Cáceres

Lord of Miracles procession

3DS PROYECTOS. Courtesy of José Antonio Vallarino

3DS PROYECTOS. Courtesy of José Antonio Vallarino

Borasino Arquitectos and José Antonio Vallarino

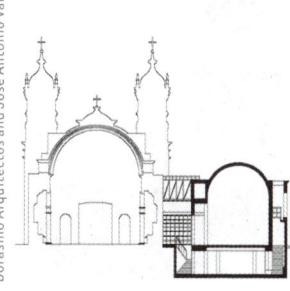

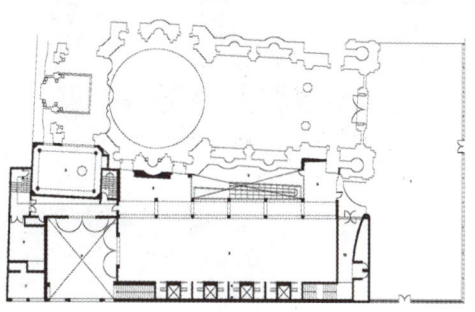

H

Lima's expansion began with the demolition of the old city walls in 1870. In the twentieth century, wide ring roads were laid where once the walls had stood and some of the narrow colonial streets were transformed into avenues such as the Avenidas Nicolás de Piérola, Tacna and Abancay, fragmenting the uniform layout of Pizarro's checkerboard plan and creating a 'centre within the centre.' Gradually, cars took over the city. In the 1980s, with the area in decay, mayor and architect Eduardo Orrego pedestrianised the section of Jirón de la Unión between Plaza de San Martín and Plaza Mayor. This emblematic street had been the recreational, social and commercial epicentre of Lima. It had even given rise to a new verb, *jironear*, meaning to stroll leisurely along the street. Although the high-end boutiques have never returned, the Jirón has preserved its status as one of the vital cores of the historic centre and is still home to major works such as the Mercedarian Convent, the Courret House and the Casa Aliaga, a large colonial mansion built on pre-Columbian remains and owned by the same family since the city was founded.

In 2014, the pedestrianisation of the Jirones Ica and Ucayali between the Avenidas Tacna and Abancay completed some sort of Cardo and Decumanus configuration that today channels most of the foot traffic in the area and which is currently being expanded through the pedestrianisation of other streets.

The Ica-Ucayali axis runs from the Monserrate neighbourhood to Calle Capón, in the heart of the Barrio Chino. The pedestrianised area is dotted with outstanding examples of different typologies and styles. However, with a more residential character than Jirón de la Unión, it largely preserves the scale and typical urban profile of the old Lima streets, with a predominance of two-storey constructions and a variety of box balconies. Several fine examples of viceregal homes can be found here. With Spanish (and therefore Moorish) roots but a distinct identity, this typology generally takes the form of buildings with an adobe ground floor and the more earthquake-resistant *quincha* for the top floor, articulated around a main courtyard and a service courtyard, both placed

Casa de la Riva
Jirón Ica 426, Cercado de Lima
Architect unknown
18th century

138 H

Candy Torres

Casa Fernandini
Jirón Ica 441. Cercado de Lima
Claude Sahut
1913

Candy Torres

on the same axis as the *zaguán* (a kind of vestibule between the entrance and the courtyard, usually separated from the latter by a barred gate) and connected by a lateral corridor with the living room and dining room located between them. The façades are painted in characteristic colours and feature a portal whose degree of complexity reflects the importance of the home, although the most outstanding

Iglesia y convento de San Agustín
Jirón Ica 2, Cercado de Lima
Architect unknown
16th–17th century

Candy Torres

Candy Torres

element is the box balcony, with its own stylistic evolution through the centuries. One of the most outstanding mansions is the Casa de la Riva (138), which dates back to the eighteenth century and whose wide façade is defined by a two-storey portal and enclosed balconies with intricate latticework. Striking a contrast with this house is the one next door, occupying a corner plot: the Casa Fernandini (139). Built in the twentieth century and featuring art nouveau decoration, it is articulated around a central space with a stained-glass roof and an arched balcony tracing the curve of the corner. Other interesting nearby constructions are the Quinta La Riva multi-family building, the Cine Central (Guillermo Payet, 1942) with its art deco façade, the neoclassical Teatro Municipal (Alfredo Viale, 1920), and the austere eighteenth-century building that houses the Asociación de Artistas Aficionados.

At the intersection with Jirón Camaná, the Plazuela de San Agustín widens. The square takes its name from the monastery complex (140) located just opposite, which has been ill-treated over the years. An outstanding feature of the church, which lost its tower in 1895 and currently presents an advanced state of neglect, is the Churrigueresque portal. In the monastery, two different sizes of arches alternate on the top floor around the main cloister; another cloister has been converted into a shopping gallery.

A sculpture by Jorge Oteiza adorns the centre of the square, while two modern constructions frame the corner. One is the Compañía de Seguros Peruano-Suiza (141), the ground floor of which is partly open to connect the square to a second public space generated by the recessed elevation on Jirón Camaná. The other is the Edificio Chavín (1965) by Enrique Seoane, who is also the architect of the Edificio Peicher (1952) located opposite. Half a block away stands the Casa Riva Agüero, with glazed box balconies.

At the intersection with Jirón de la Unión is a cluster of commercial buildings. The most notable are two twentieth-century ones with metal structures: the Casa Welsch, once a jewellery and luxury goods

Banco Mercantil
Jirón Carabaya 411, Cercado de Lima
Alfredo Montagne
1985

Casa Goyeneche
Jirón Ucayali 358, Cercado de Lima
Architect unknown
18th century

Candy Torres

Palacio de Torre Tagle
Jirón Ucayali 363,
Cercado de Lima
Architect unknown
1740

144 H

Candy Torres

Candy Torres

boutique and nowadays a Starbucks coffeeshop, and the Mansión Eiffel. In 1985, this mansion was skilfully refurbished to accommodate the headquarters of the Banco Mercantil (142), gaining a glazed void to complete the corner while respecting the proportions and giving continuity to the composition of the existing building. Diagonally across from this stands the Hotel Mauri (Héctor Velarde, 1954), somewhat modified today but whose famous bar has preserved the atmosphere of bygone days. The Casa Berckemeyer, dating back to the nineteenth century, and the former Banco Central de Reserva del Perú (A. C. Bossom, 1928) are located on the same block.

Several mansions have also survived on the other side of Jirón Lampa. The Casa Goyeneche (143), still in excellent condition, has a handsome main courtyard abutted to the party wall with an open double-flight staircase and a wooden gallery on the top floor. Although the building is now owned by a bank, it is partially visible from the *zaguán*, through

the lattice gate that separates it from the courtyard. Other examples are the Casa Aspíllaga, rebuilt in the late nineteenth century and combining the traditional organisation of two courtyards with a classicist-style façade, and the Casa Paz Soldán, nowadays Restaurante L'Eau Vive, with a unique open balcony.

Most outstanding of all is the sumptuous Palacio de Torre Tagle (144), the apogee of colonial residential architecture. The floor plan adopts the typical scheme of viceregal mansions: two courtyards on the longitudinal axis with the living room and dining room between them. The *zaguán* comprises two consecutive spaces, with segmental arches on carved stone supports. In the first courtyard, the top gallery combines two different sizes of mixtilinear arches decorated with mouldings. Other notable features are the tile claddings, the portal that frames the staircase and the elements made of carved wood. The magnificent two-storey façade has grilles at the ground-floor windows, balconies at the top-floor ones and a balustrade above the cornice. Designed in the Mudejar style, the balconies are probably the finest in the city.

The void formed by Plazuela de San Pedro and the atrium of the church of the same name provide an excellent vantage point from which to appreciate this religious building (145), one of the largest in Lima. It dates from the seventeenth century and was inspired by the Baroque Chiesa del Gesù in Rome. The monumental neoclassical façade has two large towers, rebuilt in the twentieth century. The interior combines Doric pilasters and semi-circular arches with Baroque gilt decoration and oil paintings. The church forms part of the Colegio Máximo San Pablo, which has suffered several mutilations over the years. One of the courtyards was incorporated into the Biblioteca Nacional and one of the arcades has been integrated into the building that now houses the Banco Central de Reserva del Perú. A two-storey cloister has been preserved, as well as a chapel dedicated to Nuestra Señora de la O.

Candy Torres

The former Banco Central de Reserva del Perú (1928)

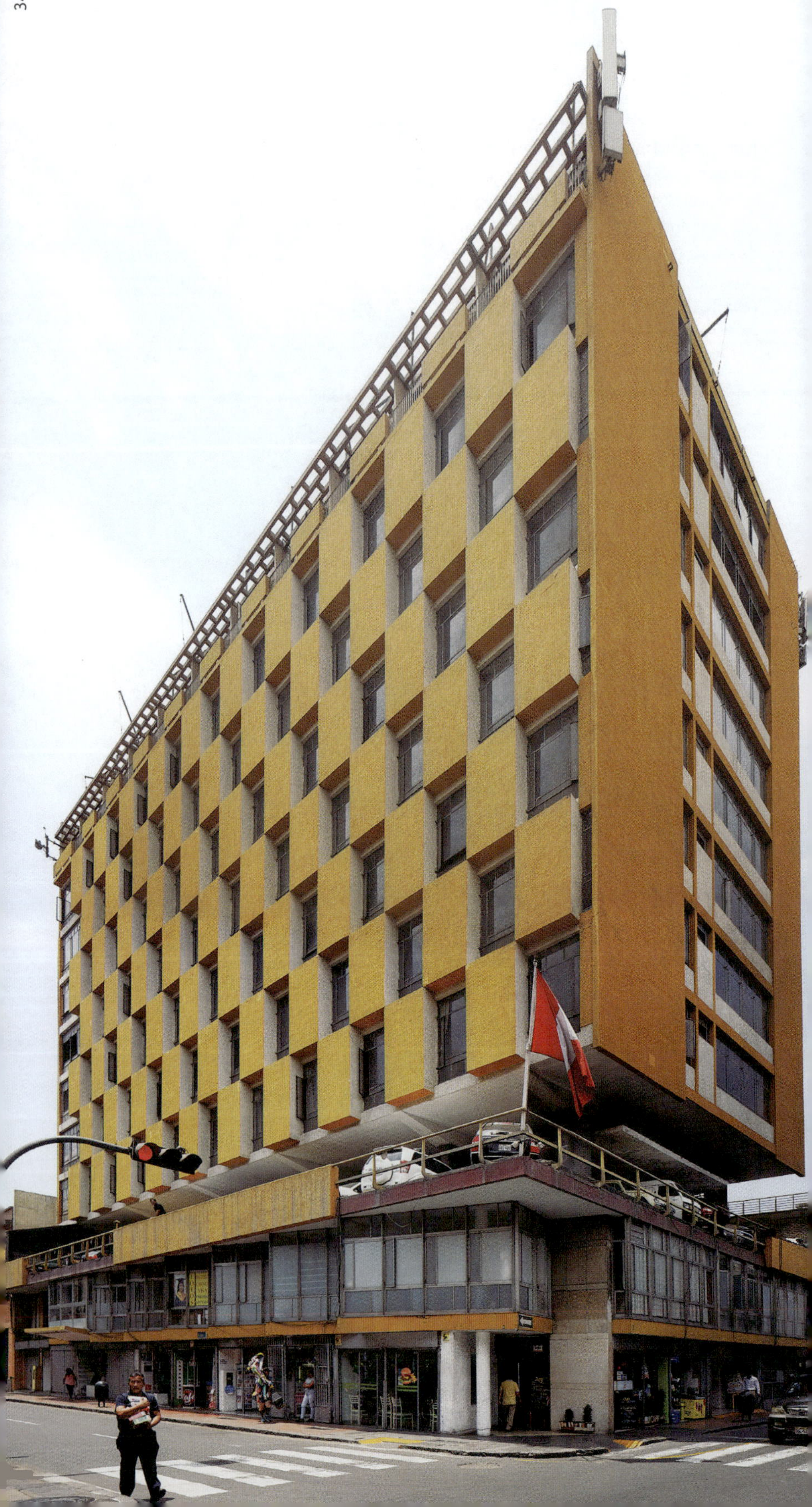

Hotel Savoy ← ↓
Jirón Cailloma 224,
Cercado de Lima
Mario Bianco
1957

146 H

During his years spent in Lima, the work of architect and engineer Mario Bianco, who had trained at the Politecnico di Torino, was crucial for the consolidation of modern architecture and urban planning in Peru. As well as contributing to the formulation of the Lima Pilot Plan of 1949, he taught in the Department of Architecture at the Escuela Nacional de Ingenieros. Bianco also deployed his skills as a designer and structural engineer in the construction of this 10-storey building. His profound interest in adapting to the immediate context of the historic centre is clearly evidenced in the volumetry: a two-storey commercial plinth preserves the line of façade and the proportions of typical Lima balconies are reinterpreted with a modern language. Above the diaphanous car park on the third level, the L-shaped block containing the hotel rooms stands apart from the volume of the base and presents a meticulously executed façade composition on the two main elevations: facing outwards, a checkerboard pattern of planes and voids, and facing the interior courtyard, an open grid of concrete window boxes supported by the parapets of the external corridors. In the 1960s, the hotel gained a reputation for its luxurious facilities and became the favourite place to stay for visiting bullfighters and international sports delegations. Following the decay of the historic centre in the 1970s, the building was abandoned and taken over by printing shops while it awaits rescue.

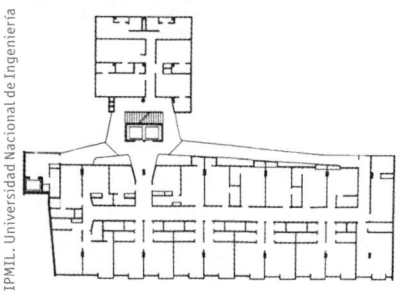

IPMIL. Universidad Nacional de Ingeniería

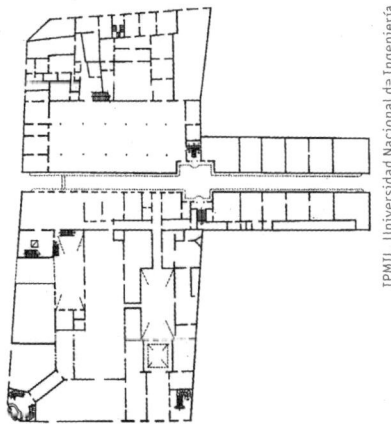

IPMIL. Universidad Nacional de Ingeniería

Pasaje del Carmen
Jirón Camaná 157,
Cercado de Lima
Raúl María Pereira
1924

147 H

The development of communication technologies at the beginning of the twentieth century prompted the extension of the old general post office completed in 1897, nowadays home of a culinary centre called La Casa de la Gastronomía Peruana. The first building, organised around three concatenated spaces and with a somewhat over-elaborate neo-Renaissance façade, was extended in the early 1920s with a new construction on the adjacent corner plot, also in a classicist style, although more austere and with access from the chamfer. When a second extension was required to meet the existing needs, a third volume with two storeys and a basement was built, increasing the administrative and storage area. This volume is articulated around a commercial gallery like the ones that emerged in Europe in the nineteenth century. It is the most characteristic part of the complex, crossing the block from one side to the other. Now known as the Pasaje Piura, it is another classicist construction, with elements like Ionic and Composite columns, semi-circular arches around openings, pilasters, friezes, garlands and mouldings. Continuous balconies with balustrades run the entire length of the passage. The roof is a metal vault-like structure whose original stained-glass window was removed after sustaining earthquake damage.

Christopher Schreier

The gallery of Pasaje del Carmen

The entrances are composed of double-height arches with a broken pediment. At ground-floor level, they were originally flanked by telamons that were subsequently replaced by the same columns as those on the top section; the mayor of Lima apparently considered them unseemly because of their nudity. Souvenir kiosks have occupied the passage for years, creating a paradoxical image in a typology usually intended for more sophisticated retail uses.

Estación de Desamparados 148 H

Jirón Ancash 207,
Cercado de Lima
Rafael Marquina, David Mutal
1912, 2007

Elsa Ramírez. Courtesy of David Mutal

In the mid-nineteenth century, during a short-lived period of economic prosperity, the Peruvian government embarked on the construction of new communication infrastructures, turning railways into the standard bearer of progress and modernity. The Polish engineer Ernesto Malinowksi was commissioned to build them and designed one of the most important feats of engineering of the day: the Trans-Andean Central Railway (1870). The Central Railway Station in Lima, built next to the Palacio de Gobierno and the now-lost Desamparados church, was inaugurated the same year but destroyed by a terrible fire in 1908. The project for the new building was the first public work by architect Rafael Marquina, who opted for an eclectic style influenced by his training at Cornell University in New York. The façade, which closes the perspective at the end of Jirón Carabaya, is a meticulously executed two-storey classicist composition crowned in the centre by a clock. The fluid spatial sequence of the interior skilfully spans the gap between the height of the entrance and the platforms below. The main concourse greets visitors with a three-storey colonnade, including an artistic stained-glass ceiling providing overhead lighting. On the ground floor, another stained-glass ceiling illuminates the waiting room. The spatial flow culminates at the boarding area, which occupies a large terrace overlooking the River Rímac. Declared a national monument in 1972, the building reopened as the Casa de la Literatura in 2009 after an austere refurbishment by architect David Mutal that won the heritage renovation prize at the 2010 Peruvian Architecture Biennial.

Juan Pablo El Sous

H

Convento de San Francisco
Jirón Ancash
Cercado de Lima
Constantino de Vasconcellos,
Manuel de Escobar
16th–18th century

149 H

When Lima was founded in 1535, a Renaissance-style grid pattern was planned around the Plaza Mayor. In contrast to this rigid distribution, the churches, convents and monasteries built by the main religious orders that arrived in Peru occupied larger plots with space to grow crops, generating open spaces on the corner of urban blocks and public squares in front of the religious buildings. The most outstanding example is this Franciscan complex, a masterpiece of Lima's Baroque style. It comprises the church of San Francisco, the monastery of El Nombre de Jesús and the church of La Soledad, all connected by a communal atrium, the Plazuela de San Francisco. The monastery was the first building in Peru to gain UNESCO world heritage status in 1988. It has always been the largest religious complex in the city and is nowadays organised around five courtyards. The main one began in 1574 as a single-storey cloister with semi-circular arches, but in the seventeenth century it was clad with *azulejos* from Seville and gained a second storey with alternating arches and oculi. The top gallery of the cloister of San Francisco Solano, built in 1732 by master builder Francisco de Sierra and reconstructed in 1940, has trefoil arches on square pillars. The exquisite wooden staircase from 1625 was rebuilt after the 1940 earthquake and has a Mudejar hemispherical dome with a magnificent geometric pattern. The library has wooden claddings and furniture and upper galleries on both sides accessed by spiral staircases. The two-storey doorway, with three openings on each level, harmonises with the adjacent churches. The original church of San Francisco was built in the sixteenth century, but the building we see today dates from the seventeenth century and was designed by Portuguese architect Constantino de Vasconcellos, who was replaced after his death by Manuel de Escobar. The outstanding features of the façade are the stone-carved, three-storey main portal with filigree details, the two-storey lateral portal with pilasters rising to the central scallop shell and the two towers, decorated with rustication and with wooden balustrades separating the three sections. The nave-and-two aisle floor plan has a central hemispherical dome and *quincha* barrel vaults decorated with intricate sgraffito geometrical motifs. One of the most singular spaces is the sacristy, which has identical vault decoration, a magnificent entrance portal and an exquisite plinth composed of carved-wood chests and niches. At the basement level, this is the only viceregal church in Lima that has preserved all the sepulchral vaults or catacombs, interconnected and open to the public. The original church of Nuestra Señora de la Soledad invaded the public square. It was therefore demolished in 1669 and rebuilt in alignment with the monastery. It has a vaulted crypt under the presbytery. Excavations carried out in the square in 2020 uncovered part of the original church as well as the original pebble-stone paving of the plaza. The conversion of Jirón Abancay into an avenue, begun in 1949, caused the progressive loss of half of the original ensemble. The Buenaventura cloister was demolished, various plots belonging to the order were expropriated and sold, and other remains were segregated. Even so, the complex is still one of the most important monuments in the historic centre.

Candy Torres

Plaza Mayor

Lima was founded atop a small pre-Columbian settlement as the new Spanish capital on the continent. Its pragmatic grid scheme, known as the *damero de Pizarro* (Pizarro's checkerboard), as well as its optimal orientation, ensuring shaded pavements and protection from the wind, reflect the urban planning experience acquired from the foundation of other Latin American cities during the colonial period. The first planned block on Lima's grid was the void that would become the Plaza Mayor (150), or main square, with commercial, religious and social functions. It remained unchanged well into the nineteenth century, when it was paved and lost its market. A series of earthquakes, including the devastating ones of 1586 and 1746, and various aggressive fires gave rise to permanent changes in the appearance of its elevations. All of these events were witnessed from one of the vertices by the Casa del Oidor (151), a sixteenth-century building defined by the corner box balcony that extends across both façades, added in the eighteenth century.

Francisco Pizarro assigned the northeast block of the square to himself when he founded the city, and after he died his house became the viceroy's palace. Extended and altered on

Evelyn Merino Reyna

Aerial view of the Plaza Mayor

several occasions, the colonial building accommodated commercial areas on the ground floor and an open gallery on the top. These all disappeared during the republican period with Cristóbal Rosas' neoclassical reconstruction in 1872. The present-day Palacio de Gobierno, completed in 1938, was begun by French architect Claude Sahut and continued upon his death by Polish-born Ricardo de Jaxa Malachowski, who introduced major changes like the courtyard of honour that recessed most of the façade. An eclectic building, its main elevation clearly demonstrates its Baroque and classicist influences.

The south-east elevation is dominated by the Catedral de Lima (153), begun in 1596 to replace the former church situated parallel to the square. Francisco Becerra's Renaissance design is organised around a basilica plan with a nave and two aisles, a row of chapels along each side and nine bays, plus two towers at the front. The original rib vaults were destroyed in 1687 and rebuilt in wood. The building has seven portals that illustrate the different phases of Lima's Baroque style. A severe earthquake in 1746 led to major reconstruction works that nevertheless preserved the original floor plan. Interior alterations, such as the relocation of the choir, were carried out in

Plaza Mayor
Cercado de Lima
Francisco Pizarro, Nicolás de Ribera, Diego de Agüero
1535

Casa del Oidor
Jirón Carabaya 1, Cercado de Lima
Architect unknown
16th–19th century

151 H

Gonzalo Cáceres

150 H

Gonzalo Cáceres

Palacio Municipal
Jirón de la Unión 3, Cercado de Lima
Emilio Harth-Terré, José Álvarez Calderón
1944

152 H

H

1895. This period also saw the demolition of part of the adjacent Iglesia del Sagrario (Church of the Tabernacle) built in 1665, which lost its original façade to align it with the cathedral. After the 1940 earthquake, Emilio Harth-Terré restored both buildings and reconstructed the church's lost façade.

The Palacio Arzobispal (154), or archbishop's palace, completes the south-east elevation. Completed in 1924, it replaced the sixteenth-century building that had been severely damaged in 1746. Jaxa Malachowski won the competition with an eclectic design whose façade consisted of neo-colonial alongside Baroque elements and Plateresque ornamentation.

In the sixteenth century, the north-west and south-west elevations had colonnades, known as the Scribes' and Buttonmakers' Colonnades. The passages that fragment them are the result of incomplete plans in the twentieth century to lay wide avenues. Initially located on the site of the present-day Palacio Arzobispal, the Palacio Municipal (152), or city hall, was relocated in the sixteenth century to the plot on which it stands today, although after a devastating fire in 1923 the municipal authorities moved temporarily to the Palacio de la Exposición. The design we see today is the work of Harth-Terré and José Álvarez Calderón, with input from Jaxa Malachowski on the interior. Completed in

Catedral de Lima

Jirón Carabaya 2, Cercado de Lima
Francisco Becerra, Juan Martínez de Arona, Diego Maroto, Juan Rehr, Santiago Rosales, Ignacio Martorell
16th–19th century

153 H

Palacio Arzobispal
Jirón Carabaya 2. Cercado de Lima
Ricardo de Jaxa Malachowski
1924

Gonzalo Cáceres

1944, the four-storey building is executed with modern materials and a neo-colonial style. The façade displays large balconies, while the interior is defined by a double-height entrance hall with an upper gallery, imperial staircase and stained-glass ceiling. The same design was repeated in the other sector of the Scribes' Colonnade, where Maximiliano Peña Prado built the Club de la Unión, and in the Button-makers' Colonnade, where Humberto Guerra added balconies to create a uniform elevation. This meant that the original colonnades were demolished. Therefore, the present-day appearance of the first space designed when Lima was founded, and collective image of the historic city, is largely a construction of the twentieth century, designed by Harth-Terré, Álvarez Calderón and Jaxa Malachowski, with the exception of the cathedral.

Gonzalo Cáceres

Noviciado Jesuita San Antonio Abad (UNMSM) `155` `H`

Avenida Nicolás de Piérola 1222, Cercado de Lima

Architect unknown

18th century

In 1746, an earthquake turned the Jesuit novitiate founded in 1605 into a pile of ruins. The reconstruction incorporated the original layout but extended it to include six cloisters with access from the church atrium. After the Jesuits' expulsion from Peru in 1767, the building became the Royal San Carlos Residence, renamed the San Carlos Student Residence after the country gained independence. Since 1866, it has belonged to the Universidad Nacional Mayor de San Marcos and today is known as the Casona San Marcos. It has undergone several alterations over the years, most of them since 1920 due to a huge increase in the student population. This led to the addition of precarious volumes and the occupation of several courtyards. Left in ruins since the 1966 earthquake, it was restored between 1990 and 2012 and converted into a cultural centre. With the urban development of the area in 1859, the property was fragmented and streets were laid around the building. Since then, the entrance has been located on the north façade. The first cloister (now 'Law Courtyard'), is one of the most handsome in the building and the only one where the top floor gallery dates from the Jesuit days. The 'Buttress Cloister' (now 'Science Courtyard') and the 'Novitiate Cloister' (now 'Letters Courtyard'), with upper galleries from the nineteenth century and 1910, respectively, are also interesting. The visual communication between the cloisters generates rich perspectives in the building's flow. The old chapel with its multifoil vault and the General Hall are two of the finest interior spaces. The restoration works largely recovered the building's original appearance. To meet new needs, a multipurpose hall has been built in a courtyard where there was insufficient evidence to retrieve the original design. The old orchard has been converted into a café and one of the courtyards has gained a somewhat debatable upper level as visual protection from the new buildings around. All three alterations are reversible.

H

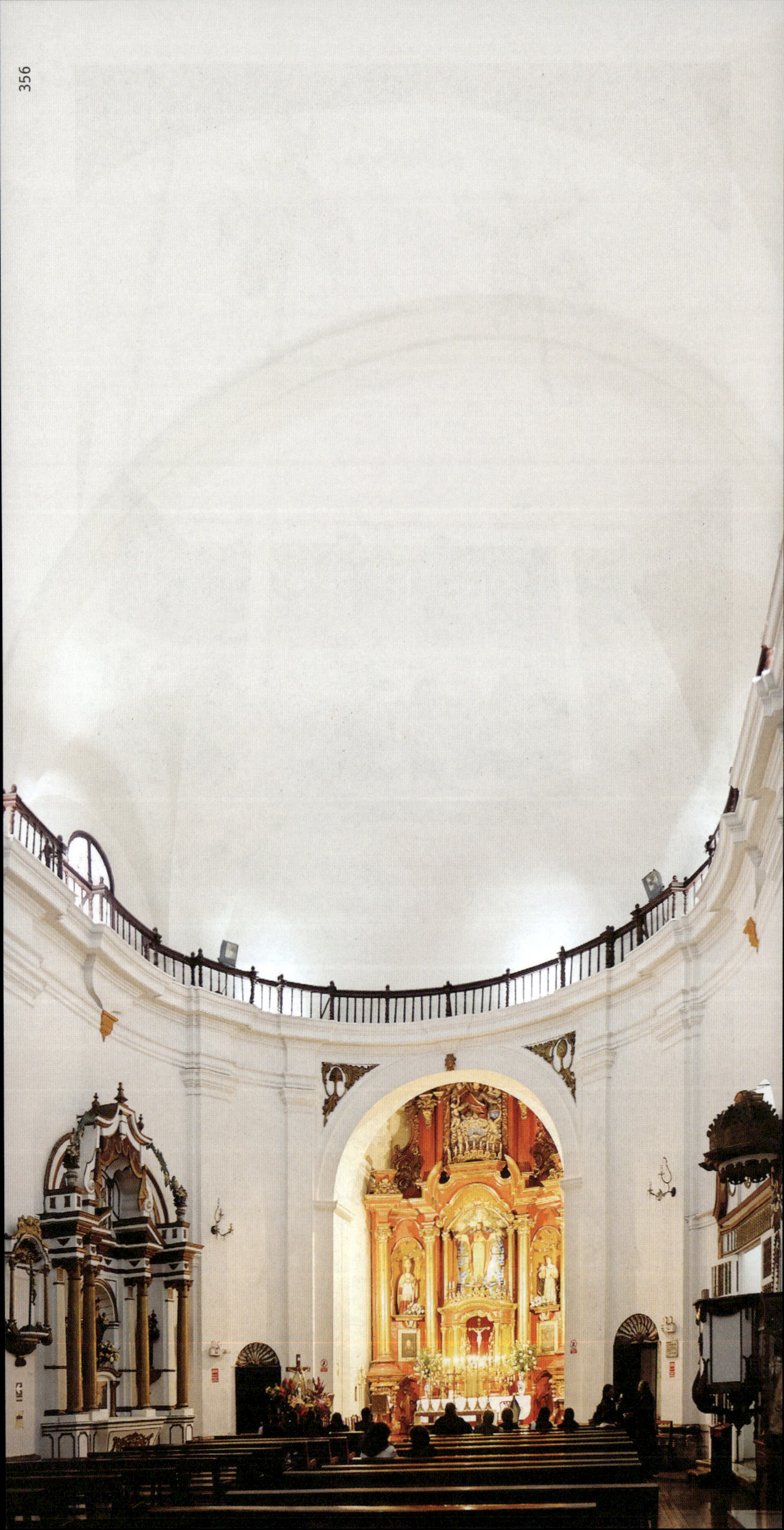

Iglesia del Sagrado Corazón de Jesús o de Huérfanos

156 H

Jirón Azángaro 776,
Cercado de Lima
Cristóbal de Vargas
1766

A few years before the 1746 earthquake destroyed the old orphanage church, work had commenced on the construction of a new adjacent church. It was officially dedicated to the 'Sacred Heart of Jesus' but came to be known by the name of the lost construction. Although there are precedents in the Spanish Baroque, the oval floor plan of this church is unique in Lima. The silhouette that envelops the single nave is emphasised by the wide entablature and continuous balustrade that run along the top of the perimeter wall. A great arch separates the nave from the main chapel. The nave walls also accommodate four niche chapels, the most prominent of which, located opposite the side entrance, has a splayed semi-circular arch. The chapel next to the altar originally had a similar design but was altered after the 1940 earthquake.

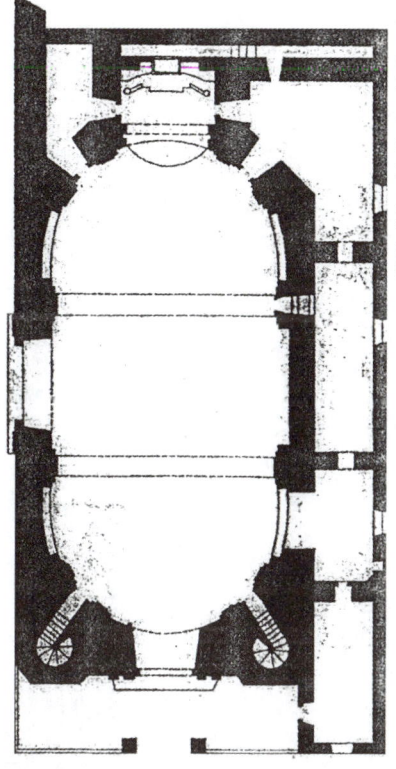

IPMIL. Universidad Nacional de Ingeniería

The roof was also modified at this time and today has only two transverse arches resting on two central pairs of pilasters. It originally had two more arches on the following pairs of pilasters, towards the altar and the front entrance, the disappearance of which necessitated larger half-domes at the ends. The baptistery chapel, built at a later date, is what makes this church the most outstanding Rococo religious building in Lima. Its defining elements are the elliptical dome and the complex caryatids with four heads on which the supporting arches rest, the profuse ornamentation of the pendentives and the alabaster window. Two basket-handle arches support the choir, one of the most characteristic features of the church with a sinuous layout that includes two small balconies at the ends. Outside, the church is defined by a two-storey main doorway and a single-storey lateral entrance that was built in the neoclassical style. The towers have an octagonal floor plan and are decorated with the same type of balustrades that are repeated around the edge of the roof.

Avenida Abancay during the COVID-19 lockdown in 2020. In the foreground: the Ministerio de Eduación and El Hueco shopping gallery

H

CENTRO COMERCIAL EL HUECO

Ministerio de Educación

157 H

Avenida Abancay 8,
Cercado de Lima
Enrique Seoane
1956

In the 1950s, the demand for raw materials from Europe and the United States boosted the growth of the Peruvian economy. General Manuel Odría's regime carried out several major works, of which this was one of the most emblematic. It took several draft projects, some of them more modern than the definitive one, to obtain the president's approval. The building finally constructed has a powerful presence and was the tallest in Peru at the time. It currently houses Lima's Superior Court of Justice. A symmetrical composition, the main volume is a curved 21-storey volume with the concave side facing the intersection of the adjacent avenues, leaving the corner free. Two 12-storey lateral volumes adjoin this central volume and all three volumes rest on a two-storey plinth, beneath which are two basements for parking. On the glazed façades, the prominence of the frames accentuates the verticality. The double-height entrance hall with a mezzanine level reflects great skill in establishing fluid relationships between the spaces and has numerous decorative elements and details, such as copper-clad columns with their quasi-star section, the impeccable design of the staircases and banisters, the ceramic floor tiles with geometric motifs and vast murals. The pre-Columbian inspiration is repeated outside in the ceramic cladding of the blind plinth walls. With its steel structure and continuous windows on one hand and symmetry on the other, the work straddles modernism and classicism. The ornamentation and vernacular references, hallmarks of Seoane's work, were very far removed from the modern canon advocated by Agrupación Espacio at the time. Today, the building is appreciated for its quest for modernity with Peruvian roots.

Galería comercial El Hueco
Avenida Abancay 8,
Cercado de Lima
*Cooperativa de Servicios
Especiales Mercado Central*
1984

158 H

The concave configuration of Enrique Seoane's design for the Ministerio de Educación was not fortuitous. It responded to President Odría's desire to create a curved plaza at the intersection of the Avenida Abancay and Avenida Nicolás de Piérola that would serve as a monumental gateway to the city centre. The architect designed two symmetrical buildings, one on either side of Avenida Abancay. The excavation and part of the basement of the twin building were carried out during the construction of the ministry, but the works were eventually halted. In the mid-1960s, Seoane submitted another draft project for this same plot, this time consisting of a new bus station with commercial areas and office spaces, but that design, based on circular geometry, also failed to come into fruition. It was not until the 1980s that the plot found the use that it has maintained to this day. At the time, the historic centre was immersed in a progressive decline and the area had been inundated by street vendors. A regeneration strategy contemplated the eviction of these vendors but they formed a cooperative of some three thousand members to negotiate with the government, finally managing to acquire the plot for themselves. The shopping gallery they built on the site is known as El Hueco ('The Gap'), a reference to the trench left when the works were halted in the 1950s and which they occupied. The difference in height is resolved by a series of staircases and a ramp that was likely the access to the car park. Precarious corrugated iron roofs protect the miscellaneous commercial establishments in a typological configuration found frequently in the city, best exemplified by the Polvos Azules shopping centre. The final use of the plot that was originally intended as the site of one of Lima's most monumental buildings highlights the difficulty of realising urban design initiatives in a city that has largely been developed without any formal planning.

H

Instituto Aerofotográfico Nacional

Ministerio de Educación under construction and twin building excavation

Ministerio de Hacienda ↓

Avenida Abancay 5,
Cercado de Lima
Guillermo Payet
1953

159 H

In the late 1940s, a series of avenues were built around the historic centre to improve the traffic in this part of the city. To make way for the new roads, numerous buildings from the viceregal period had to be demolished, including several outstanding constructions such as the convent of Santa Teresa and part of the monastery of San Francisco. One of the avenues was created by extending Jirón Abancay, on which General Manuel Odría's administration erected some of its most important buildings, such as the Ministerio de Hacienda, nowadays the Ministerio Público, or Public Prosecutor's Office. In keeping with its important role for the regime, this is an emphatic, monumental building with distinct academicist features. Designed as a regular, symmetrical volume, it has 12 floors. The first four levels occupy the entire block and the typical floor plan responds to a C-shaped scheme, reducing its scale on the rear elevation overlooking Barrios Altos. The imposing main façade is symmetrical and austere with a marble cladding. A wide flight of steps leads up to the entrance, which adopts the form of a large double-height glazed void nearly 40 metres long, framed by flat eaves and jambs and flanked by six bronze reliefs with a socialist aesthetic. The continuous windows and an approximation to a curtain wall contribute a certain degree of modernity to the overall appearance. Inside, the first three floors are articulated around the public area, onto which other administrative areas open. This high-ceilinged space has abundant light thanks to its glass vaulted roof.

Templo Kuan Kung →

Jirón Huanta 962,
Cercado de Lima
Sociedad Tung Sing
1891

160 H

In 1849, with the abolition of slavery in Peru on the horizon, Chinese labour began to arrive in the country to work at the haciendas, in the extraction of guano and on the construction of the railway. As they were gradually released from their abusive contracts, the Chinese moved to the cities. In Lima, they settled in the area where the central market currently stands, which became an important commercial hub. Many intellectuals were attracted to the Barrio Chino, or Chinatown, for the local cuisine and to engage in political debates during the days of the revolution, but in the 1930s

Margaux Eyssette

the area entered a decline. In 1999, Calle Capón was renovated, prompting a certain degree of regeneration. After the first workers were freed from slavery, the Chinese formed societies to offer mutual aid to its members and preserve ties to their culture and beliefs. One of the most important societies is Tung Sing, which was founded in 1867 and in 1880 acquired the building it still occupies to this day. Located on the rooftop terrace, as if frozen in time, is the picturesque wooden and *quincha* construction that houses the society's premises and the Taoist temple. With a façade that recalls the traditional temples found in China, the building has a rectangular, symmetrical floor plan with a stepped arrangement of concatenated spaces. The first space beyond the entrance porch is the meeting-cum-reading room. Next, an antechamber lit by an octagonal lantern invites quiet reflection and anticipates the temple itself. This is located at the rear of the building and is divided into three parts, one of which is no longer used for prayer. The other two parts each have profusely decorated altars. Many of the objects and items of furniture were brought from China in the late nineteenth century.

Mercado Central de Lima
Jirón Ucayali 615,
Cercado de Lima
Alfredo Dammert,
Gerardo Lecca
1967

161 H

Lima's commercial functions have evolved considerably since the city was founded. In the viceregal period they were centred around the street markets, located in church atriums or public squares like the Plaza Mayor and Plaza de la Inquisición, the present-day Plaza Bolívar. As time went by, concerns about the chaotic and unhealthy conditions of these places increased, leading to the decision to formalise them by means of the construction of an appropriate building. Part of the convent of La Concepción, which occupied two entire blocks in the central checkerboard district, was expropriated and demolished to make way for the building. A new street was laid to divide the plot into two parts and the Concepción market was built on the east block. Inaugurated in the mid-nineteenth century, the single-storey neoclassical building with a clock tower indicating the main entrance became the city's commercial hub. However, an outbreak of plague in the early twentieth century led to its demolition and subsequent reconstruction. This second market, a two-storey

metal structure with towers at the corners, caught fire in 1964 and burned to the ground. At this point, the authorities decided to modernise the system by creating a wholesale market on the outskirts of the city, complemented by a series of other markets. This led to the construction of a new retail market on the plot of the destroyed building to serve a densely populated sector of the city. It was designed as an exposed concrete mixed-use building, with a long office volume on a commercial base that occupies the entire block. The interior is articulated around a great triple-height void that facilitates illumination and ventilation, with scissor ramps connecting the different levels. In the following years, the local population increased exponentially. Since the market building could not be extended physically, its functions spilled out across the district. Today, what is known as the 'central market' includes the conglomeration of streets and galleries around the building. Although this hive of commercial activity forms part of the area's current identity and has a picturesque appeal, it has had a devastating impact. To service the market, clandestine high-rise warehouses have proliferated and windowless bare brick towers are gradually replacing buildings that belong to Lima's historic centre, a UNESCO World Heritage Site since 1991.

Municipalidad Metropolitana de Lima

Colegio Santo Tomás

Jirón Andahuaylas 5,
Cercado de Lima
Diego Maroto
17th century

162 H

The creation of the Universidad Nacional Mayor de San Marcos in the sixteenth century was promoted by the Dominican religious order which had academic responsibilities and therefore deemed it necessary to establish a college to train its teachers. The works were carried out in stages and over a long period of time, probably due to the irregular availability of funding. The project was initiated with a private donation but also required the use of income from the Dominican haciendas and the college itself. The complex originally occupied the entire block. The small public square at one of its corners provides access to the church, whose present-day appearance dates from the eighteenth century. The same square leads to the monastery, where the facilities are articulated around two cloisters, one rectangular and the other circular. This latter cloister is the most outstanding feature of the complex and the only one of its type in the Americas. Its layout reflects the desire of the college rector, Fray Francisco de la Cruz, to evoke the courtyard at the Palace of Charles V in Granada. Twenty-eight brick pillars support the same number of semi-circular arches and the porticoed gallery is composed of an identical number of groin vaults. A fountain in the shape of an eight-pointed star stands at the centre of the courtyard. Since Peru gained independence, the building has accommodated a wide range of uses that have altered its structure: a teacher training college, army barracks, women's prison, women's college and public administration offices. A number of earthquakes have led to partial reconstructions, but the building has still managed to retain its unique quality.

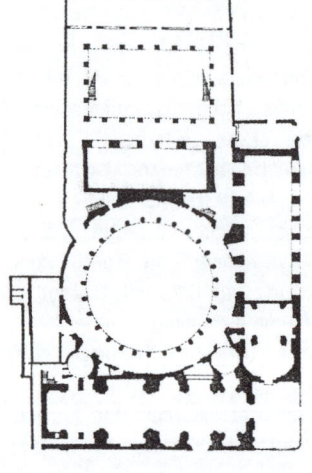

IPMIL. Universidad Nacional de Ingeniería

Gladys Alvarado

Quinta Heeren

Jirón Junín 1201,
Cercado de Lima
Architect unknown
1880

163 H

H

In the heart of Barrios Altos, in an area with an irregular layout plagued by a lack of public safety, the Quinta Heeren residential complex has survived as a silent witness to a glorious past. Hidden inside the block, it occupies the old medicinal herb garden of the Mercedarian convent, with a floor area of over 4 hectares. The complex contains a colourful group of classicist buildings that in bygone days accommodated private residences and embassies, articulated around generous open spaces that once had lush vegetation, forming a picturesque landscape. Access is from the south, via a narrow street that culminates in a small public square and a second perpendicular street that divides the complex into two sectors. The square, planted with trees and protected by railings, is decorated with sculptures of the four seasons. On the south and west elevations, the two-storey mansions have mouldings, pilasters and balustraded balconies. At the corner stands a small tower with a mansard roof. On the north side, the open space expands to form a green area with eclectic constructions of varying heights around its perimeter. The formerly exuberant garden was designed

Gladys Alvarado

The square

by Tatsugoro Matsumoto, designer of the Japanese Tea Garden in San Francisco and responsible for the presence of thousands of jacaranda trees in Mexico City. Back in the day, the complex had a pavilion viewpoint, an artificial lake and the country's first tennis court. The architecture and finishes reflect its opulent past. However, as the city's centre of gravity shifted southwards, the residents gradually changed and, little by little, the complex entered decline. Today, it is vacant, but Óscar Heeren's descendants have embarked on its progressive restoration, financing the works with guided tours.

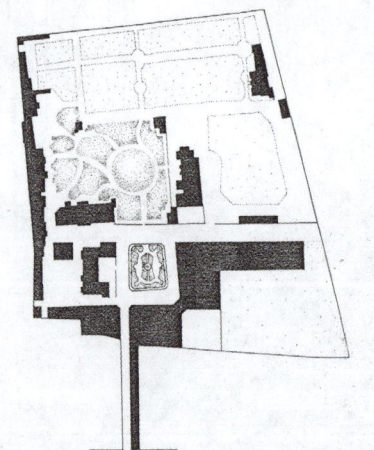

IPMIL. Universidad Nacional de Ingeniería

Gladys Alvarado

Buildings at Quinta Heeren

Plaza de Toros de Acho

164 H

Jirón Hualgayoc 3, Rímac
Cristóbal de Vargas,
Francisco Graña Garland
1768, 1945

Promoted by Agustín Hipólito de Landaburu y Rivera during the mandate of Viceroy Manuel de Amat y Junyent and inaugurated in 1768, the Plaza de Toros de Acho is the oldest bullring in the Americas and the third oldest in the world. Remodelled by engineer Francisco Graña in 1945 to increase capacity, it has cultural heritage status in Peru and was declared a UNESCO World Heritage Site in 1991. The complex is owned by Lima's Public Charity Board and in 2020 it accommodated a temporary shelter for people infected with COVID-19. Built like a fortress with a pentadecagonal perimeter, it is formed by buttresses made of adobe and wood intersected by a passage around the arena, with pebblestones for the paving and a plinth that leads to the tiered seating. This rests on a structure with a primitive appearance, in contrast to the light wooden arcade that supports the roof and shelters the boxes. The bullring also hosts the annual festival of Our Lord of Miracles, held between the months of October and November, an event that offers much more than what has now become a controversial type of entertainment. The heat of Lima in the spring, the approach from the city centre along Avenida Abancay, the viceregal air of the decaying Rímac neighbourhood,

H

Gonzalo Cáceres

iStockphoto. antorti

Aerial view of Acho and Cerro San Cristobal

Gonzalo Cáceres

The passage around the arena

the view of the outlying districts on the San Cristóbal hillside and the sound of the *paso doble* and *marinera* turn this *fiesta* into a social event from another period. It begins with the traditional lunch on Jirón Hualgayoc or at the bullring itself and moves on, after the fight, with an itinerary that starts at the *cochera* on Paseo de las Aguas. It continues with a cocktail at Café Olé, a classic of Lima design, and ends at the garden of the Country Club Hotel, where world-famous bullfighters mingle over drinks with journalists, models and other Lima celebrities. Although not to everyone's taste, it is an extraordinary experience for anyone who wants to understand the contrasts that define this city.

Alameda de los Descalzos   165 H

Jirón Atahualpa, Rímac
Cristóbal Gómez de Carrasco
1611

In 1562, a suburb was established on the other side of the river. Originally called San Lázaro, although more popularly known as 'Abajo el Puente,' the present-day Rímac neighbourhood grew up around a street that began at what was then the city's only bridge – where the Puente de Piedra stands today – and ended at the church of San Lázaro. With an irregular layout and located outside the seventeenth-century walled city,

it was an area of orchards and rustic ambiances; after various *alamedas* were developed there, it became a popular location for walks and other recreational activities. The Alameda de los Descalzos is named after the monastery located at the end of the esplanade. A longitudinal space, it forms a deep perspective against a backdrop of bare hills. Its layout emulates the Alameda de Hércules in Seville and it once had eight rows of trees and wide roads for carriages. A remodel in 1857 gave it the appearance we see today, with a perimeter fence, marble benches, urns, lampposts and statues, all brought from Europe. This second period of glory did not last long: the *alameda* fell into disuse when the city began to expand southwards. Two eighteenth-century churches, the Santa Liberata and Nuestra Señora del Patrocinio de María, can be found half-way along it. Located nearby is the Quinta de Presa, a Rococo remnant of the country houses that once populated the area. At the south end stood the house of Micaela Villegas, Viceroy Manuel Amat's mistress; it was replaced in 1876 by the old Backus brewery which now hosts interesting cultural and artistic events. Together with the simpler Alameda de los Bobos and Paseo de las Aguas, laid in 1772, this *alameda* offers a rather pleasant pedestrian route through what has unfortunately become an unsafe district.

H

Fabio Rodríguez Bernuy

Conjunto residencial Chabuca Granda

Jirón Atahualpa, Rímac
José García Bryce
1985

166 H

This apartment building with shops on the ground floor, one of José García Bryce's most emblematic works, was conceived as a pilot project for the regeneration of the Rímac historic centre. Using postmodern codes, it is skilfully integrated with the Alameda de los Descalzos, a majestic urban context steeped in tradition that forms part of a nostalgic collective imaginary. The complex combines three- and four-storey blocks and presents a uniform face to the city, preserving the alignment of the façade. Inside, it is fragmented and reveals its multi-faceted nature on a more domestic scale. The entire project is packed with references and modern re-interpretations of elements of viceregal residential architecture. Access is from the corner through a large double-height *zaguán* (a kind of vestibule between the entrance and the courtyard, usually separated from the latter by a barred gate) that culminates diagonally in the first

courtyard, an almost perfect quadrangle surrounded by exposed brick porticoed galleries that generate wide balconies for foot traffic, reached by an imperial staircase. The quadrangle is linked to a second courtyard akin to a tree-lined alley with access from the street outside through another *zaguán*. The housing blocks are articulated around both courtyards, forming setbacks and recesses that produce a dynamic rhythm while creating a certain degree of privacy. The water tanks are integrated into the volumes, generating verticality. Outside, the cantilever of the third, top level of the façade is treated like a traditional continuous enclosed balcony, painted green and decorated with geometric motifs. The two lower levels present a constant rhythm of voids – access to the shops on the ground floor, lighting and ventilation for the apartments on the floor above – interrupted by two cross-shaped holes with latticework that flank the main entrance.

H

Cerro de San Cristóbal
Avenida San Cristóbal,
Rímac

 167 H

The Cerro de San Cristóbal emerges between Cercado de Lima, Rímac, El Agustino and San Juan de Lurigancho districts. In pre-Hispanic times, it was considered an *apu*, a living mountain with the status of a deity. In the colonial period, it became a place of Catholic worship and pilgrimage. It has a powerful presence in the city skyline due to the 20-metre cross that rises from the summit and the brightly coloured informal houses on the hillside. As a genuine observatory over metropolitan Lima, it is worth taking a closer look to understand the scale and dynamics of a megapolis of nearly 11 million inhabitants, the fourth most populous in South America, after São Paulo, Buenos Aires and Rio de Janeiro. On a clear day, it is possible to make out its natural boundaries – the Pacific Ocean, San Lorenzo Island and the Morro Solar headland near Chorrillos – as well as the different urban plans: neoclassical in the case of the Presbítero Maestro cemetery, Cartesian in the case of Pizarro's checkerboard and winding in the case of the hills. Also

visible in the distance are the profiles of the Gamarra towers and the financial district. A visit to the hill is a must for anyone who wants to gain a deeper understanding of the structure of a city whose urban problems – ownership structure, inequality, informal development and transport – stem from the unplanned growth it experienced in barely three decades, from 1960 to 1990, when the population jumped from half a million to nearly nine million inhabitants. It was this 'popular overflow' that motivated nearly all the collective housing initiatives undertaken in the second half of the twentieth century, from the *unidades vecinales*, or neighbourhood units, to the PREVI experimental housing project and Villa El Salvador. Interesting as these undoubtedly were, they proved wholly insufficient to absorb the informal invasions that have been studied and documented by authors such as José Matos Mar, Hernando de Soto, John F. C. Turner, Sharif Kahatt, Reynaldo Ledgard, Bernardo Secchi, Alejandro Aravena and others. In recent years, this research field has acquired much more importance in academic and professional circles and will undoubtedly become one of the great urban planning topics of the twenty-first century.

Other Works of Interest

H01 Edificio Radio El Sol
Avenida Uruguay y Pasaje Velarde,
Cercado de Lima
Luis Miró Quesada
1953

H02 Hospicio Manrique
Plaza de Francia, Cercado de Lima
Miguel Trefogli
1866

**H03 Antigua Bodega Sanguchería
Antonio Carbone**
Jirón Cailloma, Cercado de Lima
1923

H04 Edificio Capurro
Jirón Rufino Torrico 889,
Cercado de Lima
Juan Benites, Gustavo Tode
1955

H05 Hotel Crillón
Avenida Nicolás de Piérola 589,
Cercado de Lima
Carlos Casanueva
1947

H06 Casa García y Lastres
Avenida Nicolás de Piérola 412,
Cercado de Lima
Claude Sahut
1915

H07 Edificio Ostolaza
Avenida Tacna 407, Cercado de Lima
Enrique Seoane
1953

H08 Edificio La Nacional
Avenida Emancipación 199,
Cercado de Lima
Enrique Seoane
1948

H09 Edificio Wiese
Jirón Carabaya 516,
Cercado de Lima
Héctor Velarde (refurbishment)
1924, 1940s

H10 Banco Central de Reserva
Jirón Antonio Miró Quesada 441,
Cercado de Lima
Luis Ángel Tapia, Manuel Llanos
1976

H11 Diario El Comercio
Jirón Antonio Miró Quesada 300,
Cercado de Lima
*Felipe González del Riego,
Enrique Rivero Tremouille*
1924

H12 Facultad de Medicina San Fernando
Avenida Grau 7, Cercado de Lima
Santiago Basurco/Santiago
Agurto, Javier Cayo, Eduardo Neira
1903, 1952

H13 Hotel Maury
Jirón Ucayali 201, Cercado de Lima
Héctor Velarde
1956

H14 Palacio de Gobierno
Jirón de la Unión, Cercado de Lima
*Claude Sahut, Ricardo de Jaxa
Malachowski*
1938

H15 Casa Aliaga
Jirón de la Unión 224, Cercado de Lima
Since 16th century

**H16 Iglesia y convento de Nuestra
Señora de la Merced**
Jirón de la Unión 621, Cercado de Lima
*Ventura Coco, Andrés Espinoza,
Cristóbal Caballero, Cristóbal Gómez*
17th–18th century

H17 Casa de Osambela
Jirón Conde de Superunda 298,
Cercado de Lima
1808

H18 Quinta de Presa
Jirón Chira 344, Rímac
Juan de la Roca
18th century

Casa Aliaga

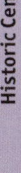

Juan Pablo El Sous

Earthquakes and the Possibilities of Architecture

Elda Cantú

Oscar Niemeyer, the legendary architect who designed Brasilia, was once asked whether there was any kind of construction that could withstand a tsunami. He said no, there wasn't. Niemeyer, who spent part of his 105 years imposing his curvilinear buildings on the planet, then declared, 'The Earth is nuts.'

Earthquake survivors tend to remember what they did to protect themselves. I find it curious that at the first sign of the earth moving, there are people who run off, terrified, and other people who stay put, terrified as well. But the element that shapes the memory is the building.

Inside or outside. Upstairs or downstairs. Architecture is a box of tricks that create the illusion that balance and stability are possible. An earthquake demonstrates that, in fact, the true order is nature's order. And when the buildings stop swaying, the rubble reveals that architecture is actually chaos.

We build to protect ourselves, to shelter, to boast. Shigeru Aoki, an expert in refining architecture, that is, in updating buildings for seismic safety, says that constructions with lightweight volumes withstand tremors better, and he recommends *genchiku*, a sort of Japanese slimming programme, to remove surplus weight and reinforce the structures of buildings. At the same time, civilisation is demanding ever-larger and heavier buildings. Construction fever is viewed as a symptom of prosperity, not of design. For visitors, cranes, builders and diggers in a city herald the optimism of progress. But a building shouldn't kill anyone. An earthquake, says Juan Villoro, renders matter, walls incomprehensible (prisons and borders do the same thing). The paradox of a seismic event is that you have to leave the house to save yourself. The architectural model of Frank Gehry's

Walt Disney Concert Hall survived the Los Angeles earthquake in 1994 but the tiny figures attending the imaginary concert couldn't escape. After a tragedy, no one blames the earth for moving; it's the concrete's fault for trapping, crushing and killing. When the Fukushima earthquake occurred, many people were saved because of ultra-sensitive alarms that sent a flurry of text messages warning of the seism seconds before it happened. But the skyscrapers were not alerted. Where would a building find shelter? Once we have paid the price of grief and memory, we should take some comfort in the destruction: Earth's tremors

Formal and informal architecture on Lima streets

humanise architecture. They remind us that everything serves a purpose and, in the heat of the moment, they force us to do some soul searching. An earthquake tests the solidarity of the people, the stamina of the rescue workers, the heritage of a country, the morality of the press corps, the meanness of the politicians and the greed of the builders. But above all, it tests the ego and generosity of the architects. Our lives are defined by seismic events: we were born before or after a particular earthquake. I wasn't there, but like all my generation I carry the wound and optimism of the Mexican tragedy in 1985. Because the temptation of a new city also invites resistance: despite their cyclical destructions, the cities of Mexico, Japan and Peru have preserved their skylines. It's as if, subconsciously, we revel in being a society of survivors, a society that every now and again is drawn to the challenge of dawn breaking over a desolate horizon, one that invites resurrection. When I decided to move to Lima, earthquakes were not on my mind. Until I put down my luggage on the ironic 13th floor of a building whose architects perhaps liked to tease faith. I understood that, at such a height, the design of a staircase loses all its beauty if the Earth goes nuts.

Appendix

Architects

Digits indicate the project number

Architects

Digits indicate the project number

Buildings

Digits indicate the project number

Buildings

Digits indicate the project number

Bibliography

As a non-academic book, it has been decided to release the texts of notes and references, necessary if you want to carry out a more exhaustive study. The bibliography that has been consulted during its preparation is listed here, from which citations, names and dates that appear in them have been extracted.

AA.VV. *Guía de Madrid: Arquitectura y urbanismo*. Madrid: Colegio Oficial de Arquitectos de Madrid. 1982.

AA.VV. *Héctor Velarde: Arquitecto y humanista*. Lima: Universidad de Lima. 2013.

AA.VV. *Mario Bianco: El espacio moderno en el Perú*. Lima: Universidad de Lima. 2017.

AA.VV. *Pueblo Libre: Historia, cultura y tradición*. Lima: Municipalidad de Pueblo Libre. 2008.

AA.VV. *Walter Weberhofer. El proyecto moderno en el Perú*. Lima: Universidad de Lima. 2016.

ÁBALOS, Iñaki. *La buena vida: Visita guiada a las casas de la modernidad*. Barcelona: Gustavo Gili. 2000.

ACEVEDO, Alejandra. LLONA, Michelle. *Catálogo arquitectura Movimiento Moderno Perú*. Lima: Universidad de Lima. Fondo Editorial. 2016.

ADRIÀ, Miquel. TSIEN, Billie. WILLIAMS, Tod. *OB+RA: Óscar Borasino y Ruth Alvarado: Desde el paisaje peruano*. Mexico City: Arquine. 2017.

ALVARADO, Gladys. *La Lima del metro*. Lima: Notaría Paino. 2014.

ALVAREZ-BUILLA, Maryan. IBAÑEZ, Joaquín. *La plaza en España e Iberoamérica: El escenario de la ciudad*. Madrid: Museo Municipal. 1998.

AUGUSTIN BURNEO, Reinhard. *Orígenes y evolución del conjunto arquitectónico de la Casona de San Marcos*. Lima: Programa de Cooperación Hispano Peruano. 2013.

BANHAM, Reyner. *Los Ángeles, la ciudad de las cuatro ecologías*. Barcelona: Puente editores. 2016.

BENTÍN DIEZ CANSECO, José. *Enrique Seoane Ros: Una búsqueda de raíces peruanas*. Lima: Universidad Nacional de Ingeniería. 2014.

BERNALES BALLESTEROS, Jorge. *Lima: La ciudad y sus monumentos*. Seville: Escuela de estudios hispano-americanos de Sevilla. 1972.

BONILLA, Enrique (coord.) and AA.VV. *Guía de arquitectura y paisaje: Lima y El Callao. Perú*. Seville: Junta de Andalucía. 2009.

CALDERÓN, Julio. *La ciudad ilegal: Lima en el siglo XX*. Lima: Punto Cardinal. 2016.

CANZIANI, José. *Ciudad y territorio en Los Andes: Contribuciones a la historia del urbanismo prehispánico*. PUCP Fondo Editorial. 2015.

CARBAJAL, Gabriel. CROMAN, Sally. CASTAÑEDA, Enrique. ZABALETA, Renzo. *Plaza de toros de Acho*. Lima: FAUA Universidad Nacional de Ingeniería. 2018

COAGUILA, Jorge. *Perú: Crónicas y perfiles*. Lima: Revuelta Editores. 2018.

COLEGIO DE ARQUITECTOS DEL PERÚ. *XII Bienal Nacional de Arquitectura del Perú*. Lima: Colegio de Arquitectos del Perú. 2006.

COLEGIO DE ARQUITECTOS DEL PERÚ. *XIII Bienal Nacional de Arquitectura del Perú*. Lima: Colegio de Arquitectos del Perú. 2008.

COOPER LLOSA, Frederick. *A house in between*. Lima: FCL ed. 2015.

COOPER LLOSA, Frederick. *Walter Weberhofer*. Revista *ARKINKA* N°237. Lima. 2015.

COOPER, Julian. MOREUIL, Francois. *Reyner Banham loves Los Angeles*. Documentary. London: BBC films. 1972.

CUADRA, Manuel. *Arquitectura en América Latina: Perú, Bolivia, Ecuador y Chile en los siglos XIX y XX*. Lima: Universidad Nacional de Ingeniería. Instituto Goethe. 2010.

DAM, P; ALVARADO, L; DEL VALLE, A; LERNER, S; LOPEZ, M; VILLACORTA, J. *Post-ilusiones: Nuevas visiones: Arte crítico en Lima (1980-2006)*. Lima: Insula editora. Fundación Augusto N. Wiese. 2006.

DOBLADO, Juan Carlos. *La arquitectura del postmodernismo en Lima: Conversos y creyentes*. Lima: Arcadia Mediática. 2020.

DRINOT, Paulo. *La seducción de la clase obrera: Trabajadores, raza y la formación del estado peruano*. Lima: Instituto de Estudios Peruanos. 2016.

ESTEBAN MALUENDA, Ana (ed.). *La arquitectura moderna en Latinoamérica: Antología de autores, obras y textos*. Barcelona: Editorial Reverté. 2016.

FLORES-ZÚÑIGA, Fernando. *Haciendas y pueblos de Lima: Historia del valle del Rímac*. Lima: Fondo Editorial del Congreso del Perú. 2008

FREIRE FORGA, Fernando. *La forma moderna en la vivienda unifamiliar peruana 1950-1970*. Lima: FFF ed. 2008.

GAVAZZI, Adine. *Lima: Memoria prehispánica de la traza urbana*. Lima: Apus Graph Ediciones. 2014.

GEBHARD, David. WINTER, Robert. *Los Angeles: An architectural guide*. Los Angeles: Gibbs Smith, Publisher. 1994.

GLAESER, Edward. *Triumph of the city: How urban spaces make us human*. New York: Pan Macmillan. Macmillan Publishers Limited. 2012.

GÜNTHER DOERING, Juan; MILTRANI REAÑO, Henry. *Memorias de Lima: Tomos I, II, III y IV*. Lima: Los portales y Empresa Editora El Comercio. 2013.

HERTZ, John. *Arquitectura Tropical: Diseño bioclimático de viviendas en la selva del Perú*. Lima: Editorial Universitaria Ricardo Palma. 2018 (Second edition).

HAMANN MAZURÉ, Johanna. *Monumentos públicos en espacios urbanos de Lima 1919-1930* (Doctoral thesis). Barcelona: Universidad de Barcelona. 2011.

HUAPAYA, José. *Fernando Belaunde Terry y el ideario moderno: Arquitectura y urbanismo en el Perú entre 1936 y 1968*. Lima: FAUA Universidad Nacional de Ingeniería. 2014.

HUNTING, Mary Anne. *Eduard Durrell Stone: Modernism's populist architect*. New York: W. W. Norton & Co. 2012.

INSTITUTO NACIONAL DE CULTURA. *Catálogo del inventario del patrimonio inmueble de La Punta y Chucuito*. Lima: Instituto Nacional de Cultura. Organización de los Estados Americanos. 1988.

JIMÉNEZ, Luis. SANTIVÁÑEZ, Miguel. *Rafael Marquina, arquitecto*. Lima: Instituto de Investigación de la Facultad de Arquitectura, Urbanismo y Artes. 2005.

KAHATT, Sharif S. *Utopías construidas: Las unidades vecinales de Lima*. Lima: PUCP Fondo editorial. 2015.

Bibliography

KAHATT, Sharif S. MORELLI, Marta. *Edificios híbridos en Lima: Estrategia proyectuales para edificios públicos en altura*. Lima: PUCP Fondo editorial. 2014.

KOOLHAAS, Rem. ULRICH OBRIST, Hans. *Project Japan: Metabolism talks...* Cologne: Taschen. 2011.

LAND, Peter. *The experimental housing project (PREVI), Lima: Design and technology in a new neighborhood.* Bogota: Universidad de Los Andes. 2015.

LAUSENT-HERRERA, Isabel. *Sociedades y templos chinos en el Perú*. Lima: Fondo Editorial del Congreso del Perú. 2000.

LEDGARD, Reynaldo. *La ciudad moderna: Textos sobre arquitectura peruana*. Lima: PUCP Fondo Editorial. 2015.

LEDGARRD, Reynaldo. FERRER Felipe. CRUZ, Gonzalo. *El proyecto urbano: Taller de proyectos fin de carrera*. Lima: PUCP Fondo Editorial. 2015.

LEGGET, GARY. POLIS. *Visiones y versiones de Lima a inicios del siglo XX*. Lima: Ediciones La Moderna. 2006.

LEÓN, Rafo. *Lima bizarra: Antiguía del centro de la capital*. Lima: Aguilar. 2006

LLONA, Michelle. NAKAMURA, Sandra. *Lecturas urbanas: Polvos azules*. Lima: Universidad Ricardo Palma. 2010.

LLONA, Michelle (ed.). MOSQUERA, Fernando (ed.). *Arana Orrego Torres: Historia de un emprendimiento*. Lima: Universidad de Lima. Fondo Editorial. 2017.

LUDEÑA, Wiley (ed.). RODRIGUEZ, Luis (ed.). *Lima(polis) 2014: Discutir, proyectar, pensar*. Lima: PUCP Fondo Editorial. 2019.

LUDEÑA, Wiley. *Lima y espacios públicos: Perfiles y estadística integrada 2010*. Lima: PUCP Fondo Editorial. 2013.

MAGGIOLO, Rafaela. *La casa peruana contemporánea*. Lima: Editorial Cosas. 2013.

MAKOWSKI, Krzysztof. *Urbanismo andino: Centro ceremonial y ciudad en el Perú prehispánico*. Lima: Apus Graph. 2016.

MARTINEZ, Virgilio. *Central*. New York: Phaidon. 2016.

MARTUCCELLI, Elio. *Arquitectura para una ciudad fragmentada: Ideas, proyectos y edificios en la Lima del siglo XX*. Lima: Universidad Ricardo Palma. Editorial Universitaria. 2017.

MATOS MAR, José. *Perú: Estado desbordado y sociedad nacional emergente*. Lima: Universidad Ricardo Palma. Editorial Universitaria. 2012.

MATTOS-CÁRDENAS, Leonardo. *Lima y la Plaza de Armas: Historia y aportes de Emilio Harth-Terré*. Lima: Universidad Nacional de Ingeniería. Colegio de Arquitectos del Perú. 2017.

MEJÍA, Léster. *La Plaza San Martín de Lima 1921–1996: proyecto urbano y espacio público.* (Master's thesis). Lima: Universidad Nacional de Ingeniería. 2011.

MEJÍA, Víctor. *Ilusiones a oscuras: Cines en Lima: Carpas, grandes salas y multicines 1897–2007.* Lima: Víctor Mejía. 2007.

MEJÍA, Víctor. CÁCERES, Roger. TORRES, Fernando. *Catálogo de la exposición: Retóricas de la línea: Gráfica arquitectónica en el Perú durante el siglo XX*. Lima: ICPNA and USIL. 2014.

MERINO REYNA, Evelyn. *Lima mas arriba: Entre los Andes y el mar*. Lima: Visart / Los Portales. 2014.

MIRANDA, Antonio. *Arquitectura y verdad: Un curso de crítica*. Barcelona: Ediciones Cátedra (Grupo Anaya). 2013.

MIRO QUESADA, Luis. *Espacio en el tiempo: La arquitectura moderna como fenómeno cultural*. Lima: Fondo editorial PUCP. 1945 (2014).

MONEO, Rafael. *Rafael Moneo: Escritos y conversaciones en el Perú*. Lima: PUCP Fondo Editorial. Facultad de Arquitectura y Urbanismo. 2009.

MONTESTRUQUE, Octavio. *Juvenal Baracco: La memoria de la ciudad, las formas de la tradición*. Lima: Universidad Ricardo Palma. 2021.

MUÑOZ UNCETA, Pablo. RODRIGUEZ RIVERO, Luis (eds.). *La ciudad de las laderas: Limapolis 2016*. Lima: PUCP Fondo Editorial. 2016.

NÓMENA. *Con posiciones: 20 aproximaciones a la arquitectura peruana*. Lima: Nómena Arquitectos. 2013.

OFICINA NACIONAL DE PLANEAMIENTO Y URBANISMO. *Estudio de parques zonales y metropolitanos*. Lima: Patronato de Parques Nacionales y Zonales. 1969.

PERROTTET, Oliver. GÜNTHER, Juan. Lima. *Una historia contada en planos*. Lima: Lima 2000. 2021.

PIMENTEL, Víctor. BEIGOLEA, José. GUZMAN, Enrique (coords.). *Inventario del patrimonio monumental inmueble – Lima*. Lima: Universidad Nacional de Ingeniería. 1994.

ROMERO Sotelo, Miguel Ángel. ROMERO Maldonado, Teresa. *Villa El Salvador: Ciudad de generaciones*. Lima. USIL Fondo editorial. 2021.

ROMERO Sotelo, Miguel Ángel. *Hábitat popular: un camino propio*. Lima: CAP and IUPP. 1992.

ROMERO, Milagros. *Barrios Altos: Historia y evolución arquitectónica*. Lima: Pakarina. 2019.

SALAZAR BONDY, Sebastián. *La ciudad como utopía: Artículos periodísticos sobre Lima 1953-1965*. Lima: Universidad de Lima. Fondo Editorial. 2016.

SALAZAR BONDY, Sebastián. *Lima la horrible*. Lima: Lápix editores. 1964.

SAN CRISTÓBAL, Antonio. *Arquitectura firme del siglo XVIII en Lima*. Lima: Universidad Nacional de Ingeniería. 2009.

SAN CRISTÓBAL, Antonio. *Arquitectura de Lima en la segunda mitad del siglo XVII*. Lima: Fondo Editorial Universidad de San Martín de Porres. 2010.

SAN CRISTÓBAL, Antonio. *Fray Diego Maroto, alarife de Lima 1617-1696*. Lima: Epígrafe. 1996.

SAN CRISTÓBAL, Antonio. *Lima: Estudios de la arquitectura virreinal*. Lima: Epígrafe. 1992.

SAN CRISTÓBAL, Antonio. *Nueva visión de San Francisco de Lima*. Lima: Instituto Francés de Estudios Andinos. 2006.

SAN CRISTÓBAL, Antonio. *Obras civiles en Lima durante el siglo XVI*. Lima: Universidad Nacional de Ingeniería. 2005.

SANTOS ARIAS, Manuel de los. *Grupos sociales diferentes en aislamiento voluntario: sobre la producción de nuevas formas de segregación socio espacial entre los distritos de Santiago de Surco y San Juan de Miraflores (1970-2006)* (Bachelor's thesis). Lima: Universidad Nacional Mayor de San Marcos. 2011.

Bibliography

SANTOS, Jesús M. *Perú sabe: La cocina, arma social*. Lima: Media Networks Latin America, Lagar de Ideas Propias, RTVE. 2012.

SOTO, Hernando de. GHERSI, Enrique. GHIBELLINI, Mario. *El otro sendero*. Lima: Editorial El Barranco. 1986.

SECCHI, Bernardo. *La ciudad de los ricos y la ciudad de los pobres*. Madrid: Los libros de la catarata. 2015.

TESTINO, Mario. *Lima, Peru: Featuring the work of over 100 Peruvian artists*. Bologna: Damiani. 2007.

TURNER, John F. *Autoconstrucción: Por una autonomía del habitar*. Logroño: Pepitas de calabaza. 2018.

VARGAS LLOSA, Mario. MEJÍA, Víctor (ed.). *Ciudad, arquitectura y paisaje*. Lima: PUCP – Fondo Editorial. 2013.

VELARDE, Héctor. *Arquitectura peruana*. Lima: Ediciones 'Studium'. 1946.

VELARDE, Héctor. *Itinerarios de Lima*. Lima: Editorial Universitaria. 1970.

VICCINA, Humberto. *Edificio Diagonal: Enrique Seoane*. Piura: Universidad de Piura. 2015.

VILLACORTA GONZALES, Carlos. *Lima escrita: Arquitectura poética de la ciudad 1970-2020*. Lima: Intermezzo tropical. 2021.

VON HUMBOLT, Alexander. *Cosmos: Ensayo de una descripción física del mundo*. Madrid: Los libros de la catarata and ediciones CSIC. *2011*.

WOLFE, Tom. *¿Quién teme a la Bauhaus feroz?* Barcelona: Anagrama. 2010.

WUFFARDEN, Luis Eduardo. *Manuel Piqueras Cotolí (1885-1937): Arquitecto, escultor y urbanista entre España y el Perú*. Lima: Museo de Arte de Lima. 2003.

Articles

BONILLA, Pamela. "Praxis en el pasado: Aproximaciones a la intervención en el patrimonio arquitectónico de Lima". *Devenir* n°3. Lima: Universidad Nacional de Ingeniería. 2015. p. 45–62

CHIARAMONTE, Gabriella. "La migración italiana en América Latina: El caso peruano". *Apuntes. Revista de Ciencias Sociales* n°13, p. 15–36. 1983.

COELLO, Antonio. "Unas notas sobre el antiguo Mercado de la Concepción, hoy Mercado Central de Lima". *Arqueología y Sociedad*, n°28. Lima: Universidad Nacional Mayor de San Marcos. 2014. p. 367–378.

DAM, Paulo. "La ocupación del desierto de la playa Asia, Lima, Perú". *ARQ n°57 Zonas áridas*. Santiago: ARQ, 2004, p. 56

GARCÍA-BRYCE, José. "Neoclasicismo y arquitectura republicana". *El Arquitecto Peruano* n°231. Lima. 1966. p. 17–29

GONZALES, Alejandro. "El campus de la PUCP: Historia, urbanismo y arquitectura". *Revista A* n°2. Lima: Pontificia Universidad Católica del Perú. 2008. p. 108–127.

LUDEÑA, Wiley; TORRES, Diana. "Del passage a las galerías populares". *ARQ* n° 88. Santiago: ARQ, 2014. p. 40–51.

MEJÍA, Víctor. "Espacio público y representación: El principal monumento a José de San Martín en el Perú (1904-1921)". *Anales del IAA*, [S.l.], v. 45, n°2, 2016. p. 181–196.

RIBAS, Nicolás de. "El tren de Lima a La Oroya: Construcción e idea de progreso en el proyecto ferroviario transandino del ingeniero polaco Ernesto Malinowski (1818–1898)". *Itinerarios*, n°14. 2011. p.251–261.

SARMIENTO, Mario. "Propuestas para un barranco de resistencia: Contextualismo y boom inmobiliario en una zona monumental de Lima". *Arquitextos* n°33. Lima: Universidad Ricardo Palma. 2018. p. 35–48.

Magazines and electronic references

ACEVEDO, Alejandra. LLONA, Michelle. *Catálogo arquitectura Movimiento Moderno Perú*. Lima 2015.

BASULTO, David. ASSAEL, David. *ArchDaily/Plataformarquitectura*. Santiago de Chile. 2008.

BASULTO, David. ASSAEL, David. *Plataformaurbana*. Santiago de Chile. 2005–2008.

BEINGOLEA, José et al. *Arqandina*. Lima: 2006.

BELAUNDE, Fernando. CRUCHAGA, Miguel. *El arquitecto peruano*. Lima. 1937–1977.

COLEGIO DE ARQUITECTOS DEL ECUADOR. *Archivo digital Bienal de Arquitectura Panamericana*. Quito: 2013.

COLEGIO DE ARQUITECTOS DEL PERÚ. *Exágono*. Lima: 2007.

CONSEJO SUPERIOR DE LOS COLEGIOS DE ARQUITECTOS DE ESPAÑA. *Bienales de arquitectura*. Madrid: 1989.

COOPER, Frederick. HERRERA, Ricardo. *Arkinka*. Lima. 1995.

CÓRDOVA, Adolfo. *1/2 de construcción*. Lima. 1987–2003.

CUADRA, Manuel. *Cultura académica en arquitectura, paisaje y urbanismo*: Ciclo de conferencias FAU PUCP. Lima. 2021.

ENTENZA, John. *Arts & Architecture*. Los Angeles. 1940–1962.

FACHO, Aldo. *Habitar: Ambiente + Arquitectura + Ciudad*. Lima. 2008.

FREIRE FORGA, Fernando. *La forma moderna en Latinoamérica*. Lima. 2008.

HAYAKAWA, José (dir.). *Devenir: Revista de estudios sobre patrimonio edificado*. Universidad Nacional de Ingeniería. Lima. 2014.

KAHATT, Sharif. *Revista A: PUCP*. Lima. 2018.

MASÍAS, Javier. OSTERLING, Rafael. *Félix*. Lima. 2018.

NÚÑEZ, Asiel. RIVERA, Carolina. BERGELUND, Erick. VILLAGRA, Mauricio. ROGRIGUEZ, Milagros. RUIZ, Olenka. *Archivo de ideas recibidas*. Lima. 2018.

ORREGO PENAGOS, Juan Luis. *Blog PUCP de Juan Luis Orrego Penagos*. Lima. 2008.

PORTA, Pool. *Arquitectura moderna - Perú*. Lima. 2016.

REYES, Roberto (dir.). MARTUCELLI, Elio (ed.). *Arquitextos*. Universidad Ricardo Palma. Lima. 1993.

VILLANUEVA CHANG, Julio. *Etiqueta Negra*. Editorial Etiqueta Negra. Pool Editores. Lima. 2002.

Authors

Laura Torres Roa

With an MSc in architecture from the Universidad Europea de Madrid and further studies in Project Management, Laura worked for Ábalos+Sentkiewicz in Madrid and Ateliers Jean Nouvel in Lima, where she was responsible for the residential towers of the Cuartel San Martín project. She subsequently joined the project management team of the Interbank Group for the same project. In 2014, she co-founded L&M Taller de Diseño with Margaux Eyssette, carrying out architecture, interior and craft design projects. Their work was awarded at the CASACOR 2017 design fair. Laura currently lives in her home city on the island of Ibiza, where she combines her professional activity as an architect with teaching at the Escola d'Art d'Eivissa. Her work Ca Na Maria, designed with Alfonso Miguel, was selected for an Architecture Award by the Official Professional Association of Architects of the Balearic Islands.

Jorge Álvarez-Builla

With an MSc in architecture from the Escuela Técnica Superior de Arquitectura de Madrid, Jorge worked for Dominique Perrault, Estudio Lamela, Ábalos & Herreros and Ábalos+Sentkiewicz, from 2004 to 2011. In Madrid, he designed the Greenspire building in Valdebebas, together with Victor Garzón and Alfonso Miguel. In Lima, he designed with Daniel Danés the master plan and urban development project for Distrito 7 in Lurín, a new neighbourhood in the south of the city. He also carried out industrial projects at various mines, the Port of Callao, the La Pampilla refinery and the airport. He currently works for consulting firm AECOM; from 2019 to 2022, he was the Project Director of Pier A at Schiphol Airport in Amsterdam. Since November 2022, he is managing an infrastructure programme for sustainable mobility at Shell.

Guest authors

Luis Martín Bogdanovich

With an MSc in architecture from the Pontificia Universidad Católica del Perú and an MA in art history from the Faculty of Letters and Human Sciences of the same university, where he won the University Social Responsibility Teaching Award, Luis Martín is the author, co author and editor of various articles and publications on Peruvian architecture and viceregal art. He has given lectures on movable and immovable cultural heritage in Peru, Latin America and Europe, and has curated several exhibitions on Peruvian viceregal and modern history and art. He has served as director of the Galería Municipal de Arte Pancho Fierro. Currently the manager of the Municipal Programme for the Recovery of the Historic Centre of Lima (PROLIMA), he is also chairman of the board of the Municipal Real Estate Company of Lima (EMILIMA) and of the Metropolitan Fund for Urban Renewal and Development (FOMUR).

Elda Cantú

An editor at the Foreign Desk of *The New York Times*, which she joined in 2018 as deputy editor of the newspaper's Spanish version, since 2019 Elda has written for *El Times*, a newsletter published in Spanish. She currently lives in Mexico City but has previously resided in Lima, where she edited magazines such as *viú!*, *Etiqueta Negra* and *Etiqueta Verde*. Born in Reynosa, Mexico, she has an MA in Latin American Studies from New York University and has taught at universities in Mexico and Peru.

Ramiro Gil Serrate

An economist by training with a PhD in economics from the Universidad de Zaragoza, Ramiro completed his post-doctoral research in urban economics at the London School of Economics from 2008 to 2011. Between 2012 and 2019, he taught at the Centrum Católica of the PUCP and in the economics departments of Universidad del Pacífico and the Universidad de Piura in Lima. He has also been a consultant for the Peruvian Ministry of Production and a teacher on the university extension courses organised by the Banco Central de Reserva del Perú.

Víctor Pimentel

With an MSc in architecture from the Universidad Nacional de Ingeniería and postgraduate studies in Urban Design at Instituto de Urbanismo de Perú and in monuments restoration at La Sapienza Universitá di Roma in Italy, Víctor has been Director of the National Museum of Anthropology, Archeology and History of Peru and Managing Director of the Instituto Nacional de Cultura, among other responsibilities. He was a drafting member of the Venice Charter and the first President of the Peruvian Committee of ICOMOS. He has served as a consultant on different projects for UNESCO and OEA and is currently professor emeritus at UNI. Awarded with the Hexágono de Oro and the Premio América, he was recognised as a 'meritorious personality of the culture' by the Ministry of Culture in 2012.

Contributors

Margaux Eyssette

With an MSc in architecture from École
Nationale Supérieure d'Architecture de
Paris-Belleville, Margaux worked for
Abalos+Sentkiewicz and Herzog & de
Meuron in Madrid. In 2011, she relocated
to Lima as a member of the team at
Ateliers Jean Nouvel that designed the
Cuartel San Martín project. She subse-
quently worked for Alejandro Shell on the
UTEC project. In 2014, she co-founded
L&M Taller de Diseño with Laura Torres,
carrying out architecture, interior and
craft design projects. Their work was
awarded at the CASACOR 2017 design
fair. She currently lives in Madrid, where
she runs her own real estate agency,
Adelante Prime Real Estate.

Fabio Enrique Rodríguez Bernuy

With an MSc in architecture from
Universidad Nacional de Ingeniería,
Fabio Enrique has contributed to the digital publication *ArchDaily* and worked
with Allende Arquitectos and Plan
A0100 on housing, education and office
projects. At the third National Conference
on Architecture and Urban Planning
Research, organised by the Universidad
Nacional de Ingeniería, he delivered
a paper entitled 'CREALIMA Centres:
Cultural infrastructures, participatory
design and appropriation of public spaces
2011–2015).' He is an active member
of urban planning, history and culture
groups such as Iniciativa Libre, Recorre
Lima and TVRobles.

Ricardo Herrera Ruiz

With an MSc in architecture from the Faculty of Architecture and Urban Planning of the Universidad Ricardo Palma, Ricardo was nominated for the MCHAP Student Award in 2016 and has worked as an assistant teacher of architectural design at FAU URP, under Juvenal Baracco, and on the mathematics for architects courses at the Faculty of Architecture at UCAL, under Laurín León. He currently works in the field of computer-aided conceptual design and is an editor of the magazine *ARKINKA*, run by Frederick Cooper.

Juan Caycho

With an MSc in architecture from the Faculty of Architecture and Urban Planning of the Pontificia Universidad Católica del Perú, graduating with honours for his final degree project, Juan has worked for Román Bauer Arquitectos, Poggione+Biondi Arquitectos, Samadhi Perú and Jorge Álvarez-Builla. In 2018, he won first prize in the public competition for the Plaza Paz Soldán in San Isidro, following it up in 2019 with first prize in the competition for the SumaqWasi building in Huancayo.

Delia Bayona

With an MSc in architecture from the Faculty of Architecture and Urban Planning of the Pontificia Universidad Católica del Perú, Delia has edited *ArchDaily* in Peru and published several articles there. She was involved in the design of the DisfrutARTE project, in association with Lima Cómo Vamos and PUCP, and has delivered papers at the second Foro de Intervenciones Urbanas (FIU) and at the 'Lima muchas miradas' event organised by UNESCO.

Carlos Vadillo

With an MSc in architecture from the Escuela Técnica Superior de Arquitectura de Sevilla, including university studies in Nuremberg, Carlos has also studied music and plays the saxophone. He has worked for the studio ARX Portugal and for Allende Arquitectos in Lima, where he has lived since 2013. He is currently a project manager at the company RH10, where he develops hotels and mixed-use buildings. He is a lover of nature and outdoor sports such as surfing.

Roger Miranda

A photographer and editorial designer, Roger has been an editorial designer for *Revista de Crónicas Latinoamericanas Etiqueta Negra*, a graphic designer at the design studio Partn&rs and lead designer at the Instituto Peruano de Publicidad. He currently organises Behance Portfolio Reviews in Lima and is a consultant on design projects for companies such as BBVA, the World Bank, BCP, TedxTukuy, Visual City and TECHO.

Judith Wilcock

With a degree in Spanish and French from the University of Bradford and a post-graduate diploma in translation from the Chartered Institute of Linguists in the UK, Judith relocated to Spain in 1985. She has worked as a full-time translator since 2001, specialising in the fields of architecture, tourism and the arts, and has translated numerous documents and architectural guides for the regional government of Andalucía.

Photographers

Leonardo Finotti

Leonardo's work can be found in the collections of the Bündner Kunstmuseum Chur (Switzerland), the Fundação EDP (Portugal), the Harvard Art Museums (USA), the Cité de l'Architecture et du Patrimonie (France) and Itaú Cultural (Brazil). He has represented Brazil at three editions of the Venice Architecture Biennial and won an award at the 15th Buenos Aires International Architecture Biennial. He took part in *Latin America in Construction: Architecture 1955–1980* (2015), an exhibition organised by the Museum of Modern Art in New York, whose permanent collection features several of his works.

Juan Solano Ojasi

With a degree in architecture from the Universidad Nacional de Ingeniería, since 1995 Juan has been actively disseminating architecture and design in Peru by photographing architectural and interior design projects, editing and designing specialised publications and monographs, and organising competitions and exhibitions. His work in these fields has led to collaborations with numerous architecture studios, universities and media organisations.

Gonzalo Cáceres

After studying communication sciences at the Universidad de Lima and then photography at the Istituto Europeo di Design (IED) in Milan, Gonzalo spent a large part of his career in Barcelona, working in the fields of publishing and advertising. A decade ago, he returned to Lima, his home city, where he has specialised in photographing architectural and interior design projects for leading professionals in the sector and specialised media. He has exhibited his work at various group shows.

Billy Hare

A disciple of Minor White and Aaron Siskind, Billy obtained a master's degree from the Rhode Island School of Design (1977–1978) courtesy of a grant from the Fulbright Commission. In 1992, he was awarded a Guggenheim Grant. The founder of the Photography Department at the Instituto Gaudí, of the Centro de la Fotografía and of the galleries Secuencia and El Ojo Ajeno, he has taught at PUCP, USIL and UPC. His work has been exhibited in Peru and abroad at both solo and group shows. In 1997, the Fundación Telefónica organised a retrospective of his work and published a catalogue entitled *Billy Hare Fotografías*.

Christopher Schreier-Barreto

With a degree in architecture from the Universidad Ricardo Palma, a master's degree in architectural history, theory and criticism from the Universidad Nacional de Ingeniería, and a diploma in photography from the Instituto Peruano de Arte y Diseño, Christopher is a registered teacher and researcher at Scopus and a full-time lecturer in the Faculty of Architecture at the Universidad de Lima. He has contributed to a variety of academic and professional publications with articles on architectural theory and analysis, as well as photographs of architecture.

Candy Torres

With a degree in social communication from the Universidad Nacional Mayor de San Marcos, Candy specialises in corporate events, portraiture and fashion photography. Since 2011, she has worked with various mainstream media organisations across Peru. Previously, she was also a member of the national volleyball team.

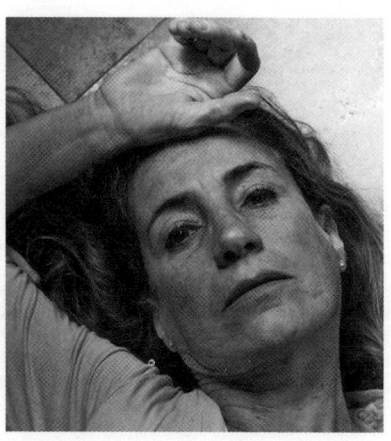

Eleazar Cuadros

With a degree in architecture from the Universidad Nacional de Ingeniería, Eleazar is a self-taught photographer. He is co-founder of Coordinadora de la Ciudad en Construcción (CCC) and Ciudad Transdisciplinar (CITIO), teacher of urban photography and creator of *Presbicia del Andar*, an urban photography blog. He won first prize at the competitions 'Lima Foto Libre,' organised by the Centro de la Imagen, and 'FotoEnsayos,' organised by the Housing Institute of the Universidad de Chile. With CCC, he won the 2021 Architecture for Development Prize at the Lima Architecture Biennial.

Gladys Alvarado

Trained in photography at Centro de la Imagen, Lima, Gladys also studied Administration and Control at the Universidad del Pacífico and has a master's degree in Documentary Photography and a Latin American master's in Contemporary Photography (MALDEFOCO). She took part in the *Estratos de un Paisaje* show at the Casa de América in Madrid, organised as part of the 2019 edition of the contemporary art fair ARCO, and she has also held solo shows at the Centro de la Imagen and at the Lima Photography Biennial.

Christian Declercq

With a degree in audiovisual communication from the Pontificia Universidad Católica del Perú and a master's degree in wildlife documentary production from the University of Salford in Manchester, Christian has worked in a variety of formats for institutional, corporate and fiction productions, documenting landscapes, culture and inhabitants across Peru. He is currently a member of KmCero, a Lima-based consultancy team specialised in communication, tourism and sustainable development.

Renzo Rebagliati Beltroy
With a degree in architecture from the Universidad Peruana de Ciencias Aplicadas and professional experience at Malachowksi Taller de Diseño and Leondelima, Renzo also trained at the International Center of Photography (ICP) in New York and has been dedicated exclusively to architectural and design photography since 2013. He likes to photograph buildings by isolating parts of them and focusing on the details, leaving the rest to the viewer's imagination. His work has been published extensively in specialised books and magazines.

Evelyn Merino Reyna
Evelyn is an aerial photographer and director of VISART Photography & Producciones. She is the author of *Lima Más Arriba* and producer of the documentary *Pacificum: Return to the Ocean*, now available on Netflix. She studied plastic arts and architecture in Peru and Switzerland. Her photographs have been exhibited at art fairs including Art O'Clock in Paris, Kunst in Zurich, SCOPE and Lima Photo. Her work is part of the permanent collection of the Museo Metropolitano de Lima. In 2018, she received the Medal of the Order of Merit for Women.

Edi Hirose
A photographer trained at the Instituto Gaudí, Edi's interest in landscape photography has given rise to a long-term research project on the Peruvian territory and its transformation as a result of the economic boom of the last two decades, focusing on themes related to real estate development, self-construction and mining. His work has been exhibited at biennials in São Paulo and Istanbul, the Museo de Arte de Lima, the Museum of Modern Art in New York and other venues.

Acknowledgements

This book is dedicated to all those who have played a role in the construction of Lima: to the architects of the selected works and of others that ultimately could not be included who gave us access to the drawings and documents to study them; also, to the people who developed the works, the technicians and workers who built them, as well as those who live in and maintain them.

To the architects and experts who advised us during the preparation of the book, bringing new ideas and nuances: Héctor Abarca, Diana Álvarez-Calderón, Marian Álvarez-Builla, Rodrigo Álvarez, Miguel Anguita, César Becerra, Susel Biondi, Luis Martín Bogdanovich, Edgar Bravo, Andrés Bretel, Miguel Ángel Calle, Carlos Casabonne, Frederick Cooper, Jean Pierre Crousse, Miguel Cruchaga, Paulo Damm, Aldo Facho, Felipe Ferrer, Pauline Ferrer, Fernando Freire, Rafael Freyre, Joaquín García Calderón, José García Calderón, Arturo and Gustavo Ghezzi Novak, Ramiro Gil Serrate, Joaquín Ibañez, Gary Leggett, Alexia León, Javier Lizarzaburu, Michelle Llona, Lucho Marcial, Javier Masías, Henry Mitrani, Marta Morelli, David Mutal, Asiel Núñez, Elisabet Olivares, Víctor Pimentel, René Poggione, Fernando Puente, Marco Rosales, Miguel Eugenio Romero Sotelo, Jorge Sánchez, José Antonio Vallarino, Fernando Vela. And especially to Sharif Kahatt, who has been very generous with his time.

To the institutions that collaborated in the publication, dedicated time to us, provided access to their archives or gave us documents.

To our parents, who encouraged us to travel and live adventures. And, of course, to all our friends in Lima, to whom this book owes so much.

Panoramic view of Lima from the Port of Callao, 1840 (FitzRoy and Belcher)

FitzRoy and Belcher.
Biblioteca Nacional
de España

Photo credits
Non-credited pictures are the property
    of the authors of this book

Archives and other sources
Aldo + Hannie van Eyck Foundation
Aldo Facho Arquitectos
Alejandra Acevedo
Archive of Antenor Orrego
Archivo de Arquitectura de la PUCP
    (Michelle Llona, Karen Yarlequé)
Archivo Digital de Arte Peruano. MALI
Archive of Emilio Soyer
Archivo Fotográfico del Ministerio de
    Defensa del Perú
Archive of Miguel Rodrigo Mazuré
Archive of the Weberhofer family (Heinz
    Weberhofer)
Arquitectónica
Arquitectura Moderna – Peru. Blog of
    Pool Porta
Asociación Amigos de Villa
Autoridad Portuaria Nacional del Perú
Barclay & Crousse Arquitectos
Biblioteca Nacional de España
Canadian Center for Architecure (Caroline
    Dagbert)
Carlos Palomino
Carlos Villavicencio
Central Restaurante / Mater Inciativa
Chano Palomino
Cooper, Graña, Nicollini Arquitectos
David Mutal
Diego La Rosa
Editorial Universidad Ricardo Palma
    (Jorge Ramos, Lourdes Chang)
Enrique Bonilla
Enrique Ciriani
Enrique Santillana
Fernando Freire
Hunerwadel Arquitectos (Victor Pazos)
IDOM
Instituto Aerofotográfico Nacional del
    Perú
Inventario de arquitectura de Lima. FAUA
    UNI (Shirley Chilet)
Jaime Ortiz de Zevallos
Jean Paul Getty Trust. Getty Research
    Institute
Jose Antonio Vallarino, Arquitecto

José Barreda
Juvenal Baracco
Kikutake Architects (Mutsuko Smith
    Kikutake)
Leonmarcial Arquitectos
Librería Metrópolis (Arturo Aguirre)
Llonazamora Arquitectos
Llosa Cortegana Arquitectos
Los Portales
Luis Martín Bogdanovich
Mario Lara Arquitectos
Martín Dulanto
Marzio Kogan Arquitectos
Miguel Eugenio Romero Sotelo
Ministerio de Cultura del Perú
Monumental Callao
Museo de Arte Contemporáneo de Lima
    (Naisha Vergara)
Museo de Sitio Antonio Jiménez Borja –
    Puruchuco
Museo de Sitio de Ancón
Museo de Sitio de Pachacamac
Museo Larco Herrera
Museo Naval de Madrid
Museum of Modern Art, New York
Municipalidad Metropolitana de Lima
National Archives of Modern
    Architecture, Japan (Naoko Kato)
OB+RA Arquitectos
Octavio Montestruque
Peter Land Foundation (Marietta Land)
Plataforma Urbana
Poggione+Biondi Arquitectos
ProLima. MML
Rafael Freyre
RAMSA Architects, New York
Restaurante El Mercado (Claudia Cortez)
Revista ARKINKA
Revista CASAS (Laura Alzubide)
Revista El Arquitecto Peruano
Revista Vitrubio
Reynaldo Ledgard
Royal Museum Greenwich
Scala Archives (Elvira Allocati)
Servicio de Parques de la MML
Universidad de Lima (Moses Abensur)
Universidad Nacional de Ingeniería
Universidad Ricardo Palma
V.Oid Arquitectos
Victor Pimentel and Alfonso Huamaní
51-1 Arquitectos

Next double page: Manchay, Pachacamac

The Deutsche Nationalbibliothek lists this publication in the
Deutsche Nationalbibliografie; detailed bibliographic data
are available at http://dnb.d-nb.de

ISBN 978-3-86922-648-4 (English)
ISBN 978-3-86922-871-6 (Spanish)

© 2023 by DOM publishers, Berlin
www.dom-publishers.com

Proofreading
Reuben Ross

Design
Roger Miranda

Maps
Juan Caycho

Printing
Tiger Printing (Hong Kong) Co., Ltd.
www.tigerprinting.hk

DOM
publishers